question-answer
seeking
Description
not Prescription
dutybased society
Commandbased

aadesh
updesh

HINDU DHARMA AND THE CULTURE WARS

HINDU DHARMA AND THE CULTURE WARS

KOENRAAD ELST

RUPA

Published by
Rupa Publications India Pvt. Ltd 2019
7/16, Ansari Road, Daryaganj
New Delhi 110002

Sales Centres:
Allahabad Bengaluru Chennai
Hyderabad Jaipur Kathmandu
Kolkata Mumbai

ISBN: 978-93-5333-405-5

First impression 2019

10 9 8 7 6 5 4 3 2 1

Printed Nutech Print Services, Faridabad

Contents

Introduction

The present volume is a collection of my papers from 2012 to 2018. All of them, tangentially or centrally, pertain to India's ongoing culture wars. They are not about ancient or medieval history (where I have mainly been writing about the Indo-European homeland theories and the genesis and intra-Hindu status of Buddhism, therefore about religious conflict), except insofar as it impacts current debates.

'Culture wars' is a term that dates back to the nineteenth century and to the German nation-builder Otto von Bismarck, who started a struggle with the Church for control over education—the *Kulturkampf* (culture war). Though he lost the struggle, the term gained currency in the United States (US) as the debate between modern and religious worldviews. In the broader sense, it can refer to any non-economic controversy. To the men who think that only economic matters are 'the real issue', these cultural controversies are but a distraction.

The array of issues at stake sometimes largely overlap between the US and India, and sometimes not. Thus, unlike the US, India has hardly known a debate around abortion. Yet, Hindu scriptures explicitly and sharply condemn abortion, classing it as the worst kind of sin. That is why, in 1996, when the Vishva Hindu Parishad (VHP) presented the political parties with a 'Hindu agenda'*, among the forty points listed was a demand for prohibiting abortion. A section of less scripturalist but more politicized Hindu activists supported this demand, but for demographic reasons—to stem the downward evolution of the Hindu birth rate. But no political party, not even the

*http://vhp.org/organization/org-hindu-agenda/

Bharatiya Janata Party (BJP), has attempted to make this demand its own, if only because of India's enormous population pressure.

As for euthanasia, to which a level-headed approach has prevailed in India, let me first state that I come from one of the few countries that have legalized it—Belgium. I have, in general, been opposed to the former prime minister Guy Verhofstadt's government, but I greatly welcomed this move, which took place in 2002. And so did the overall population—even the Catholic segment, which initially opposed it—because the predicted abuses never materialized and it turned out to be beneficial for families and the elderly. It helps prevent suicide, because people who are assured they can end their life when the need arises, no longer feel pressured to do so by, say, throwing themselves in front of a train. And not even a devout Catholic would want his suffering mother—whom he sees begging for an end to her ordeal—to go through more pain.

With our own history of Christian pangs of conscience over this taking control of one's own death (as had once been common among the pagan Romans, where Stoic philosophers such as Seneca justified it), we should understand that Hindu society has always accepted euthanasia—not suicide by a lovesick Romeo but a mature end to life by a person who has his or her reasons for doing so. Hinduism has a more relaxed attitude to death, seen through the larger perspective of reincarnation, and appreciates the renunciation that death brings. This is where the fundamental values of civilization come into play and where, as American culture warriors are wont to say, 'ideas have consequences'. Except for advanced yogis who are said to be able to control their own life force and hence their time of passing, the usual procedure is fasting unto death. Some well-known modern cases are V.D. Savarkar in 1966 and Vinoba Bhave in 1982. Among Jains, it is, in fact, quite common.

When Bhave lay on his deathbed, he was visited by then prime minister Indira Gandhi. Immediately, secularist editorials had written about how he was entitled not to Indira's respect but to a time in jail and force-feeding, because he was trespassing against the law of the land. But this law, which prohibited a gentle death, had been enacted by the British and had its roots in the colonial era, in which the savage natives were 'civilized' by imposing on them Christian-inspired beliefs. Only God, not man, should have control over life and death—such was the Christian view. Here, as elsewhere, secularists, without any proper reflection, had just expressed their knee-jerk opposition to anything that was remotely Hindu. They were identifying with colonial rule, and had internalized a Christian position without even realizing it. (They were also exhibiting an anti-democratic mentality, as if the law of the land is something imposed on us rather than something we ourselves can evaluate and modify.)

In recent years, the issue has come to a head, not in the political arena but in the courts. When a citizen was prevented from fasting unto death (*santhara*, *sallekhana*), the Jain community went to court over its right to uphold this humane tradition.* The Supreme Court eventually supported the Jain position and upheld the ancient right to take control of one's own death. On a very small scale, this was a culture war—though the commotion raised was minimal, it could have earth-shaking consequences. In the long run, the pro-tradition and pro-dignity outcome is bound to influence the relevant policies in other countries as well.

Another culture war took place around the normalization of homosexuality in the West. In India this has mostly taken the form of opposition to Article 377 of the Indian Penal Code, another British-made and Christian-inspired prohibition. It was rendered ineffective by the Supreme Court in 2018 and the issue did not cause the kind of commotion it did in the West. However, interestingly, it did show how numerous Hindus were defending a fairly recent British law as part of their own tradition, while other Hindus took

---

*Ghatwai, Milind, 'The Jain Religion and the Right to Die by Santhara', *The Indian Express*, 2 September 2015, accessed 31 January 2019, indianexpress.com/article/explained/the-jain-religion-and-the-right-to-die-by-santhara/

a completely different view, claiming that homosexuality had always been accepted by Hinduism.

To be sure, Hinduism has never stoned homosexuals to death, as happens in the Muslim world, nor has it ever locked them up as criminals, as the Christian world did with author Oscar Wilde or mathematician Alan Turing. But tolerating or even accepting something as a fact of life does not mean institutionalizing it. Thus, the Shastras acknowledge eight forms of marriage, but 'gay marriage' is not one of them. Traditional societies have often accepted homosexuals but not conceded their modern demand for equality. The fact that they had a certain right did not imply that homosexuals, too, could claim this right, such as the right to marriage and child adoption. Thus, among some Native American communities, homosexuals had a legitimate role in society and could function in 'soft' professions, but not be part of the martial endeavours of 'real' men.

In early 2018, there were calls for banning Professor Bharat Gupt, a retired art historian, then an invited speaker at a conference in Hawaii, for his nuanced views on homosexuality. In the West, things are more black and white, with a recent swing from total criminalization of 'sodomy' to making the least afterthought about the normalcy of homosexuality taboo. It took forceful intervention of the leading India scholar Ramdas Lamb, more at home in really existing Hinduism than most American academics, to ensure his admission. The incident illustrates the shrill and ultimately totalitarian approach of American 'liberals' (since when is censorship 'liberal'?) with the more moderate but comparatively enlightened Hindu approach.

This difference between the separate legitimate identities of different groups and the total equality envisaged by modern liberalism is most readily visible in the largest cultural shift around: women's emancipation. In the US army, women now have the right to every job that men do, including frontline combat duty. Even the Israeli army, for long the yardstick of women's participation in national defence, has never gone that far. Likewise, India has a more realistic approach to women's rights than the American variety of feminism. Madhu Kishwar's periodical, *Manushi*, is the pioneer of this rooted and more mature form of feminism in Indian society.

So these are all important debates in 'culture wars'. They are often not as black and white as in the West, where Christianity, with its monolithic doctrines and mobilizing power, mounts a stronger and more focused opposition to these views. In India, the culture wars that get the most attention (but I admit that this could be a subjective impression because of my own interests) are those that take place within the Hindu community, between conventionalists and secularists. They mainly concern religious and national symbols, the definitions of Hinduism and secularism, caste, history and, like for Bismarck, the school curriculum. These themes are, of course, also in focus in the West (which is why this collection contains several articles originally directed at Western readers, though those with an interest in Indian culture), but not deemed as consequential as in India. Here, the warring parties foam at the mouth and even indulge in 'divisive' or 'anti-national' activities that can ultimately cause civil war and the nation's disintegration.

The definition of 'secularism' is a uniquely Indian concern. Muslims and Christians, no matter how radical or obscurantist, call themselves secularists, even if their counterparts abroad may abhor secularism. Many Nehruvians, too, consider themselves secularists, even if they are not sure of the right definition of the nebulous ideology they swear by. And those in the Hindutva brigade do the same, but make use of a more qualified term—'real secularism' or 'positive secularism'.

Within their discourse, however, a conspicuous evolution has taken place, one towards Nehruvian secularism, with Narendra Modi extolling 'development' (from infrastructure and digitalization to toilets) at the expense of specifically Hindu priorities, thus echoing Jawaharlal Nehru's praise of hydroelectricity generators as 'our new temples', discarding the need for the classical sort. At the time of writing, the Nehruvians and their foreign allies are still suppressing the acknowledgment that the erstwhile Hindutva forces have indeed, for better or for worse, evolved in the direction of secularism. Considering the fanciful foreign reporting in 2014–19 about a non-existent fanatical Hindu government, they are still succeeding in their disinformation.

It is in these debates that the present book contains a small contribution by me. Most chapters are based on journalistic articles and essays, two are of a scholarly nature, with references and scientific transcriptions of the Sanskrit words used, and one is a hybrid. They are sometimes located in the West, because NRI-PIOs (Non Resident Indians-Persons of Indian Origin) are often faced with similar debates as their counterparts in the Indian homeland. Let's take the conversation forward.

I dedicate this collection to the Vedic foremother *Ilā*, and to all first-born sisters, including my own.

Koenraad Elst
18 February 2019, Delhi

Hindu Fearlessness through the Ages*

Hindus are often confined to the Gandhian niche of being infinitely tolerant. They are expected to take everything lying down. If they show some self-respect, they are told that this isn't 'really Hindu'.

One hears it all too often: 'Hindus are cowards, they only deserve what they are suffering.' Mahatma Gandhi said it clearly enough: 'The Muslim is a bully, the Hindu a coward.'** But Hindus are by no means cowards. Hindus as such have their problems, but lack of bravery is not one of them.

Look at the Bangladesh war of 1971. The Pakistani army was brave enough as long as its job consisted of, among other things, perpetrating crimes against Bengali women, but as soon as the Indian Army appeared on the scene, all they could do was flee and surrender. The Indian Army liberated the oppressed Muslims and the persecuted Hindus of Bangladesh. Or look at the Kargil War of 1999. Though politicians forbade Indian soldiers from taking the war into enemy territory by crossing the Pak border, the Indian Army besieged the Kargil mountain which the Pak invaders had taken, and reconquered it.

Let us look at the historical record. First off, the *Vedas* and

---

*Published on Hindu Human Rights, 23 October 2012

***Hindu-Muslim Tension: Its Cause and Cure,* Young India, 29 May 1924; reproduced in M.K. Gandhi: *The Hindu-Muslim Unity*, pp.35–36

the Hindu epics, like most ancient writings, extol bravery. The *Bhagavad Gita* also underpins its plea for bravery on the battlefield with a typically Hindu (at least very un-Christian and un-Islamic) philosophy, namely the belief in reincarnation. Cicero and Caesar had noted the Gallic men's battlefield bravery and its connection to their belief in reincarnation. This was equally true of the Hindu warriors: they were not afraid of death.

Then, Hindus stopped Alexander the Great. To be sure, this is old history, we have a paucity of reliable sources about what really happened. At any rate, Alexander's soldiers were uniquely far from home and understandably unwilling to go farther even if they could. But the fact remains: the great Alexander was satisfied with the Iranian provinces of India's frontier and declined to enter India proper. That was no mean achievement of the Hindus.

Then the Shakas, Kushanas and Hunas managed to gain a foothold in India's Northwest. The Shakas were defeated—the Vikram calendar begins with this victory. These conquering foreigners were not fully expelled, but at least they were absorbed. There is no distinct Shaka, Kushana or Huna community today, much less do they demand minority privileges.

The Muslims entered Indian history with a naval attack north of present-day Mumbai a few years after Prophet Mohammed's death. It was repelled. Then for half a century, they sent a number of expeditions overland from Mesopotamia to Sindh. Each expedition was defeated.

While conquering North Africa was a cakewalk, there was a caliph who expressed his reluctance to send another army to Sindh, because those expeditions only cost the lives of so many good Muslims. But, of course, if you keep trying, you will break through one day. So eventually, Mohammed bin Qasim occupied Sindh in AD 712. But even then, his successor was soon defeated.

Meanwhile, the Muslim armies conquered Central Asia, and their next attack was through Afghanistan and the Khyber Pass. Afghanistan was ruled by the Hindu Shahiya dynasty, which gave them a long-drawn-out fight. But towards the year AD 1000, the

Muslims finally won, and the Shahiya king killed himself when he found himself unable to defend his subjects. From Afghanistan, Mahmud Ghaznavi entered India proper for what his court chroniclers described as raids.

In fact, he would have been happy enough to occupy India permanently, but the Hindus were still too strong for that. However, what the Hindus had in bravery, they lacked in alertness. They didn't realize that Islam was a new type of enemy, much more difficult to digest than the earlier invaders. In the peripheral Kashmir region, the king acted 'secular' and gave Muslims positions of power and confidence, which then gave them the opportunity to take steps towards the Islamization of the region. This scenario would be repeated many times, down to the present.

Thus, the kings of the Vijayanagar empire showed off their broad-mindedness (now mis-termed 'secularism') by hiring Muslim troops, only to find in the battle of Talikota that their Muslim armies defected to the Muslim opponent camp and inflicted defeat on their erstwhile Hindu overlord. (For doubting Thomases, this inconvenient fact has even made it past Nehruvian controls into standard textbooks such as K.A. Nilakanta Sastri's *A History of South India: From Prehistoric Times to the Fall of Vijayanagar*, or Hermann Kulke's and Dietmar Rothermund's *A History of India*.)

Meanwhile, Mahmud's nephew Salar Masud Ghaznavi made a successful foray into the Ganga basin. The Hindu kings in the neighbourhood got together to stop him. Led by Maharaja Sukh Dev, and including the famous philosopher-king Raja Bhoja, they defeated Ghaznavi in the battle of Bahraich near Ayodhya in AD 1033.

It is a different matter that sentimental Hindu sleepwalkers of later years joined their Muslim neighbours in worshipping at Salar Masud Ghaznavi's grave, not appreciating the bravery and foresight of the Hindu kings and soldiers who had defeated him. There are certain things very wrong with the Hindu mentality, but again, lack of bravery is not among them. For more than a century and a half, the people of the Ganga basin considered Islamic invasions a thing of the past.

But then, the breakthrough came. It was not due to Hindu cowardice, but due to Hindu magnanimity and overconfidence. A year after being defeated by Prithviraj Chauhan, who had spared him, Mohammed Ghori did battle again and took his erstwhile victor captive. After blinding and executing Prithviraj, he and his generals conquered the entire Ganga plain, using newer battlefield strategies.

From there, they would extend their power southwards to cover almost the whole subcontinent in due course. But for five centuries and a half, the Hindus had prevented this, while West Asia, North Africa and Spain had fallen within eighty years.

The age of Muslim expansion was again marked by endless Hindu resistance. Wise Muslim rulers opted for a compromise with this unbeatable foe (misinterpreted by secularists as 'secularism'), but more zealous rulers depleted their forces in endless wars.

In this endeavour, they were helped by a stream of West-Asian adventurers and African slave-soldiers who came to India to increase the Delhi Sultanate's large standing armies. The Muslim states were totally geared to warfare, something rare in Hindu history. For this reason, we can say with the comfort of hindsight that the Muslims could finally have conquered all of the subcontinent had they remained united.

Even Hindu bravery could probably not have prevented it, any more than the brief acts of North African bravery could stop the Islamization of North Africa. But fortunately, Muslim states or Muslim ethnic lobbies within a state also fought each other, which gave Hindus a chance to regroup and mount another counter-attack.

Also, some Hindu kings did what they thought best under the circumstances, viz. they surrendered without war, paid tribute and retained sufficient autonomy to house rebels from other areas or become rebellious themselves once circumstances allowed it.

For a comeback, it was important to have these free territories (just like the reconquista of Spain was possible only because its Asturian region had managed to remain free since the beginning). Their collaboration was not cowardice but a ruse to gain time. All the same, this meant that many Hindus enlisted in the armed forces of sagacious Muslim rulers.

Akbar, who had consolidated his power by defeating the Hindu ruler Himu, was smart enough to keep enough of the Hindus on his side to overpower rival Muslim claimants and to fight Hindu freedom fighters. Famously, the rebellious Rana Pratap was countered by Man Singh, who wielded the sword of the Moghul empire. Hindu bravery was employed by Muslim rulers.

Finally, in the seventeenth century, a rebellious Shivaji, born in a family of collaborators, would arise and restore Hindu sovereignty. Where his Maratha army appeared, defeat of its enemies was a certainty. The Moghul empire became a mere shadow of its former self, while military power rested with the Marathas.

In 1817, the Peshwas, who had taken over the Maratha confederacy, were terminally defeated by the British. But again, this was not for Hindus' lack of bravery. They fought like lions, and on the other side, other Hindu divisions fought like lions for the British, who could conquer and rule India without doing too much fighting themselves.

If something can be held against the Marathas and their Peshwa successors, it is not lack of bravery or military prowess, but lack of proper ideological motivation. This is why they spilt their energies in predatory raids against other Hindu populations, it is why their leader Mahadji Scindia prostrated before the powerless Moghul emperor in 1771, it is why some Peshwa descendants could be enticed into a Hindu-Muslim or Moghul-Maratha cooperation (which was really a case of mutual deception) in the Mutiny of 1857.They lapsed from Shivaji's sense of mission as the liberator of the Hindus.

One constant for at least eight centuries was that Hindus didn't use their brains to update their warfare. They didn't learn from their enemies' successes. Also, they were sentimental and too overly attached to the person of their leader. They could bravely fight all they wanted, but if the leader was killed, there was no second person, much less a collective plan, to take his place. When you look at today's Hindu politicians and Internet warriors, you find exactly the same defects.

In a hostile sense too, Hindus are too focused on persons. They have wasted their energies attacking Sonia Gandhi and her family, and failed to dismantle the secularist dispensation established by her grandfather-in-law, Jawaharlal Nehru, given a Marxist slant by the aides of her mother-in-law, Indira Gandhi.

They haven't emulated the techniques by which the secularists, like the British of yore, exercise power totally out of proportion to their numbers. They haven't figured out how to stop the phenomenon of 'Hindus wielding the sword of Islam', in which Akbar exulted, but which has become so commonplace under the guise of secularism. For that, an analysis of all the factors in the field is necessary.

This is not too difficult—it only takes a normal degree of involvement and will. But so far, Hindus have not mustered up the will to win.

Is Yoga Hindu? The Court Verdict*

In the debate over the definition of Hinduism, it is often asked whether yoga is Hindu.

A county judge in San Diego, California, has ruled that yoga is not always religious (*Washington Post*, 2 July 2013). Parents in a San Diego school district had complained that yoga was intrinsically intertwined with the Hindu religion and that its practice in a public school setting violated the constitutional separation of church and state. The court ruling means that these parents had it wrong: It is possible to divorce yoga from Hinduism, and that is how the local school authorities have gone about their yoga classes.

While yoga may be religious in some contexts, and then notably Hindu, it can also be practised and taught purely for its benefits. Modern school authorities see these benefits mostly in the form of strength, suppleness and nervous relaxation, as well as combating aggressiveness and bullying. Therapists might add the benefit of restoring or at least improving normalcy in individuals afflicted with burnout, nervous breakdown, certain complexes and other mental disorders. Serious practitioners would invoke calmness, renunciation, even liberation (howsoever defined), as worthy goals for human beings who are perfectly healthy from the beginning. But all of them would do so without reference to Shiva, or Ganesha, or whichever God it is that Hindu yogis invoke.

---

*Published on Hindu Human Rights, 7 July 2013

YOGA IS INTRINSICALLY HINDU

This judgment is part of a broader struggle over the origins and nature of yoga. Some Christians, apparently including the litigating parents from San Diego, object that yoga is intrinsically Hindu and that it serves as a conduit for Hindu polytheistic god worship and even for 'evil Hindu social mores' such as caste discrimination, arranged marriage and widow-burning. It is, of course, also debated on how far these mores and this polytheism are bound with Hinduism, but it is universally agreed that, at least as a system of worship, Hinduism is different from Christianity.

For the same reason, these circles had in the past opposed Transcendental Meditation, a simplified form of mantra meditation, for being obviously Hindu, even though advertised as 'scientific'. They had hired specialized lawyers (or 'cult busters') to show that the various gurus who seduced Americans into yoga were salesmen of Hinduism-based cults.

These Christians find odd allies in the Hindus who insist that yoga is indeed naturally Hindu, and that the bead-counting and incense-waving and greeting gestures and, indeed, prayers that Hindu yogis practise, all come with the yoga package and cannot be divorced from it. They criticize American yoga aficionados, such as many showbiz stars and, indeed, the San Diego yoga schoolteachers, for reducing yoga to a fitness system without its cultural roots.

YOGA IS UP FOR GRABS

On the other side of the divide are those Hindus who say that yoga is scientific and universal, so that it is only normal for it to take on local cultural forms wherever it goes. The motorcar was invented in Germany, but few people driving a Japanese car still remember this. The aeroplane was invented in America, but this invention is now available to travellers all over the world. The Chinese don't put a sign 'invented in America' on their planes, nor do they pay intellectual property rights on them. Of course, Chinese textbooks have a line or two on the aeroplane's invention by the Wright brothers, and that nod to American honour will suffice. As the late Bal Thackeray used to say: 'You cannot take the swadeshi ("national produce") policy too far, for then Indians would have to do away with the light bulb.' So Hindus should be happy that Americans are willing to practise their yoga, and apart from a historical detail of origins, India or Hinduism no longer come in the picture.

And this still is a neutral rendering of the viewpoint of a sizable number of Hindus. We don't even mention moneymakers like Deepak Chopra, who try to obscure yoga's Hindu origins in order to claim certain yoga techniques as their own.[*] Aseem Shukla aptly calls him the front runner of 'how to deconstruct, repackage and sell Hindu philosophy without calling it Hindu!' Chopra likens the Hindu rejection of his appropriation of yoga as 'the resentment of an inventor who discovered Coca-Cola or Teflon but neglected to patent it', thus explicitly subjecting Hindu tradition to American commercialism.) Some yoga schools, whether manned by native Hindus or by Christian-born Westerners, have patented their own brand name and techniques, so that nobody, and certainly not Hindu tradition, can claim these.

This tendency is strengthened by the attempt of some Hindus to deny a Hindu identity even to the worldview they themselves are advertising, e.g. as I have witnessed several times, the Hare Krishnas worship Krishna, a Hindu god par excellence, yet tell Western audiences that they are not Hindu; or the Ramakrishna Mission, founded in the late nineteenth century under the motto 'Say with pride, we are Hindus', now says that its message is 'universal' rather than 'narrowly Hindu' (as analysed in detail by Ram Swarup in *The Ramakrishna Mission: In Search of a New Identity*, 1986).

Again, these Hindus find odd allies in many Christians, both

---

*'Shukla and Chopra: The Great Yoga Debate', accessed 31 January 2019, https://www.onfaith.co/onfaith/2010/04/30/shukla-and-chopra-the-great-yoga-debate/4379

the lukewarm and the activist kind. Lukewarm Christians, as well as New Age ex-Christians, see yoga as a neutral and universal commodity. For them, it can be practised as a fitness system without having any serious implications on their worldview or religion. Just as the European colonizers used the compass and gunpowder without bothering that these were Chinese inventions, American yogis have taken yoga for its tangible benefits without bothering about its Hindu origins. Even the Sanskrit names of the yoga exercises have been translated, so that you can become an accomplished yogi without even being reminded of its exotic origins.

Activist Christians, by contrast, admit that yoga is not religiously neutral. They want to adapt yoga because of its inherent attractiveness, and transform it into 'Christian yoga', as they themselves call it (e.g. Yogafaith.org or Christianspracticingyoga.com). To them, yoga has indeed historically been linked with Hinduism, but can be delinked from it and tied to another religion. We have even reached the stage where some Christian centres and schools back in India offer classes in 'Christian yoga'.

YOGA HAS HINDU ROOTS

So, the San Diego verdict was a victory for lukewarm Hindus and adaptable Christians, and a defeat for serious Hindus and doctrine-conscious Christians. But what do we ourselves make of the issue?

First off, it is a matter of course that yoga is Hindu. The word 'Hindu' is a very general term encompassing every Indian form of pagan religion, no matter how old. It is, therefore, simply silly to say 'yoga is older than Hinduism', as Deepak Chopra does (for example, in his just-cited debate with Aseem Shukla). The question, then, becomes whether yoga can be divorced from Hinduism and given a neutral universal identity, as claimed by the San Diego yoga teachers, or even relinked to another religion, as is claimed by the adepts of 'Christian yoga'.

A system of physical fitness, if it is only that, can certainly be integrated in modern Western or purportedly global culture. The *Shetashvatara Upanishad* already says, and the later hatha yoga classics more colourfully assert, that the yoga practitioner develops a healthy and lustrous body. They even lure the readers into practice by intimating that one becomes irresistible to the opposite sex—the very reason why most modern Americans take up yoga. Like the aeroplane or the light bulb, a system of physical fitness can be exported and inculturated, divested of its original *couleur locale*.

However, it is worth emphasizing that yoga, and even particularly hatha yoga, does have Hindu roots, because this seemingly trivial knowledge is now being challenged. A few academics have claimed that Chinese 'internal alchemy' (Neidan) travelled overseas to coastal India and influenced Indian siddha yoga and siddha medicine. A few techniques of hatha yoga do seem similar to older Daoist exercises from China. The influence has been posited but by no means proven. I am willing to consider it probable, but even then it was only an influence on a few exercises in a long-existing native tradition. It is nobody's case that the *Rig Vedic* reference to 'munis', wandering ascetics with ashes over their naked bodies (still recognizable as the Naga sadhus), or the Upanishadic glorification of the breath as the key to consciousness and self-mastery, or Patañjali's description of a whole yoga system, is due to foreign influence.

Very recently, the American media has gone gaga over a new theory claiming that hatha yoga is very recent and is essentially a gift from the British colonizers. This can, of course, not be said for the breathing exercises so typical of hatha yoga, but many of the postures are said to be standard exercises of British soldiers, or to be part of Western systems of gymnastics. Even in this limited form, the claim is ridiculous. The essence of hatha yogic postures is relaxation and allowing a steadily held pose to take its effect over time. By contrast, Western gymnastics pride themselves on being 'dynamic', of emphasizing movement and muscle strength. Further, a very physical circumstance comes in the way: Yogic exercises are mostly done on the floor. In cold England, the floor is avoided, witness the generalized use of chairs and of the 'English' water closet. Any influence would have to be confined to the standing exercises. At any rate, if at all there was Western influence, it can never have been more than an influence touching the skin of an already old native tradition.

But even hatha yoga sees its physical and breathing exercises only as a means to a higher end: liberation. A fortiori, the ancient yoga synthesized by Patañjali was totally geared towards liberation, howsoever defined. The definition of his *kaivalya* ('isolation' of consciousness from its objects, his supreme state) is: quieting the mind so that it consciously rests in itself and is not absorbed by its usual objects. It doesn't matter whether you believe in reincarnation, or an afterlife, or nothing at all: it suffices to let the self rest in itself, right now. Whatever liberation may be, it is definitely different from, and incompatible with, Christian salvation.

But this is a goal not pursued in most American yoga studios. They aim to make singers better singers, caregivers better caregivers, workers better workers. This has been done before: After the Buddhists had familiarized the Chinese with meditation, some Confucians still rejected the Buddhist philosophy of renunciation and liberation, but embraced the practice of meditation, just to 'tune their instrument', to function better in society. You can do this, but it is not the fullness of yoga. Also, all the Western therapeutic adaptations of yoga, as a treatment of physical or mental ailments, are designed to make a defective human being normal; while the original yoga was meant to make normal people liberated. So, by commodifying yoga, Americans are importing something from India, but not the whole package.

Did Ramakrishna Also Practise Other Religions?

Modern anglicized Hindus, both 'secularists' and loyally practising Hindus, are overwhelmingly under the spell of the colonial-age current of thought known as the Bengal Renaissance, sometimes more broadly as the Hindu Revival. A key idea that germinated during this movement and became a mantra under Mahatma Gandhi and an unassailable dogma in secularist India today, is that 'all religions are equally valid', often even 'equally true'. This idea was pioneered within the Kolkata-based Brahmo Samaj, and became the received wisdom among educated Bengalis even before 1900. A case in point was the Ramakrishna (RK) Mission, launched by Ramakrishna's disciple Swami Vivekananda.

Part 1*

When the RK Mission sought recognition as a minority ca. 1990, its central argument for its non-Hindu character was that, unlike Hinduism, it upheld 'equal truth of all religions' and 'equal respect for all religions'. The latter slogan was popularized by Mahatma Gandhi as *sarva-dharma-samabhâva,* a formula officially approved and upheld in the BJP's constitution. In 1983, RK Mission spokesman Swami Lokeshwarananda said: 'Is Ramakrishna only a Hindu? Why did he then worship in the Christian and Islamic

*Published on Hindu Human Rights, 2 August 2013

fashions? He is, in fact, an avatar of all religions, a synthesis of all faiths.'*

The basis of the Swami's claim, as per Swarup, is a story that Swami Vivekananda's guru, Paramahansa Ramakrishna (1836–1886) once, in 1866, dressed up as a Muslim and then continued his spiritual exercises until he had a vision, and likewise as a Christian in 1874. If at all true, these little experiments shouldn't be given too much weight, considering Ramakrishna's general habit of dressing up a little for devotional purposes, e.g. as a woman, to experience Krishna the lover through the eyes of His beloved Radha (not uncommon among Krishna devotees in Vrindavan); or hanging from trees to impersonate Hanuman, worshipped as the monkey god and a close ally of Rama.**

But is the story true? Author Ram Swarup finds that it is absent in the earliest recordings of Ramakrishna's own talks. It first appears in a biography written twenty-five years after Ramakrishna's death by Swami Saradananda,*** who had known the Master only in the last two years of his life. Even then, mention (on just one page in a 1,050-page volume) is only made of a vision of a luminous figure. The next biographer, Swami Nikhilananda, ventures to guess that the figure was 'perhaps Mohammed'. In subsequent versions, this guess became a dead certainty, and that 'vision of Mohammed' became the basis of the doctrine that he spent some time as a Muslim, and likewise as a Christian, and that he 'proved the truth' of those religions by attaining the highest yogic state on those occasions.

It is hard not to sympathize with Swarup's scepticism. In today's cult scene, there are enough wild claims abroad, and it is only right to hold their propagators guilty (of gullibility, if not of deception) until proven innocent. In particular, a group claiming experimental

*Full discussion in Ram Swarup's *The Ramakrishna Mission: In Search of a New Identity*, 1986

**Ibid

***Swami Saradananda. *Sri Ramakrishna: The Great Master*, Sri Ramakrishna Math Chennai, 2011

verification of a religious truth claim as the unique achievement of its founder, should not be let off without producing that verification here and now. Shady claims about an insufficiently attested event more than a century ago will not do. It is entirely typical of the psychology behind this myth-making that a researcher can make such claims. Neither Swami Vivekananda, nor any other monk known to the author, ever carried out his own experiments. They all accepted the truth of all religions on the basis of their master's work. This is the familiar pattern of the followers of a master who are too mediocre to try for themselves that which they consider is the basis of the master's greatness, but who do not hesitate to make claims of superiority for their sect on that same (untested, hearsay) basis.

WAS RAMAKRISHNA A MUSLIM? OR A CHRISTIAN?

For some more polemical comment, let us look into one typical pamphlet by a Hindu upholding the Hindu character of the Ramakrishna Mission: *The Lullaby of Sarva-Dharma-Samabhâva* by Siva Prasad Ray (included as chapter 7 of his book *Turning of the Wheel*, Houston 1985). The doctrine of 'equal respect for all religions' (in fact, even a more radical version, 'equal truth of all religions') is one of the attributes claimed by the RK Mission as setting it apart from Hinduism.

This doctrine is propagated by many English-speaking gurus, and one of its practical effects is that Hindu girls in Westernized circles (including those in overseas Hindu communities) who fall in love with Muslims feel justified in disobeying their unpleasantly surprised parents, and often taunt them: 'What is the matter if I marry a Muslim and your grandchildren become Muslims? Don't these babas to whom you give your devotion and money always say that all religions teach the same thing, that Islam is as good as Hinduism, that Allah and Shiva are one and the same?'

When such marriages last (many end in early divorce), a Hindu or Western environment often leads to the ineffectiveness of the formal conversion of the Hindu partner to Islam, so the children are not raised as Muslims. Yet, Islamic law seems to impose on the Muslim partner the duty to see to this, and in a Muslim environment, there is no escape from this Islamizing pressure. Thus, after the Meenakshipuram mass conversion to Islam in 1981, non-converted villagers reported to the effect that there had been marriages between Hindu harijans and the converts. Whether it was the bride or the groom, the Hindu was expected to convert to Islam.*

Even when the conversion is an ineffective formality, such marriages or elopements which trumpet the message that Hindu identity is unimportant and dispensable do have an unnerving effect on vulnerable Hindu communities in non-Hindu environments. They also remain an irritant to Hindus in India, as here to writer Siva Prasad Ray. More generally, the doctrine that all religions are the same leaves Hindus intellectually defenceless before the challenge of communities with more determination to uphold and propagate their religions.

To counter the facile conclusion that Ramakrishna had practised Christianity and Islam and proven their truth, Ray points out that Ramakrishna was neither baptized nor circumcised, that he is not known to have affirmed the Christian or Islamic creed. Likewise, he failed to observe Ramzan or Lent, he never took Christian or Islamic marriage vows with his wife, and he never frequented churches or mosques. This objection is entirely valid: Thinking about Christ or reading some Islamic book is not enough to be a Christian or a Muslim.

Equally to the point, he argues: 'Avatar' or incarnation may be acceptable to Hinduism but such is not the case in Islam or Christianity. In Christianity, one might say that the notion of divine

---

*Reported Mass Conversion of Harijans to Islam in Tamil Nadu and other parts of the country and the reaction of the Government of India thereto, accessed 8 April 2019, http://rsdebate.nic.in/rsdebate56/bitstream/123456789/384004/1/PD_119_15091981_22_p241_p353_7.pdf

incarnation does exist, but it applies exclusively to Jesus Christ; applying it to Ramakrishna is plain heresy. Sitting down for mental concentration to obtain a 'vision' of Christ or Prophet Mohammed is definitely not part of the required practices of Christianity or Islam. Neither religion has a notion of 'salvation' as something to be achieved by practising certain states of consciousness. In other words: Before you claim to have an agreement with other people, check with them whether they really agree.

The same objection is valid against claims that Swami Vivekananda was 'also' a Muslim. As Kundrakudi Adigalar, the forty-fifth head of the Kundrakudi Tiruvannamalai Adhinam in Tamil Nadu, has said: 'He had faith and confidence in Hinduism. But he was not a follower of Hinduism alone. He practised all religions. He read all books. His head bowed before all prophets.' But 'practising all religions' is quite incompatible with being a faithful Christian or a Muslim: As the Church fathers taught, syncretism is typical of pagan culture (today, it is called the 'New Age').

Leaving aside polytheistic Hinduism, the mere attempt to practise both Islam and Christianity, if such a thing were possible, would have stamped Ramakrishna as definitely not a Christian, nor a Muslim. Moreover, it is simply untrue that Swami Vivekananda ever 'practised' Christianity or Islam: He was not baptized or circumcised, did not attend Church services or Friday prayers, never went to Mecca, never observed Ramzan or Lent. But he did practise vegetarianism (at least in principle) and celibacy. Worst of all, he did worship Hindu gods, which by definition puts him outside the Islamic fold, Islam being based on the rejection of all gods except Allah.

Ramakrishna was quite satisfied worshipping Goddess Kali, but as Ray says: 'There is no respectful place for deities in female form in Islam. Rama Krishna engaged in the worship of Kali was nothing but an idolater in the eyes of the Muslims. Islam says that all idolaters will finally end up in Islam's hell. Now, I want to ask these eggheads of *sarva-dharma-samabhâva* if they know where exactly the place for Ramakrishna in Islam is? The fact is that Ramakrishna never truly worshipped in the Islamic fashion, neither did he receive Islamic salvation.'

Ray challenges the RK Mission monks to try out their assertions on a Muslim or a Christian audience: 'All this is, thus, nothing but creations of confused and boisterous Hindu monks. No Christian padre or Muslim maulvi accepts Ramakrishna's salvation in their own religions. They make snide remarks. They laugh at the ignorance of the Hindu monks.'

Ray makes the snide insinuation explicit: 'Only those Hindus who do not understand the implications of other religions engage themselves in the propagation of *sarva-dharma-samabhâva*; like stupid and mentally retarded creatures, such Hindus revel in the pleasures of auto-erotism in their wicked pursuit of the fad.' This rude comparison means that they pretend to be interacting with others, but it is a mere fantasy, all inside their own heads, with the assumed partners not even knowing about it.

Finally, Ray wonders what happened to the monks, those of the RK Mission and others, who talked about 'equal truth of all religions' and chanted 'Râm Rahîm ek hai' ('Rama and Rahim/ Allah are one') and 'Ishwar Allâh tere nâm' ('both Ishwar and Allah are Your names') in East Bengal before 1947. As far as he knew, they had all fled across the new border when they suddenly found themselves inside Pakistan, but then he said: 'Many a guru from East Bengal (who) has been saved by the skin of his teeth, once in West Bengal, resumed his talk of *sarva-dharma-samabâva*. But the point still remains that if they really had faith in the message of *sarva-dharma-samabhâva*, they would not have left East Bengal.' As so often in Indo-Pakistani and Hindu-Muslim comparisons, the argument is reminiscent of the inequality between the contenders in the Cold War: you could demonstrate for disarmament in the West, but to demonstrate for this in the East Bloc (except if it were for unilateral disarmament by the Western 'war-mongers') would have put you in trouble.

'ALL RELIGIONS' VS THE ETERNAL RELIGION

Ray also mocks the RK Mission's grandiose claim of having evaluated not just a few popular religions, but all religions. 'Did Ramakrishna ever worship in accordance with Sikh, Buddhist, Jain, Saurya or Ganapatya principles? No, he did not. Neither did he worship in accordance with the Jewish faith of Palestine, the Tao religion of China, the religion of Confucius, or the Shinto religion of Japan. Empirically verifying the truth of each and every religion is a valid project in principle, but a very time-consuming one as well.'

According to Ray, the slogan of 'equal truth of all religions' is nothing but a watered-down sentiment that means nothing. It is useful only in widening the route to our self-destruction. It does not take a genius to realize that not all paths are good paths in this life of ours; this is true in all branches of human activity. Unlike the RK Mission monks, Ray has really found some common ground with other religions, and with rationalism too: They all agree on the logical principle that contradictory truth claims cannot possibly all be right—at most one of them can be right.

To sum up, Ray alleges that the RK Mission stoops to a shameful level of self-deception and ridicule, that it distorts the message of Ramakrishna, the Kali-worshipping Hindu, and that it distorts the heritage of Swami Vivekananda, the Hindu revivalist. Yet, none of this alleged injustice to Hinduism gives the Mission a place outside Hinduism. After all, there is no definition of 'Hindu' which precludes Hindus from being mistaken, self-deluding or suicidal. Regardless of its fanciful innovations, the RK Mission remains a Hindu organization, at least by any of the available objective definitions. Alternatively, if the subjective definition, 'Is Hindu he and only he who calls himself "Hindu"', is accepted, then of course the RK Mission, unlike its founders, is no longer Hindu—but then it is no longer Ramakrishna's mission either.

The larger issue revealed by the incident with the RK Mission is a psychology of self-repudiation which is fairly widespread in the anglicized segment of Hindu society, stretching from actual repudiation of Hinduism to the distortive reformulation of Hinduism itself after the model of better-reputed religions. In a typical symptom of the colonial psychology, many Hindus see themselves through the eyes of their once-dominant enemies, so that catechism-type books on Hinduism explain Hinduism in Christian terms, e.g. by presenting many a Hindu saint as a 'Christ-like figure'. Modern translations of Hindu scriptures are often distorted to satisfy non-Hindu requirements such as monotheism. This can take quite gross forms in the *Veda* translations of the Arya Samaj, where entire sentences are inserted to twist the meaning in the required theological direction. (For example, the Houston Arya Samaj website translates the *Gayatri Mantra* thus: 'The literal meaning of the mantra is: "O God! You are Omnipresent, Omnipotent and Almighty. You are all Light. You are all Knowledge and Bliss. You are Destroyer of fear, You are Creator of this Universe, You are the Greatest of all. We bow and meditate upon Your light. You guide our intellect in the right direction."'* Sentences 2 to 4 are nowhere in the Sanskrit original.) The eagerness to extol all rival religions and be unsatisfied with just being Hindu is one more symptom of the contempt in which Hinduism has been held for centuries, and which numerous Hindus have interiorized.

In Ramakrishna's words: 'Various creeds you hear about nowadays have come into existence through the will of God and will disappear again through His will. Hindu religion alone is Sanâtana dharma', for it 'has always existed and will always exist.'

Part 2**

RKM IS HINDU

One person scolded me for even thinking that the Ramakrishna Mission is non-Hindu. He cites the Hindu atmosphere and the many

---

*https://www.aryasamajhouston.org/resources/articals/veda-sudha/scientific-meaning-of-gayatri-mantra

**Published on Hindu Human Rights, 17 August 2013

Hindu rituals and practices at the Mission centres. I might add the fact that the Mission only recruits among Hindus. No Christian or Muslim would join this pagan outfit. That fact alone refutes the Mission's own claim that it has somehow embraced all religions. The Mission is a typically Hindu group, and even its pompous claim of validating all world religions is a claim made by many Hindus. When Mahatma Gandhi said: 'I am a Hindu, I am a Muslim, I am a Sikh, I am a Christian', Mohammed Ali Jinnah dryly commented: 'That is a typically Hindu thing to say.'

But I am surprised to hear that the Ramakrishna Mission has not disclaimed Hinduism. Not only has the organization shouted from the rooftops and on all kinds of public forums that 'universal Ramakrishnaism' is superior to 'narrow Hinduism', it has even gone to court to be officially recognized as a non-Hindu minority.*

LOGIC

Then there were some who, expectedly, took the opposite position, viz. that the RKM follows its saint Ramakrishna in embracing non-Hindu religions and their founders. One of these, by a self-proclaimed Ramakrishnaite, deserves a closer and more detailed reply. Not that he had said much beyond several lengthy e-mails full of personal abuse. He belonged to a type I have become sadly familiar with on the Internet: born Hindus who muster endless argumentation, often cleverly twisting issues and deploying a sophisticated discourse, all to defend a case that is downright silly and, moreover, harmful to Hinduism.

For instance, I've had to face endless argumentation in favour of the belief that Jesus lived and died in India. This belief stems from the 1894 book *La Vie Inconnue de Jésus-Christ* ('The Unknown Life of Jesus Christ') by the Russian aristocrat Nicolas Notovitch,

*It lost in this bid with the 1995 SC verdict ruling the RK Mission to be 'Hindu', as reported in *Hinduism Today,* https://www.hinduismtoday.com/modules/smartsection/item.php?itemid=4427

who claimed to have found notes about Jesus's stay in India in a monastery in the Himalayas. This manuscript was never found and the monastery's abbot denied ever having had or seen such a text. The contents of the text, which Notovitch claimed to have seen, were also very suspect: The themes of Jesus's alleged controversies with Brahmins are typical for the late-colonial age, not at all for the first century.

In the present case too, we have a learned display of rhetoric in the service of an illusion. Of course, our RK follower doesn't try to prove his claim. Either this claim has not been proven, as we maintain, or it has been. In the latter case, it would be well worth the extra trouble to spell out this proof clearly, once and for all. But, alas, this proof is not forthcoming. According to Ram Swarup's booklet, this proof is *not* that according to a second person, RK had 'had a vision', then according to a third person years later, this vision was 'perhaps of Mohammed', and according to a fourth person, later again, it is dead certain that he 'saw Mohammed'. For the founding moment of a religion, 'Ramakrishnaism', one is entitled to expect proof of a higher quality than testimony at several removes.

Even if this very flaky and very suspect sequence were to convey the truth, such a 'vision' would in no way be what the RKM now claims, viz. the 'practice' of Islam/Christianity. As a Muslim commented, you cannot take a holiday and be a Muslim for a while, then revert to goddess-worshipping. Neither Christianity nor Islam consist in having a 'vision' of their founder.

Nonetheless, this RKM sympathizer's reformulation of the challenge to non-Ramakrishaites is interesting: 'The scope of my discussion is quite limited and is focused on only one thing: Ramakrishna believed in the divinity of Jesus Christ and he did practise some discipline of Christianity, on the results of which his belief was based. The same can be said of his feeling for some discipline of Islam—that he practised it and derived divine/spiritual satisfaction from it. I think it is for Koenraad Elst to spell out his clear position on this observation once and for all.'

As a matter of walking the extra mile, I will spell out my position. However, let it be understood that I am under no obligation to explain anything or give proof for anything, as I am not putting forward any claim. I am merely sceptical of a claim made by the RKM and this fellow. Because it is he who has put forward a claim, it is up to him to prove his point. Even if nobody comes forward to offer any kind of counter-proof or refutation, the mere fact that the claim is put forward does not annul its need for proof. As long as the claim is not proven, it is right for sterling Hindus like Ram Swarup and Siva Prasad Ray to express scepticism of it. The burden of proof is 100 per cent on the maker of this challenge.

BELIEF IN JESUS

Now, my position. If Ramakrishna had found that his own Hinduism was insufficient, if he had founded a new religion, which the RKM calls Ramakrishnaism, if RK had found Christianity and Islam to be 'part' of this new religion and if he had personally 'verified the truth' of these religions by means of 'visions', then this would be such a momentous revolution that he would have spent the rest of his days discussing and elaborating on it. Instead, there was absolute silence, and Kali. So this already pleads against the RKM's claim.

Now that we are discussing this, it strikes me that in the twenty-four years that I have followed this debate, I have not seen the RKM come up with an actual quote from the master in which he claims Jesus's divinity. Surely, such belief would have been big news to his Hindu and non-Christian followers. Our critic, too, has eloquently beaten around the bush in several replies and has spurned the occasion to present to us the only thing that would finish this debate, viz. proof (as opposed to mere claims) that RK worshipped Jesus as a divine being. The best proof would be a statement to this effect by RK himself, but this time, too, it is not forthcoming.

But to really evaluate Ramakrishna's beliefs about Jesus, it would be useful (from a scholarly viewpoint) to get the facts straight about Jesus himself. I have not brought Jesus into this discussion, it is the RKM (from Swamis Saradananda and Nikhilananda, cited by Ram Swarup below) that insists Ramakrishna had a vision of Jesus and believed in Jesus's divinity. So let's discuss Jesus. But let me warn you: Hindus by their upbringing may know everything about puja or other Hindu things, but their knowledge of Jesus tends to be very hazy. I, having gone through the whole Catholic education system and, moreover, having made a purposeful study of the character Jesus, know more about this subject than the RKM sympathizer will ever know in his lifetime.

I have studied Jesus, he has not. That is not some colonial utterance—in fact, two Hindus sceptical of the RKM claims set me on this path—but it is simply a fact that someone who has assimilated the scholarly findings on Jesus knows the subject better than religious types who have only interiorized some missionary sermons calculated to fool a gullible audience. Conversely, Hindus who have not made a specific study of comparative religion, and especially of Christianity, are ill-equipped to pontificate about Jesus.

So, what I know about Jesus is that he was no more divine than you or me. He was a wandering healer, with his ears open for the wisdom going around, which he relayed in his own *logia*, sermons with parables—a few of them good—but still revered by the people mostly because of his reputation as a healer. To be sure, his friends and relatives, who knew him, saw through his act, which is why he performed no 'miracles' in his hometown (Matthew 13:57, Mark 6:16, Luke 4:1-24). Elsewhere, he could often pull them off, but still he was less powerful than proper medicine would have been. Thus, he healed someone of epilepsy (deemed ghost possession, e.g. Mark 9:14-29, Matthew 17:14-20, Luke 9:42), making him rise after his epileptic seizure—but such fits always subside and end in a return to normalcy. And in one case, the gospel says in so many words that the disease later reappeared (Matthew 12:3-45). There's nothing scandalous, but nothing divine either, about false beliefs in healing powers.

Jesus had what I would consider a rather big idea about himself, just like Prophet Mohammed and some other religious leaders. Thus, he believed that he was the Messiah. He repeatedly made the prediction that he would return within the lifetime of some in his audience (Matthew 16:27-28; 24:25-34; 26:63-64; Mark 13:26-30; Luke 21:27-32; John 16:16). Today we are 2,000 years and dozens of generations down the line, yet Jesus has not come back. Now, wrong predictions are human—in fact, they are ten a penny. Jehovah's Witnesses put their feet between your front door to predict the end of the world, but it didn't come in 1914, nor in 1975.

But at least Jesus overcame death by his resurrection. This is the core of the Christian belief system. Now, the difference between the living and the dead is that you can run into the living, not into the dead. But, like the dead, Jesus is beyond meeting. People have reported 'seeing' Jesus in visions, but no one has met him in person. So his condition is the same as that of other mortals. The wages of the original sin are mortality and childbearing in pain, and it would be somewhat divine if Jesus had overcome mortality to live endlessly and still be among us. But no, he's gone. The New Testament writers have spirited him away through the trick of the 'Ascension'. Though somewhat spectacular, he did the same thing as the rest of us mortals: he went to heaven. So, nothing particularly divine about mortality.

I have said enough to underpin the conclusion: Jesus was not divine. If Ramakrishna was a Muslim, as the RKM claims, then he was already convinced of Jesus's non-divine status, which is a basic belief of Islam (and in that respect, Islam is more rational than the cult of personality that I believe Christianity is). If, however, as our RKM sympathizer claims, RK believed in the divinity of Christ, then he was badly informed, not to say that he was mistaken.

In fact, this sympathizer wants you to venerate a gullible Ramakrishna who believed the sob stories of the missionaries, to the point of self-hypnotizing and seeing a vision of Jesus. By contrast, I (or rather Swarup and Ray) give you a Ramakrishna who was discerning enough to keep the missionaries at a distance.

He was not a Christian, nor a Ramakrishnaist, but simply a Hindu, worshipping Krishna and Hanuman and, most of all, Kali. You, too, can live a happy, healthy, holy life while staying a Hindu and ignoring Jesus.

BEING A CHRISTIAN

The second claim is that Ramakrishna 'practised a Christian discipline', and that, as a result, he found that Christianity is equally true and yields the same results that he had already reached through his Hindu sadhana. Now, 'being a Christian' or 'being a Muslim' has a precise definition, which RK did not fulfil. He was not recognized as one of theirs by any known maulvi or padre. The missionaries sent bulletins home, in which they reported the conversions they had achieved—surely they would not have neglected reporting the Christianization of a leading Hindu saint? And the RKM has had more than a century to get and show the document that proved their case, viz. that Ramakrishna turned his back on 'narrow Hinduism'.

Even in the different sects of Hinduism, you only become a member by going through a formal ceremony. You are given a yajnopavit (sacred thread) or you get diksha (initiation) or shaktipat (transmission of energy). Ramakrishna never went through the formal ceremonies making him a Christian or a Muslim. He was not circumcised and never uttered the Islamic creed. He was not baptized and never uttered the Christian creed. No matter what vision he had, it did not make him either Christian or Muslim.

Further, there is no such thing as 'practising' Christianity or Islam. Either you are in or you are out. Imitating the behaviour of a Muslim/Christian all while remaining pagan does not make you a Muslim/Christian. In fact, we would like to know what these practices were. Our RKM sympathizer has repeatedly spurned the occasion to spell this out. Did RK observe Ramadan, or did he prefer Lent? Did this vegetarian offer sheep sacrifice, as is prescribed for Muslims? Did he eat fish on Friday, as Catholics do? Did he condemn caste, which is an intrinsic attitude of Christianity, at least according to contemporary missionaries? And again, was he baptized? Which worthy Christian accepted him as a Christian? We would like some straight answers to these questions.

Not that they would make any tangible difference. Ramakrishna may have been pure gold, but even his acceptance of the quintessential Christian belief in Jesus's divinity would not make Jesus divine—at least not more than you and me. If, after all these years, the RKM were at last to prove that Ramakrishna did worship Jesus, we would have to conclude that he was mistaken—surely not the conclusion the RKM would like us to draw. Fortunately, there is no indication that he did.

SOME FURTHER PROBLEMS WITH THE RKM'S CLAIM

Another problem: A Christian cannot be a Muslim, and a Muslim cannot be a Christian. Leaving aside Hinduism and 'Ramakrishnaism', please focus only on Christianity and Islam. How could Ramakrishna be a Christian while also being a Muslim? No Christian or Muslim authority would accept his being one while also being the other. Christians believe Jesus was the son of God, both God and man, while Muslims consider him just a man. Christians believe he was resurrected, while Muslims disbelieve that he even died on the cross. How did RK combine these mutually exclusive beliefs?

Finally, RK is known to have died while worshipping Kali. By Christian and Islamic definition, he was a goddess-worshipper, hence an out-and-out pagan. If he ever was a Muslim or a Christian, his dying as a pagan meant that he was an apostate. If being an ignorant pagan is bad enough, being a wilful apostate, who has known but rejected the truth and reverted to the false belief of paganism, is demonic and a sure ticket to the fires of hell. So, according to the RKM, RK has spent the last century braving the fires of hell. For that is what Islam and Christianity (which the RKM holds to be 'true') promise to a pagan like Ramakrishna.

The RKM professes a syncretism, combining elements of different religions. Ramakrishnaism is a syncretism par excellence, affirming 'all' religions to be true. As the Church fathers wrote, syncretism is typical of paganism; and as the numerous interreligious as well as intra-Christian persecutions of even very slightly different doctrines show, Christianity was by contrast very intolerant of doctrinal pluralism. The Roman-Hellenistic milieu in which the first Christians had to function was full of syncretism, with Roman matrons worshipping Isis with the babe Horus (an inspiration for the image of Mary holding the babe Jesus), legion soldiers worshipping Persian-originated Mithras, and imperial politicians worshipping the Syrian-originated Sol Invictus, the invincible sun. Against this syncretism, the Church fathers preached religious purity*: extra ecclesiam nulla salus* (outside the Church, there is no salvation). They had no problem admitting that paganism was naturally pluralistic, but, they reasoned, what is the use of choosing between or combining different kinds of falsehood?

They, as Christians, had something better than pluralism, viz. the truth. And once you have the truth, you are no longer interested in any other religion. So from the Christian viewpoint, the RKM's dissatisfaction with 'mere' Hinduism is an admission that Hinduism doesn't have the truth.

SWAMI VIVEKANANDA'S CLAIM

The best argument in favour of the RKM's claim is a statement apparently made by Swami Vivekananda. According to our correspondent: 'The next desire that seized upon the soul of this man (RK) was to know the truth about the various religions. Up to that time he had not known any religion but his own. He wanted to understand what other religions were like. So he sought teachers of other religions. (...) He found a Mohammedan saint and placed himself under him; he underwent the disciplines prescribed by him, and to his astonishment found that when faithfully carried out, these devotional methods led him to the same goal he had already attained. He gathered similar experience from following the true religion of Jesus the Christ.'

Our RKM sympathizer wants to 'point (out) to KE that the burden of proof is on him to disprove the observations of RK's chief disciple (and official spokesman?), as otherwise, by default, they should be assumed to be true. (...) Would KE care to share his compelling reasons to believe that SV lied?'

Once again, he has got things backwards. It is he who makes a claim, and the burden of proof is thus 100 per cent on him. Swami Vivekananda was not an eyewitness and made this statement (which I will, for now, assume to be genuine; Ram Swarup was a great reader of Swami Vivekananda's *Complete Works* and doesn't mention it even when discussing such claims), many years after the fact. Nothing of the above loses any of its force by this early version of a claim later made into the official line of the RKM, but for which any proof is missing.

It is no surprise that somebody ignorant of the rules of logic should use an 'argument of authority' as his trump card. He plays upon the expected indignation of the Indian-born majority of the readership if I dare to say that Swami Vivekananda 'lied'. But, in fact, I don't need to put it down as a 'lie'. In the world of religion and the occult, I have rarely seen anyone who deliberately said something that he knew to be untrue. But I have met or witnessed or read thousands of people who spread falsehoods which they believed to be true.

Even Swami Vivekananda was just a fallible human being—a statement which may scandalize his followers but which he himself would wholeheartedly accept. The processes that have led the RKM to believe and propagate the falsehood about Ramakrishna's visions may have taken him in too. Or he may simply mean that Ramakrishna had that commendable Hindu attitude of curiosity and respect for whatever other religions drew his attention. At any rate, while we don't know which processes were at work in Vivekananda's case, we have his naked statement and this, at least, we can evaluate. And I find it, if taken literally, to be simply false.

'Liberation', the goal of the Upanishadic seers and most Hindu schools since, is not the (or even a) goal of Christianity. No Christian ever claimed to have achieved it, nor was any Christian claimed by fellow-Christian observers to have done so. The case applies even more bluntly to Islam: The goal of the five pillars of Islam is simply to obey Allah's commandments as given in the *Quran*, not any 'Liberation'.

The goal of a Hindu sadhana will not be achieved by a Muslim or a Christian 'sadhana', and vice versa. If someone said that a Christian discipline 'led him to the same goal he had already attained', he was most certainly wrong. However, it is possible that the state of consciousness that Ramakrishna had already attained in his Hindu sadhana remained with him when he practised whatever the Muslim master who is claimed to have taught Ramakrishna gave him to do. But would that state still be so easily achieved if he had practised *only* these Islamic or Christian exercises?

CONCLUSION

Sita Ram Goel once said that 'Hindus think they know everything about everything'. Thus, while it is hard enough to study a handful of religions, numerous Hindus routinely make claims about the equal truth of 'all' religions, as if they had studied them all. In this respect, at least, the RKM monks are certainly Hindus.

The RKM's ambition to outgrow Hinduism and be 'universal' is a form of hubris. In Greek religion, hubris, or man's will to be equal to the gods, is the cardinal sin. In Christianity too, Adam and Eve committed hereditary sin, not by lust (as many superficial people think) but by hubris: Initially innocent creatures, they wanted to be equal to God, who knows good and evil. In this respect, at least, many (it would be hubris to assert 'all') religions agree—and they happen to be right. So let us stop this bad habit of making claims about 'all' religions, including those that we know only hazily or not at all. One thing that initially attracted me to the Hindu cause was the humbleness and simplicity of the ordinary Hindus I met. It would be nice if all megalomaniacs climbed down from their high horses and rediscovered this simplicity.

Secondly, I find it sad and not spelling anything good that Hindus who are so laid-back about the enemies of and the challenges before Hinduism get so worked up when their own little sect is challenged. I think Arya Samaj spokesmen don't have 1 per cent of their forebears' concern with the Christian and Islamic threats, but they really get into the act when defending against other Hindus their pet beliefs about Vedic monotheism and non-idolatry.

The ISKCON people, I believe, never confront Christianity or Islam, but they get really nasty against fellow Hindus who are not as Krishna-centred (such as the pre-Krishna Vedic rishis) as they themselves are. And here, too, the RKM is alarmed when some Hindus disbelieve its pet doctrine of Ramakrishna's visions of Jesus and Mohammed. It would be good if they shed this obsession with their sectarian 'unique selling proposition' and return to a broader consciousness, one that would be recognizable to all Hindus.

Hinduism existed before Jesus and Mohammed. It was good enough for the Vedic seers and non-Vedic sadhus, and it didn't need those two. I think Hinduism will only survive if it forgets about this version of Ramakrishna. The RKM ultimately has no choice but to admit that for the past so many decades, it has been spreading an erroneous and harmful belief—the divinity of Christ and Mohammed, and the 'equal truth' of Christianity and Islam. It should announce out loud that all struggles over its exact identity are over, because it owns up to its natural Hindu identity. Indeed, it should rediscover and second its founder, Swami Vivekananda, who declared: 'Say with pride, we are Hindus!'

Aum In or Out for International Yoga Day?*

As a member of the Yogafederatie der Nederlandstaligen in België, or the 'Yoga Federation of the Dutch-Speakers in Belgium', I received a copy of the booklet the Government of India issued for the United Nations' first Yoga Day. It falls on 21 June, Summer Solstice, a day of mixed feelings: It is the longest day alright, but it is also the start of the Sun's decline—the converse of the beginning of the Sun's rise on Winter Solstice, considered a reason for celebration.

Now the booklet. It has a non-traditional drawing on the front page, and as was widely expected, no Aum sign is included anywhere in the logo. Not too important in itself, but significant when it comes to the mindset of the dominant faction within the ruling government: to appease a certain section of society. In the secular worldview, India is a neutral entity, and its government has no business promoting Hindu traditions such as Aum, the first word of the *Rig Veda*. As we know, the *Vedas* mention neither Christ nor Mohammed, let alone Macaulay or Marx, so it was a communalist book denying the minorities a place in the sun. There you have it: a secular taboo rests on the Aum sign.

I noted this in a message on social media, and prompt came the reply from the Indian Embassy in Belgium: Please look at the prayer on p.9, it has the Aum sign at the beginning of the Devanagari text. Even people who can't read Devanagari, like most Western practitioners of yoga, will recognize the Aum sign.

*Published on Hindu Human Rights, 15 May 2015

Indeed, Western yogis are very used to the Aum sign and adorn their halls and clothes and front pages with it. They don't know any better than that this is the sign of yoga, and have no suspicion about the sinister communal reputation it has acquired among the various anti-Hindu lobbies in India. And though they would have expected an Aum sign on this brochure (of all places), they won't suspect that the brochure writers have omitted it out of ideological compulsions.

So they had not entirely omitted it: It appears in a prayer they had copy-pasted in the brochure. Alright, that is something: They didn't censor the prayer. Just imagine Christians printing the Lord's Prayer without any mention of the Lord. The good thing about it is that at least the brochure contains a prayer, a sign of yoga's embeddedness in a not-to-be-named culture. So, for Hindus, there is a consolation prize: The link with Hinduism (of which the Aum sign serves as a token) is in the brochure, though tucked away in the small print on an inside page.

For the secularists, this would still make the brochure into a no-no. Hindus try hard to be secular and efface their own culture, but they should try harder.

So what has the BJP-controlled government of India achieved by engineering the brochure the way it did? For the secularists and minorities, it remains government promotion for a Hindu practice, ill-concealed by a non-Hindu logo. For the Hindus, it turns out to be a disappointment: The first Yoga Day, moreover under what is widely considered a Hindu nationalist government, should have been an occasion for showing the world just what Hindu civilization has contributed to it. Instead, Hindu civilization is pushed out of the picture and falsely delinked from yoga.

And all for nothing: There is nothing threatening about the Aum sign for the minorities, no genuinely secular purpose is achieved by this manipulation, except for the further deconstruction of Hinduism.

In my opinion, this is the real goal of the lobbies that swear by 'secularism': the annihilation of Hinduism. Those who thought the

BJP was aggressively pro-Hindu will be surprised to learn that the BJP is supporting this project. The result is that the BJP is having the worst of both worlds: It surely manages to displease its Hindu constituents, and it still fails to please its secularist masters.

I am aware of the laws of diplomacy, which are different from the laws of logic. Sometimes it is necessary to make a compromise; to concede something in order to acquire something else. In that case, it would have been defensible if yoga had been promoted at the cost of a mere sign, not even present for yoga masters living in Himalayan caves or for Vedic seers practising an oral culture and doing without the stylized alphabet signs that have made up the classical Aum sign.

But that is not the case here: The present brochure is still too Hindu for the secularists, is Hindu in spite of itself, and is at the same time uninspiring for Hindus, desirous of a proud self-assertion. Like so much in Hindu nationalist discourse, it is neither here nor there.

Is Yoga Hindu? The Question at Face Value*

Part of the secularist project is to belittle Hinduism: Anything Indian that is bad or deemed to be bad is blamed on Hinduism, whereas anything good or deemed good is delinked from Hinduism. Since yoga has been embraced in the West and threatens to give Hinduism a good name, a lot is invested in proving that 'yoga is not Hindu'.

A much-discussed topic in the context of cultural appropriation is whether 'yoga is Hindu'. The argument is so heated because Westerners often aggressively argue that yoga is separate from Hinduism, so that Hindus cannot lay claim to it and have no say when foreigners allegedly distort it. In reply, the Hindu American Foundation has waged a campaign to 'take back yoga'.

In this argument, much of the history of yoga is trotted out, mainly to deny that it ever was Hindu in the first place. About modern postural yoga, developed by Tirumalai Krishnamacharya, it is asserted (David Gordon White, Mark Singleton) that it owes more to British army drills than to tradition. Yet, many exercises are from the well-attested hatha yoga repertoire dating back to ca. the eleventh century. This tradition, in turn, starts against the background of the introduction of the notion of Kundalini, not older than AD 400, and the concomitant need to remove 'energy

*Talk by the author in Ghent, Belgium, on the occasion of the first UN Yoga Day, celebrated worldwide on 21 June 2014

blockages' in the spine by means of postures and breathing techniques. There are strong indications, starting in Joseph Needham's famous research, that this innovation itself owes a lot to the Chinese tradition of 'internal alchemy' (Neidan, a system of breathing and physical exercises linked with Chinese medicine), more than 2,500 years old, or centuries older than the birth of Kundalini in India. An early case of 'cultural appropriation', so to speak.

However, these colourful and headline-friendly forms of yoga are only a supplement that came to enrich the heart of yoga, which itself was already attested since Harappa, ca. -2500. A number of Harappan seals depict yogis in meditation, though never in hatha yogic contortions. Yoga as meditation is already described in the *Bhagavad Gita* and the *Katha Upanishad*, up to -1000. There is absolutely no indication that they ever got this fundamental doctrine and practice of yoga anywhere else. And even if they had done so, it would still make yoga a central part of Hindu civilization for far longer than, say, the matrioshkas (of Korean provenance) have become proverbially Russian.

Then you can further argue that any culture this early cannot be called 'Hindu' because the word didn't exist yet. True, it is a late exonym stemming from the Persian for 'Indian', but it has always, and especially since the Muslim invasions introduced this Persian term in India, referred to precisely the native culture that distinguished its practitioners from the Muslims and other outsiders. This predated the word, which came to designate a culture that already existed, and that is indeed continuous with ancient Indian culture. At this point, we must highlight Nick Allen's finding (in his pathbreaking article 'The Indo-European Origins of Yoga', *International Journal of Hindu Studies* 2 (1):1-20, 1998) that cognate myths and literary motifs in the Greek and Indian epics differ by having a yogic component in the Indian but not in the Greek version.

The ancient link of yoga with Hindu culture is simply a fact. But that doesn't imply it is not meant for outsiders to that culture. Indeed, the reincarnation doctrine implies that people who have thoroughly imbibed the yoga tradition may take birth within a different culture, and yet be destined to continue their yogic path. This partly explains why Hindu and related teachers (including Sikh, Tibetan Buddhist and Lingayat) have fairly smoothly accepted Western disciples, have started coming to the West and even adapted their teachings to (what they assumed to be) Western sensitivities. Some of these disciples have become masters in their own right, and the indigenization of yoga in most countries is in full swing. The problematization of Western yoga has come about not as a second thought in the minds of gurus, but in circles of non-resident Indians and people of Indian origin.

The reason why they didn't like what they saw of the Western 'digestion' (as author Rajiv Malhotra calls it) of yoga is what they perceived as disrespect to yoga itself and to its origins in a Hindu milieu. Disrespect to yoga is, for example, its mixing with Western psychotherapies (themselves often borrowed Indian techniques and insights in disguise, such as transpersonal psychology), its mixing with hedonism (e.g. naked yoga practice), and its use for more mundane purposes (such as to control high blood pressure, for relaxation and for better concentration on one's job) than to reach awakening. Disrespect for Hindu origins is found in their very concealment, for example, by translating the Sanskrit names of exercises, by the denial of their assumed philosophical background or even the latter's replacement with non-Hindu worldviews, for example 'Christian yoga'. These demanding Hindus form an unexpected de facto alliance with purist Christians who recognize yoga as intrinsically un-Christian, just as many (not all) Muslim authorities reject it as un-Islamic.

Though anyone can take the airplane, and though this invention was never meant for the exclusive use by the Wright brothers' fellow countrymen, it is irrevocably an American invention. This should not endlessly be repeated, but it should not be denied either; and many Hindus think that this is now increasingly happening with yoga. A slippery slope leading to this 'digestion' is the assertion by the leading yogi Jaggi Vasudev that 'yoga is not more Hindu than that Isaac Newton's law of gravity is Christian'. This papers over a fundamental difference: The discovery of physical laws is not dependent on a Christian background (see Archimedes' law, Euclid's theorems, the Indian numerals, the Chinese discovery of magnetism, etc.), whereas the discovery of yoga is at least more favoured by some cultures than by others. Indeed, it is naturally in conflict with Christianity, which can accept hatha yoga as a physical discipline on a par with gymnastics but imperatively links salvation with baptism and belief in Christ, not with the mere 'funny feeling' triggered by yoga practice.

So the situation is that many so-called 'moron swamis' welcome this 'digestion' (with Western culture as the tiger swallowing the goat and thereby strengthening itself), allegedly because they have little discernment and because they enjoy being flattered by the interest Westerners take in their 'product'. If Hindus denounce the 'cultural appropriation' of yoga, you can immediately cite a great many fellow Hindus who approve of it and cooperate with it.

My conclusion can't be black and white. As a historical fact, the 'Hindu' origin of yoga is, in our present state of knowledge and with the necessary qualifications about the meaning of the term 'Hindu', undeniable. But the implications of this fact are limited, and the universal dimension of yoga ensures its unstoppable spread not just in the West but also in cultures without any colonial history in India. I expect the problem to solve themselves as Western yoga circles progressively become better acquainted with yoga's real purpose and start focusing on its genuine roots, which are obviously ancient Hindu.

The Modi Government as an Exponent of BJP Secularism*

The annual conference of the American Academy of Religion (AAR) takes place every November in a North American city. The proposals have to be sent in February: First an ample explanation, then an abstract for publication. This piece draws attention to an important phenomenon with a strong and hitherto unrefuted predictive power, viz. the BJP variety of secularism. The AAR's 'experts' were not interested, preferring their prestigious delusions about the BJP's imaginary Hindu fanaticism to hard facts. The reader can judge for himself/herself whether the facts before that time and ever since have proven me wrong.

Atal Bihari Vajpayee's NDA government (1998–2004) heavily disappointed the experts who had predicted 'all Moslims into the Indian Ocean' or similar doomsday scenarios—or rather, it put them squarely in the wrong. Hindu 'fascism' as a threat to democracy? When Vajpayee narrowly lost a confidence vote, he meekly stepped down. War against Pakistan? Though Pakistan unilaterally invaded India (Kargil, 1999), Vajpayee forbade the Army to strike at the invaders' base across the border, and later opened a peace process, making symbolic concessions which the Congress had always refused. Isolationism? He threw the Indian

*Explanation sent by the author sometime in February 2015 for the annual conference of the American Academy of Religion

media market open to foreign media ownership, a move opposed by India's entire political spectrum. The only 'Hindutva' thing the NDA ever did was HRD Minister M.M. Joshi's clumsy overhaul of recommended history schoolbooks, changing nothing dramatic and easily reversed. When the government created a Chair for Indic Studies in Oxford ('saffronization!'), it selected an outspoken opponent for the job, in the vain hope of receiving a pat on the back from its declared enemies.

With the hindsight knowledge of historical reality, it would be embarrassing to reproduce the predictions by Indian and foreign experts. Today, anti-BJP discourse is less shrill, but still confidently classifies the BJP among the 'Hindu right'. This implies a prediction that once in power, the BJP will pursue distinctly pro-Hindu policies. However, in the light of our experience with the Vajpayee government, it is no surprise that the present government led by Narendra Modi fails to live up to this learned prediction, at least for now. (Of course, this paper will be updated by November as new developments take place.)

In spite of having a more homogeneous majority, it is reluctant to do anything pro-Hindu or perceivable as anti-minority. On the contrary, one of its first acts was to decree a new subsidy to Islamic schools. The stray Hindutva statements by loose cannons* were followed by retractions, condemnations by government spokespersons and indignant innuendos by Modi-friendly journalists. Public reconversions by the allied VHP, heavily publicized and demonized by the media, were promptly discouraged by the government. Having learnt from Vajpayee's 2004 defeat, though, Modi does 'keep the pot boiling', does regularly throw crumbs of inconsequential Hindu symbolism to his support base, all while not formally changing anything.

---

*'After abusive rant, Union minister Sadhvi Niranjan Jyoti expresses regret in Parliament', *India Today*, 2 December 2014, accessed 31 January 2019, https://www.indiatoday.in/india/north/story/niranjan-jyoti-narendra-modi-parliament-ram-controversial-remarks-229437-2014-12-02

However, if many BJP workers are disappointed with this government, it is not for what it does but mainly for what it persistently fails to do. Thus, it inducted no figure with a strongly ideological profile (Arun Shourie, Subramanian Swamy). Likewise, some public figures who had crossed the floor (e.g., Madhu Kishwar) were conspicuously not rewarded—a fact not considered here for disgruntled ego reasons but for illustrating the BJP's lack of strategy: It doesn't put people who have actually sacrificed for the BJP to any use, while awarding positions of influence to unreliable newcomers motivated by sheer opportunism. While some things on the Hindu agenda are either useless to Hinduism (e.g., declaring a 'Hindu rashtra') and others would arouse violent protests, for which the media is sure to blame Modi (e.g., a common civil code, though 'secular' par excellence), others are perfectly feasible and, moreover, turn out to be the most consequential for the flourishing of Hinduism.

In particular, the potential amending of Constitutional articles 28 and 30, which (de facto) discriminate against Hinduism in education, does not take away any rights from the minorities, yet lifts an enormous burden from Hindu organizations investing in education and eliminates a major reason for Hindu sects (Arya Samaj, RK Mission, Jains, Lingayats) to have themselves judicially declared non-Hindu minorities. Similarly, eliminating the legal basis of the discrimination against Hinduism in temple management, with rich temples (but not mosques or churches) nationalized and their income pocketed by politicians or diverted to non-Hindu purposes, would give an enormous boost to Hindu religious and cultural life, without impinging upon the rights of the minorities.

It has to be noted, however, and it buttresses my case for 'BJP secularism', that temple management is partly a competence of the States, and that BJP state governments have not made the difference. At any rate, there are meaningful things a BJP government could do specifically for Hinduism without endangering its non-religious agenda (development, cleaning India, etc.) or its international standing—yet it chooses not to do them.

As for the Hindutva fits and starts of some BJP members, now considered extremists but, in fact, only representative of what the erstwhile Jan Sangh (1952–1977, predecessor of the BJP) stood for, it should be easy to bring them in line around a more reasonable but still credibly pro-Hindu programme. It is here that the BJP is most conspicuously failing—conspicuous at least to insiders, for 99 per cent of the outside literature about the BJP never mentions this phenomenon. Contrary to a consensus among academic and journalistic India-watchers, the supposed 'Hindu extremist' party has no Hindu agenda. As I see it, the party relies on pro-Hindu workers to do the campaigning legwork, but once in power, it cold-shoulders them, publicizes and pursues an agenda of economic development only, and tries to curry favour with the secularists.

The main reason is the long-standing deliberate lack of investment (pioneered by M.S. Golwalkar) in an intellectual and strategic vision of its own, the spurning of any analysis of the forces in the field and of the potential and limitations of the situation. It, therefore, also lacks competent personnel for the ideological struggle, e.g., for a textbook overhaul or, now, for nominating politically friendly new vice-chancellors. Consequently, most BJP leaders have an enormous inferiority complex vis-à-vis the secularists and, even when in office, try to live up to the norms laid down by their opponents.

This is hardly the impression created by most experts; but the primary data, the only source to which this paper pledges loyalty, tell a clear story: The present BJP is only termed a Hindu party in deference to the distant memory of its initial orientation.

Debating the Hindu Right*

How does the West look at India? The Western public is completely, and the professional India-watchers largely, dependent on information filtered by a Delhi bottleneck under firm Nehruvian control. This is not a matter of 'sepoy' intellectuals blackening India and Hinduism at the behest of an American conspiracy. It is a two-way influence, with Indians trying to live up to Western fashions and Westerners trying to align with Indian ideological norms.

An important new book exemplifies this American-Indian cooperation against any political mobilization in the name of Hinduism—*Pluralism and Democracy in India: Debating the Hindu Right* (Oxford University Press, New York, 2015). It is a collection of twenty essays, mostly based on updated versions of contributions to a 2005 conference in Chicago. The editors are religious historian Wendy Doniger and law scholar Martha Nussbaum, both from the top-ranking University of Chicago. Doniger's name has gained some currency in India ever since her book *The Hindus: An Alternative History* was withdrawn by the publisher under Hindu pressure (affair discussed in detail below, ch.20). This way, a biased, flippant and error-ridden book, already exposed in detail in Vishal Agarwal's counter-book, was given a false aura of martyrdom. The episode also confirmed her enmity for any Hindu self-assertion, as is obvious from the introduction she co-authored with Nussbaum.

About the outspokenly partisan perspective of the book, we can be brief because no attempt is made to hide it. Thus, if we are

---

*Published as 'How the West Looks at India' in *The Pioneer*, Delhi, 6 September 2015

going to discuss 'democracy in India', it should be hard to leave the Emergency and the Sangh Parivar's opposition to it unmentioned; yet these are carefully and completely hushed up. The year Zero of the book's time horizon is explicitly said to be 2002, because of the Gujarat riots. On these, the old progressive party-line is still strictly observed, assuming 'Modi's complicity in the riots' (p.14). Herewith, they consciously overrule the fact that 'he has not been convicted in court' (p.1), though not for want of trying. But if riots are deemed so important, surely attention is paid to the far larger killing of the Sikhs in 1984 by Congress secularists; or to the East Bengali massacre of Hindus in 1971 that dwarfed all Indian communal killings since Independence combined? No, this book only notices killings when Hindus are (or can be portrayed as) the perpetrators.

The Ayodhya controversy is mentioned a number of times, but without the decisive information—quite new to the American target audience—that the temple argument has a strong claim to legitimacy, according to several findings (discussed elsewhere). The whole lambasting of the centuries-old pro-temple consensus, challenged by the secularists in 1989 and rebaptized the 'Hindu fundamentalist claim', was carried through American academe—yet it was wrong. The paper specifically about 'the road from Ayodhya' has forty footnotes, all referring to partisan anti-Hindutva sources except for one in which BJP stalwart Ram Madhav provides some hard data. And that count is representative for most papers, but then Hindus should admit that they themselves have produced few intellectual works worth quoting.

The editors call Narendra Modi's accession to power 'ominous for India's very future as a democracy' (p.1). In American academe, the demand of objectivity, on which scholarly authority is based, is candidly suspended in works about Hindu politics.

The subtitle could suggest that a debate with the so-called Hindu right is being envisaged. That is not the case. The debate is, in fact, between different sections of the secularist Left (with its American extension), as exemplified by Amartya Sen's response to

Ramachandra Guha's review of his book *The Argumentative Indian*. The Hindu right is only an object. The token contribution from Ved Nanda as former head of the Hindu Swayamsevak Sangh (US section of the RSS) has no argumentative thrust—it merely details all the historical and numerical facts about Hinduism in the US.

Yet, many of the separate papers in this book are certainly worth reading. Most papers require a review in themselves, but to settle for one example, Mushirul Hasan's paper on the BJP's reforms on textbooks provides interesting data on the BJP's intellectual agenda *as seen by the secularists*. Once you have accepted that this is not a scholarly account but a veteran's memoir giving the view of one of the warring camps, it becomes a very worthy read. Incidentally, on p.255, Hasan labels Hindu history-rewriting an 'attempt to Talibanize India's history', thus holding up an Islamic movement as the level to which Hindus could stoop. Thereby, he implicitly admits that the ideologically streamlined textbooks which he fights in India are a routine fact of life in Pakistan.

A serious drawback of this book is that it narrows its focus to the Sangh Parivar, all while announcing a treatment of the 'Hindu right'. Perhaps this was still passable in 2005, but anyone moderately informed about the ideological scene should know that it is not so in 2015. At the mass level, scholars ought to have noticed that the Hindu self-defence network in West Bengal, Hindu Samhati, has been set up by a dissatisfied ex-Swayamsevak because the RSS was just not living up to its promises. The Sangh's enemies portray it as a formidable Hindu force, but insiders know better. It might have numbers, and today it might even hold office, but its commitment to Hindu victory is wobbly and lackadaisical. More and more, Hindus are locally organizing outside the Sangh. They even continue to do so now that 'their' side is in power in Delhi and proving to be no more than time-servers. Mostly they are happy that Modi is at the helm, but for an actual Hindu dimension to politics, more will be needed.

While this trend is still marginal, it is already very visible on the media front, where Internet papers have become the arteries of new communities shedding the Sangh baggage and trying to serve the Hindu cause through new analyses: VijayVaani, India Facts, Hindu Human Rights, *Swarajya*, *Bharata-Bharati* and the India Inspires Foundation. These people have no power yet, but they do have ideas. More up-to-date and more aware of international trends in political thinking than the gerontocratic Sangh, their thought is far more interesting. It also is more rooted, more Hindu than the Hindutva current, which is stuck in the 1920s' borrowed nationalist paradigm. If 'debate' with the Hindu side is what you want, it is they who are the ones to talk to.

The Confabulated Murder of Saint Thomas*

*There was an article by David Green propagating the Christian claim that 'Thomas the Apostle was murdered in India',*** *viz. by Brahmin priests of Kali. In the brief letter below, I set the record straight. Since this myth is standard fare among secularists and Gandhian Hindus in India, and since their attention span is notoriously short, it will be useful if they read the following summary.*

So your source is 'common Christian tradition'? Fortunately, we are past the stage where we believe a story just because 'tradition' says so. Therefore, we don't believe the blood libel against the Jewish people any more (i.e. that it is responsible for the killing of Christ, and by extension also for other deadly crimes), even though for centuries it has been supported by 'common Christian tradition'. Likewise, we don't believe the blood libel against the 'priests of Kali' either.

Nothing of this legend is proven. The only written source for it is already some fifty years younger than this Thomas's supposed martyrdom: the apocryphal *Acts of Thomas*. There, he is presented as coming to 'India', then a very large term (when Columbus landed in

---

*Published on koenraadelst.blogspot.com on 11 March 2016

**Published in *Haaretz* on 21 December 2015, accessed on 29 March 2019. http://www.haaretz.com/israel-news/this-day-in-jewish-history/1.692829?date=1457643796561

what he thought was Zipangu/Japan, he called the natives 'Indians', meaning Asians), in a part that was desert-like and where the people had Persian names. This describes Afghanistan or western Pakistan well, but not the lush and rich tropical landscape of south India. When he has committed several crimes against society, the king asks him to leave, and only when he refuses this diplomatic solution does the king have him executed.

I first learnt about the hollow mythical nature of the St Thomas story while studying in Leuven Catholic University, from a Jesuit professor of Comparative Religion, Frank de Graeve. Not exactly a 'fanatical Hindu' source. More recently, Pope Benedict XVI publicly declared that St Thomas had come to western India, and that from there, after an unspecified period of time, Christianity, not Thomas, reached south India.* I am aware that Indian Christians have raised hell against this scholarly assessment, and have pressured the Vatican into removing this statement from its website. But that is not going to alter the verdict of scholarly historiography: There is no evidence at all to support this story.

And when Christians did reach the coastal area of south India, probably as fourth-century refugees from the Persian empire that had turned hostile after the Christianization of its Roman rival, they were welcomed rather more cordially than any treatment given by Christians to pagans. Far from being 'murdered by the priests of Kali', they were given hospitality and integrated into Hindu society, without any questions asked about the contents of their religion. Hindus have extended their hospitality more recently to Parsis, Armenians and Tibetan Buddhists; and more anciently to the Jews. That glorious record is the target of gross injustice in the fictional story of St Thomas.

*Pope's General Audience of 27 September 2006

Pluralism in Ilā's City*

In 2016, the Sanskrit department of the Allahabad University hosted an international conference on the Rig Vedic verse 'Ekam sad viprā bahudhā vadanti', *meaning 'the wise express the one reality in many ways'. I was invited to participate in the opening ceremony, before the serious work began. My talk strikes a lighter note but, nonetheless, makes a few points, one even fully original and appreciated as such by the audience.*

Bhadrajanāḥ,
Mama nāma Kūnrāḍ Elst asti, aham Pascimadvīpād Beljamdeśād āgatosmi

Unfortunately, that is about all the Spoken Sanskrit I can muster. I only learnt the Devabhāśā as a literary language, a storehouse of political and philosophical insights and terminology, but not as a daily medium of communication. For anything more sophisticated, I will have to switch to a language in which I can express my thoughts more comfortably. *Isliye, mein abhī Angrezī me bol dum̐ gā. Kṣamā kījiye.* (It is for this reason that I will switch to English, forgive me.)

However, I do have the intention of learning spoken Sanskrit properly after my retirement, so that I have mastered it by the time I die. That way, when I go to heaven, I will be able to converse with Varuṇa, Mitra and the other gods shining brightly up there.

---

*Talk by the author at an international conference hosted by the Sanskrit department of the Allahabad University in 2016

PLURALISM

We are gathered here to ponder the Rig Vedic verse *Ekam sad viprā bahudhā vadanti*—'Reality is one, the sages formulate it in many ways', or 'Truth is one, the sages give it many names.'

We are here in the city of Allahabad, founded in 1575 by Moghul emperor Akbar, who was posthumously turned into the patron saint of Indian secularism. More recently, it became famous as the home base of the first prime minister Jawaharlal Nehru, the theoretician and propagator of 'secularism'. The temptation must be palpable to treat this maxim as the cornerstone of this uniquely Indian ideology. Indeed, whenever it is brought up in public debate nowadays, it is as an argument of authority for secularism. Yet, it voices a rather different idea: pluralism. Let me explain.

In its European countries of origin, secularism (French: *laicité*) wanted to be a way to contain the Christian churches, to make and keep the state free from interference by the church. In the budding United States, the emphasis was slightly different: to keep the churches free from interference by the state. At any rate, the core idea was separation of church and state. The most fundamental characteristic of a secular state is the equality of all its citizens before the law, regardless of religion.

In that sense, India is not a secular state at all. Its Constitution mandates quite a bit of state interference in religious laws and institutions, at least those of the Hindus, and formally as well as effectively discriminates against its religious majority.

It does not satisfy the very first criterion of a secular state, viz. the legal equality of all citizens regardless of religion. On the contrary, in family matters, there are different sets of laws for Hindus, Muslims, Christians and Parsis. The most famous example is, of course, that a Muslim man can have four wives, others cannot. The discrimination lies not only in the state's perpetuation of a consequential inequality, but also in the genesis of that inequality through state intervention, viz. by the abolition of polygamy where it existed in Hindu society versus its deliberate non-abolition among

Muslims. One can recognize an incompetent India-watcher by his pompous claim that 'India is a secular state'. It is not. Period.

Fortunately, that is not what our verse is about. It is not about secularism, whether genuine or Nehruvian. It is all about pluralism, not plurality and coexistence of different law systems, but legitimate coexistence of different viewpoints.

Thus, a person may be given a passport name at birth. In intimate circles, he also acquires a house name. Among his friends, he may get a nickname. When he succeeds in life, he may be given a title or be named after an award he earns. If he is a writer, he may be known by a pen name. In China and other civilizations, he may later receive a posthumous name. Moreover, he may be described as someone's son, someone's brother, father, boss, employee or neighbour. But all these names refer to the same person. Many names, one reality. And likewise with Ultimate Reality.

QUOTATIONS OUT OF CONTEXT

If I hear a famous quotation, I would want to know its context: both the phrases surrounding it and its place in life (German: *Sitz im Leben*). For famous quotations have a way of, let us say, emancipating themselves from the author's original intention. They may even come to mean the very opposite.

Thus, having come all the way from the West, I am often reminded here of Rudyard Kipling's verse: 'East is East and West is West, and never the twain shall meet.'

It is one of the most famous poems in English but was written in India—Kipling was a native Mumbaikar. However, as it stands here, the verse means just the opposite of what he had in mind, and this becomes clear from the context:

> 'But there is neither East nor West, Border, nor Breed, nor Birth,
> When two strong men stand face to face, though they come from the ends of the earth!'

So, in simple prose: The eastern point and western point of the compass will never meet, alright, but when two people of calibre encounter each other, the accidents of birth are not of much consequence any more.

Ahiṁsa paramo dharma—'non-violence is the highest ethic/righteousness'—is another quotation cut in half to suit contemporary purposes. In a Gandhian context, it has come to stand for absolute pacifism. But in the original *Mahābhārata* version, it is only half the picture: The other half is *dharma hiṁsa tathaiva ca*, or 'righteous violence'. So, non-violence in some situations, but righteous violence in others. And that happens to be far more realistic.

Suppose you are walking in a quiet forest lane, and suddenly you are set upon by a gang of rapists. Before the worst can happen, a knight in shining armour appears on the scene, beats up the rapists and puts them to flight. Wouldn't you be grateful for this bit of 'righteous violence'? Wouldn't you at once trade all the Gandhian pieties for this bit of forceful salvation? To be sure, it is still the lesser evil, we have to keep striving for a system in which violence is completely unnecessary. Yet provisionally, in the real world, violence may still be the lesser evil compared to full *adharma*, or unrighteousness.

Vasudhaiva kutumbakam—'the whole world is one family'—is a very oft-quoted verse, and very much taken out of context. It nowadays functions as the creed of Hinduism, at least for public consumption. Hindus often think it has been taken from the *Vedas* or from the Bhagavad Gītā, but it comes from a fable collection, the *Hitopadeśa*. And there, its meaning is not that positive.

When a jackal targets a deer for his meal and cleverly wins its trust, a crow gets alerted by the sinister sight of this sudden interloper. However, the jackal protests that suspicion is misplaced: *vasudhaiva kutumbakam*! The crow has to bow out, but remains vigilant from a distance. When the jackal finally tries to strike, the deer is saved by the crow's intervention. Moral of the story: Only a knave would assert, and a fool believe, that 'the whole world is one family'. Fortunately, there are still a few clever sceptics who don't let down their guard and see through this unrealistic maxim. I wonder what it says about modern Hindus that they all run away with this saying and even advertise it as the essence of their worldview.

Instead, I stand by another Sanskrit maxim. It is one that can't be shaken by any possible context, because it is always a reliable guiding principle: *Satyameva jayate*—'truth verily triumphs', 'truth shall prevail'. This is from the *Muṇḍaka Upaniṣad*, and nothing in the context gives a different or contrary message. It has become India's national motto, and I feel so strongly about it that I have put it on my calling card. When it conflicts with more popular phrases, I will drop those others any time.

And now, let us see what this care about the context would mean for the maxim that we have thematized for this conference.

POLYTHEISM

The oft-quoted part of our mantra (RV 1:164:46) is *Ekam sad viprā bahudhā vadanti*, or 'the wise ones speak the one truth in many ways', and is nowadays read as an affirmation that a single reality underlies seeming plurality. But the mantra further says (and then sums up in the quoted part) that they worship this reality as Indra, as Yama, as Mātarīśvan, as Garutman, as Agni and other gods. That is to say: It affirms a form of religion we know as polytheism. According to this verse, it is perfectly alright to picture the divine as a heavenly bird, Garutman, or as fire, Agni, or as any of many other forms.

This bears emphasizing, since during the last two centuries, there have been many Hindu 'reformers' and 'modernists' who contrived to define Hinduism as 'monotheistic' too. That is to say, monotheistic like the Christian or Islamic role model. In evaluating a doctrine, most people are guided not by its truth but by its effectiveness as a social passport, as a gateway to status. So, when monotheism became prestigious, many Hindus started saying: Hinduism, too, is monotheistic. Indeed, this very verse is often given as proof of the *Vedas*' 'monotheism'. See, the seeming manifoldness of the Vedic gods hides an underlying 'one God', so we are as good as them!

It seems that Hindus (at least the unrooted ones who try to live up to borrowed ideals) are eagerly appropriating words which they do not properly understand, such as 'monotheism'; and which they would not consider so desirable if they did understand them. In the *Bible* and the *Quran*, it is said that there is only one God and others are false. Is that what you would want to venerate as the Vedic doctrine? In this verse, however, there is no such thing as a 'false god', on the contrary. In the *Bible* and the *Quran*, there is said to be only one God and no other, but here it is said that He is the same as the others, and that they are all legitimate. After all, the sages use many names, right?

Underlying this polytheism, there is a oneness, a common essence, 'one reality' indeed. And yet, the more conformist Hindus who try to live up to the norm set by Christianity or Islam, are wrong to deduce that 'Hinduism is also monotheist'. They are 'me too' monotheists—at least, *if* they are monotheists. Like the *Ārya Samāj*, which translates every one of the Vedic god names as 'God' and thus declares itself monotheistic. Hopefully it simply hasn't realized that monotheism would mean you do not allow pluralism. That is what it has always meant for Christians and Muslims: Smash the statues and temples and rituals reminding the people of Jupiter, of Apollo, of Horus, of Ishtar and Marduk. Is that Hinduism? Is that (and I will now use it positively) secularism?

The *Vedas* would say: 'They call it Jupiter, they call it Apollo, they call it Horus, they call it Ishtar, they call it Marduk: the sages call the one reality by many names.'

Really becoming monotheists would mean for Hindus rewriting the (say) *Hanumān Chālīsā* and inserting into it an injunction: 'Hanumān wants you to go and destroy the temples of *Śiva*! And destroy the statues of Sarasvatī too, and the sculptures of the rest of them. Hanumān alone!' For a 'monotheist' is not someone who worships one god—sticklers for precision in the science of religion would call that a 'henotheist'. A Hindu who worships a chosen deity is not a 'monotheist' but a henotheist. (And usually a 'serial henotheist' at that, sometimes worshipping other gods as well.) A monotheist worships one god to the exclusion of all others: They are deemed false and/or evil.

The Greek word *monos* does not mean 'one'—it means 'one alone'. It is not inclusive, but exclusive. It is the very opposite of what our Vedic verse expresses. That mantra is not directed against anything, but if at all you want to bring monotheism into the picture, then it is against monotheism.

DĪRGHATAMAS

The verse we are considering was written by one of the earliest Vedic seers, the ṛṣi Dīrghatamas, in the last one of his twenty-five hymns, the *Riddle Hymn* (RV 1:164). His name means 'long darkness' and this is sometimes explained as referring to blindness. However, he is also known for his astronomical insights (including the first division of the heavenly circles in 360°, on top of that in twelve parts), and it is hard to do astronomy when you're blind. Rather, 'blindness' seems to have been an accepted circumlocution referring to a certain attitude of deep concentration and piercing research. The Greek poet Homer was likewise described as 'blind'.

Two very basic ideas pervading Hindu thought first find expression in Dīrghatamas: renunciation and monism. To be sure, these may even be older—it is by no means certain that he invented either of them. But he has the distinction of being the first to articulate them in a form that has survived.

Renunciation is the guiding idea of the verse (RV 1:164:20), where he contrasts two birds in a tree: one eats the berries, the other merely looks on. One man enjoys life, the other merely contemplates. This is the foundation of the entire science of meditation, India's greatest gift to the world. Numerous later thinkers developed it further and founded their own schools of meditation, but its essence is already encapsulated in this verse.

Monism is what finds expression in the verse under consideration: *Ekam sad viprā bahudhā vadanti*. It characterizes what underlies the multiplicity of viewpoints and ways of understanding as a single reality. It is unity in diversity. It is the integration of the many into the one. The belief that a visible plurality masks a deeper oneness was part of the Vedic outlook since the very beginning.

A third idea that may also stem from the *Riddle Hymn*, and that has strongly marked Hindu tradition throughout, is Dīrghatamas' notion of the 'syllable', apparently the Aum sound. Given the context, with mother cows expressing their tenderness (*vatsalya*) for their young by lowing at them, and the young lowing back, it looks like the unspoken syllable is another vocalization of 'Mooh'. But I am confident that this august company of Sanskrit scholars has a loftier explanation. Then again, the Vedic sages must have had a lot more humour than their bookish descendants.

In the West, it is said that the whole tradition of philosophical thought is but a series of footnotes on the Greek philosopher Plato (whom you might know from Urdu sources as *Aflatūn*). Here, you could say that all Indian thought is but a series of footnotes on Dīrghatamas.

ISLAM

Now we come to the point where I should start saying the very thing you have gotten me here for. I came thousands of miles to brook the subject that all Hindus seem to be afraid of. Well, not all Hindus, but at least those who are into interreligious dialogue. That subject is Islam.

Tomorrow, this conference, this hall, this very table, will feature an interreligious forum. There will be a Buddhist and some other Dharmics, as if they are the ones with whom problems of coexistence have to be resolved. There will be a representative of Christianity, already a bit touchier. But the real elephant in the room is, of course, Islam. When it is emphasized before a Hindu audience that *ekam sad viprā bahudhā vadanti*, it means effectively: Don't you Hindus dare to harbour suspicions against Islam! Hindus have to suspend their opinions on Islam, but no one dares formulate just what opinions Muslims should suspend regarding Hinduism.

Frankly, I wonder just what they sermonize on these occasions against Muslims to make them more appreciative of Hinduism. Hindus always justify their acts of 'Muslim appeasement' by saying: 'But we have to live with them!' It seems they never think about its logical counterpart: Teach them to live with us. And I wonder what verse from the *Quran* they intone to propagate an interreligious understanding among Muslims.

I will not embarrass anyone by asking the question whether such is also the intention behind this conference, and, of course, I remain perfectly willing to get convinced otherwise. But until then, I believe the Hindu psychology of Muslim appeasement is so strong that even the present organizers have not been able to escape it. Indeed, a Hindu present here in the audience asked me this very morning not to go into the Ayodhya controversy, about which I have published, as there would also be one Muslim present. (I certainly am going to mention Ayodhya, but not the controversy.)

One Muslim among hundreds of Hindus, and already Hindus want to conceal their opinions. Already all those Hindus are ready to bend over backwards to please that one Muslim, without even asking him! This must be an underground society, used to living in hiding. And yet, what for? Are they 'Islamophobic', meaning 'afraid' of Islam?

Well, I am not. I don't think Muslims are a bunch of humourless touch-me-nots who freak out as soon as you mention the rougher edges of pluralism. I will not alter my speech just because one Muslim is present, or many Muslims, or only Muslims. They are our own countrymen, they are fellow human beings born with the same capacities and propensities. A certain conditioning by a certain religious doctrine has formed a surface layer, but deep down they are the same. So, address Muslims not at the level of their indoctrination, but at the deeper level of their general humanity.

I am here to join in this effort and make everybody feel that we are in the same boat together. Since we have already done so much to satisfy Hindu tastes (lighting lamps, garlands, coconuts, a Sarasvatī statue), let us now say certain things that Muslims would feel good about.

People who know my critical work on Muḥammad (Arabic: 'The praised one') would not lend me any credibility if I started praising him. Yet, there is one merit of his that I greatly recommend. As you might know, he was an orphan, brought up by relatives. While they looked after him with one hand, they deprived him of his parental inheritance with the other. And so, Mohammed remained very sensitive to this problem and always emphasized that you should not deprive children of their inheritance. Well, in this respect, at least, we should all be followers of Mohammed: Don't lose your rightful inheritance. Don't let them make you embrace any artificial imposition instead of what is naturally yours. Stay true to your legacy, to your roots.

Otherwise, I may have my second thoughts about Mohammed, but for now, let us focus on Allah. Indeed, I am all for Allah. If there is one thing great about Islam, it is Allah. Nay, He is not merely 'great', he is 'greater'.

ALLĀH, THE ILĀH

Let us analyse the word Allāh, as students of the Devabhāśā would. You may know that deva, 'god', literally means 'the bright one'. Now, the bright ones living in heaven are, of course, the stars. And, indeed, in Sumerian hieroglyphics, 5,000 years ago, the concept of 'god' was rendered as a radiant star. This sign was pronounced *Dingir* in Sumerian, and *Ilu/El* in Akkadian Semitic. It is the same *El* that we find, through Hebrew, in Gabriel ('My strength is God'), Uriel ('My light is God') or Michael ('Who is like God').

Now, this *El* is rendered into a generic substantive (compare it with God/godhead, deus/deity, deva/devatā): Hebrew *eloha*, Arabic *ilāh*. In Arabic, then, this generic noun is coupled with the article *al* to become *al-ilāha*, 'the deity', 'the god par excellence'. This expression is contracted to become a name again: *Allāh*, 'thé god', 'God'.

As you all know, Allah is great. And even greater: *Allāh akbar*, 'Allah is greater'. The phrase has gained a bit of a bad name, but, in fact, it is quite profound. Muslims often use it as a reminder that their plans and designs may ever be so clever, but it is God who has the last word. In those instances, it is a sign of humility. No matter how important a given concern may be, it is always dwarfed by the divine.

The name Allāh acquired the monotheistic meaning of 'only God' with the Islamization of Arabia in the 620s. Before that, it had a generic meaning. Thus, it is described how someone kneels down before a statue of the moon god Hubal and then 'prays to Allāh', i.e., 'prays to *the deity* before him', viz. Hubal. So, the word Allāh belongs in the polytheist landscape.

This moon god Hubal presided over the Kaaba, the shrine built around a meteor stone fallen from heaven. In an unsculpted stone, Hindus will readily recognize the *Śivaliṅgam*, the symbol of the moon-carrying god (Candradhāra), the Lord of the Moon (Somanātha), *Śiva*. Hubal's or *Śiva*'s crescent has become the main symbol of Allāh. And like *Śiva*, 'the deity' Hubal comes with a triad of goddesses: In India they are Pārvatī, Durgā and Kālī; in Arabia, al-Lāt (al-Ilāhat, 'the goddess', the sun), al-Uzza ('the strong one', the planet Venus) and al-Manāt ('fate, doom', the night). Remark how in Arabic, like in German, the word 'sun' is conceived of as female, the word 'moon' as male, which facilitates the personification of the moon as the god Hubal, and of the sun as the goddess al-Lāt.

I don't know if Hindus and Muslims are all that different, but Indians and Arabs clearly are not. Their religious imaginations have generated very parallel families of gods.

Among Hindus with an excitable fantasy, this has led to the belief that 'the Kaaba used to be a *Śiva* temple'. This is exaggerated, but through the theme of the moon- god, *Śiva* does have a link with the Kaaba. Indian traders visiting Arabia used to worship there, and Arabs used to worship at the Somnāth temple on the Gujarat coast. Later, Mahmud Ghaznavī believed that the Arab goddesses, chased out of Arabia by the Prophet, had found refuge there.

So, it is not at all far-fetched to sing: *Īśvar-Allāh tere nām*, or '*Īśvara* (= *Śiva*) and Allāh are equally your names'. The Gandhians and Nehruvians have churned out a lot of nonsense, such as the absurdity that 'all religions are equally true', but they are right to repeat this songline. Nor is it weird to go on pilgrimage to the Kaaba in Mecca, just as Hindu pilgrims go to Ayodhyā, to Sabarimalai, to Mount Kailāś, or indeed, at the time of the Kumbha Melā, to *Ilāhābād*. The *hajj* existed since long before Islam, which has only borrowed it, and it deserves to be perpetuated. (This should not be done through a 'hajj subsidy', though, not at taxpayers' expense, for that defeats the whole purpose of a pilgrimage, intended as a form of sacrifice.)

In the West, some anti-Muslim crusaders are saying that we should bomb the Kaaba. On the contrary, we should ensure that it remains unharmed and honoured as a sacred site. Indeed, like Gurū Nānak before us, we should go there ourselves. An armed expedition will do no more good than the Western military interventions in Iraq and Libya, which have turned out disastrous and counterproductive. What the Muslim world needs is not even more polarization and war.

What it needs is a thaw. In a situation of peace and prosperity, the minds can evolve. People can then expand their perspectives and learn about the spirituality that their neighbours have to offer. For starters, they can practise the meditation techniques that Sri Sri Ravi Shankar is now offering across the Middle East. So, as an unapologetic Islam critic, I am nonetheless emphatically wishing the Muslims *salām*, 'peace'.

THE DĪN-I-ILĀHĪ

Emperor Akbar, already at age 13 a *ghazī* ('raider against the infidels') reputed to have killed the Hindu emperor Hemacandra with his own hands, gradually grew away from Islam. He started his own private and non-dogmatic religion, the Dīn-i-Ilāhī, the 'religion of the deities' or the 'divine religion'. A Sanskrit translation could be Daivika Dharma. And who could be against that? Not Mitra, the lord of the day sky, nor Varuṇa, lord of the night sky. Nor Uśā, lady of the dawn, for that matter. All the thirty-three Vedic gods smiled when crude monotheism had to make way for this Daivika Dharma, this Dīn-i-Ilāhī.

This step was not without risks, however, since court cleric Aḥmad Sirhindī denounced it as 'blasphemy'. After Akbar's death, it would wither away under the reassertion of orthodoxy. Yet, it was based on a commendable and correct observation: that no religious doctrine can claim a monopoly of the truth. This observation was very close to our maxim *Ekam sad viprā bahudhā vadanti.*

In the spirit of this new religion, he called the city he founded Ilāhābād, 'city of the deity' or 'the divine city'. It lay on one of the most sacred places of Hinduism, the saṅgam (confluence) of Gaṅgā and Yamunā. The British interpreted the name wrongly as Allāhābād, with the Arabic article *al-*. But another explanation is possible, and we will invent it herewith.

THE FOREMOTHER ILĀ

'On the saṅgam is a city / where the girls are so pretty /...'

At least 5,000 years before *Akbar*, this area was the habitat of Ilā, the daughter and eldest child of Manu. He, in turn, was the founding patriarch of mankind, or at least of a part of it. His daughter, in spite of her primogeniture, had to leave the succession to the throne to her younger brother, Ikṣvāku, who stayed in the paternal capital, Ayodhyā, and founded the Solar dynasty. Being myself an eldest son but second child, I know how it must have felt: Ikṣvāku always looked up to his elder sister and felt a bit indebted to her.

On her part, Ilā moved out to Pratiṣṭhānapura, next to the virgin land where Akbar was to build his divine city. This is where her son Purūravas founded the Lunar dynasty.

One descendant of theirs, Nahuśa, moved westwards to the Sarasvatī valley, where one of his own descendants was Yayāti, after whose five sons the 'five tribes' were named. Of these, Pūru headed the central Paurava tribe. One of his progeny was Bharata, after whom India is still called Bhāratavarṣa. In his clan grew a tradition of composing hymns, and these were collected in the *Vedas*. Later sources describe Dīrghatamas as his court priest. The Vedic seers rightly glorified their ancestress, Ilā, who became a goddess and member of a typical goddess triad: Ilā, Bhāratī and Sarasvatī.

So many cities have already been renamed, and I will presently propose to rename Ilāhābād as well, viz. as, well, Ilāhābād. It can retain its name—that saves us all the renaming on road maps, street signs and letterheads. Only, it would get a new interpretation: 'city of Ilā'. So, after her, this city's name should be re-analysed as *Ilā*-h-*ābād*, 'city of Ilā'. Normal rules of phonetic harmony would contract this into Ilābād, but that could also refer to an *ābād* founded by a man named Ila (short -a). So to make sure that we know a lady is being eternalized in this divine city, we intersperse an /*h*/ sound, like a sigh of joy, and make it into Ilāhābād.

Hospitable people of Ilāhābād, and especially you, ladies of Ilāhābād, I salute you as carriers of the heritage of the Vedic grandmother Ilā. Without her, no Dīrghatamas would have been there to compose the verse, *Ekam sad viprā bahudhā vadanti.* As the Prophet has enjoined: Don't let your rightful inheritance be snatched away from you. Revive Ilā's memory and continue the work she began—the Vedic civilization, no less.

Thank you all.

The Sati Strategy*

Among the hostile stereotypes of Hinduism is that it forces wives on to the funeral pyre of their husbands. This custom of sati was always limited to a few castes and, even then, subject to certain conditions. It was outlawed almost two centuries ago. Nevertheless, the topic still bedevils many debates with or about Hinduism.

After making history with her book on the Ayodhya controversy, *Rama and Ayodhya* (2013), Professor Meenakshi Jain adds to her reputation with the present hefty volume, *Sati: Evangelicals, Baptist Missionaries, and the Changing Colonial Discourse* (Aryan Books International, New Delhi, 2016). In it, as a meticulous professional historian, she quotes all the relevant sources, with descriptions of sati from the ancient through the medieval to the modern period. She adds the full text of the relevant British and Republican laws and of Lord William Bentinck's *Minute on Sati* (1829), that led to the prohibition on sati. This book makes the whole array of primary sources readily accessible, so from now on, it will be an indispensable reference for all debates on sati.

But in the design of the book, all this material is instrumental in studying the *uses* made of sati in the colonial period. In particular, the missionary campaign to rally support for the project of mass conversion of the Indian heathens to the saving light of Christianity

---

*Published on Bharata-Bharati, 24 March 2016; and Hindu Human Rights, 27 March 2016; review for *Sati*, by Meenakshi Jain, a History professor at Delhi University

made good use of sati. This practice had a strong in-your-face shock value and could perfectly illustrate the barbarity of Hinduism.

INDIGNATION

In the preface, Professor Jain surveys the existing literature and expresses her assent to some recent theories. Thus, Rahul Sapra found that Gayatri Spivak's observations—e.g., that the nineteenth-century British tried to remake Indian society in their own image and used sati as the most vivid proof of the need for this radical remaking—don't take into account the changing political equation during the centuries of gradual European penetration. In the seventeenth century, European traders and travellers mostly joined the natives in glorifying the women committing sati, whereas by the nineteenth century, they posed as chivalrous saviours of the victimized native women from the cruel native men. This was because they were no longer travellers in an exotic country and at the mercy of the native people, but had become masters of the land and gotten imbued with a sense of superiority.

Indians in large numbers, and especially the many indefatigable but amateurish 'history rewriters', tend to be defective in their sense of history, starting with their seeming ignorance about the otherwise very common phenomenon of *change*. When I hear these history rewriters fulminate against the West with its supposed evil designs of somehow dominating India again, it seems that in their minds, time has frozen in the Victorian age. Similarly here, there is not one monolithic Western view of sati but, apart even from individual differences of opinion, there are distinct stages, partly because of the changing power equation and partly because internal changes in the Western outlook have influenced the Western perception of things Indian. So it takes a genuine historian to map out precisely what has changed and what not, and which factors have effected those particular changes.

Then again, it is, of course, interesting to realize the continuity between the present-day interference in Indian culture by Leftist scholars like Wendy Doniger and Sheldon Pollock and that of the British colonialists: 'We know best what is wrong with your traditions and we come to save you from yourselves.'

In this respect, the changes in the Western attitude to sati run parallel to that regarding caste. Until the early twentieth century, caste was seen as a specifically Indian form of a universal phenomenon, viz. social inequality. Around the time of the French Revolution, the idea of equality started catching on, but only gradually became the accepted norm. At that point, it became problematic that people's status was said to be determined by birth. In this case, determination by the inborn circumstance of being a woman, unequal in rights compared to men, and never more radically unequal than in committing sati. After the Second World War, the norm (henceforth called human right) of absolute equality and increasingly of absolute individual self-determination made the tradition of caste and of sati too horrible to tolerate. Therefore, the indignation about sati is far greater today than when Marco Polo visited India. Today, sati is already a memory, but the commotion around the exceptional sati of 1987 gave an idea of the indignation it would provoke today.

EVANGELIZATION

In this case, an extra factor came into play to effect a change in British attitudes to sati. In parliamentary debates about the East India Company charter in 1793, there was no mention yet of sati, though it had been described many times, including by company eyewitnesses. But by 1829, sati was forbidden in all company domains. This turnaround was the result of a campaign by the missionary lobby.

Ever since the missionaries set out to convert the pagans of India, they made it their business to contrast the benignity of Christianity with the demeaning atrocities of heathenism. This was an old tradition starting with the biblical vilification of child sacrifice to the god Moloch by the Canaanites. The practice was also attested by the Romans when they besieged the Canaanite (Phoenician) colony of Carthage. The *Bible* writers and their missionary acolytes present child sacrifice as a necessary component of polytheism, from which monotheism came to save humanity. And indeed, we read here how Reverend William Carey tried to muster evidence of child sacrifice too (but settled for sati as convincing enough, p.178)

In reality, the abolition of human sacrifice was a universal evolution equally affecting pagan cultures such as the Romans. In the case of Brahmanism, it is speculated that the Vastu-Purusha concept (a human frame deemed to underlie a house) is a memory of a pre-Vedic human sacrifice. Even if true, the fact is that in really existing Brahmanism, human sacrifice has not been part of it for thousands of years; if it had, we would be reminded of it every day. In this respect, Brahmanism was definitely ahead of the rest of humanity.

Not to idealize matters, we have to admit that, like the biblical writers, who used the vilification of the child-sacrificing Canaanites as justification to seize their land (and even to kill them all), pagans who had left the practice behind equally used the reference to it to score political points. The Romans had practised human sacrifice within living memory and then abolished it, so they were acutely aware of it and tried to exorcize it from their own historical identity by rooting it out in conquered lands as well. (This is the same psychology as among modern Westerners who remember their grandfathers' abolition of slavery and therefore feel spurred to support or engineer the 'abolition of caste' in India.) Using that mentality, Roman war leaders would emphasize this phenomenon of child sacrifice among the Carthaginias to portray them as barbarians in urgent need of Rome's civilizing intervention. Later, Caesar would also demonize as human-sacrificers the Druids of Gaul, another 'barbarian' country the Romans 'liberated' from its own traditions after conquering it. Likewise, the Chinese Zhou dynasty justified its coup d'état (eleventh century BCE) against the Shang dynasty by demonizing the Shang as practising human sacrifice.

This way, sati came in very handy to justify an offensive

in India. Mind you, in a military sense, India had partly been conquered already, and British self-confidence at the time was such that the complete subjugation of the subcontinent seemed assured. The offensive in this case was not military, its target was the Christianization of the East India Company, to be followed by the conversion of its subject population. Around 1800, the company was still purely commercial and even banned missionaries: Their religious zeal might have created riots, and those would be bad for business. So, the Christian lobby had to convince the British parliamentarians that the Christianization of India was good and necessary, and therefore worthy of the company's active or passive support, namely to free the natives from barbarism. To that end, there was no better eye-catcher than sati.

Here I will skip a large part of Professor Jain's research, namely details of the specific intrigues and events that ultimately led to the success of the missionary effort. While these chapters are important for understanding the Christian presence in India, and while I recommend you read them, I have decided to limit my attention for colonial history, as it is presently eating up too much energy, especially of the Hindus. The study of colonial history is instructive and someone should do it, but for the many, it is far more useful to study Dharma itself, to immerse yourself in Hindu civilization as it took shape, rather than in the oppression of and then the resistance by the Hindus. India is free now and could reinvigorate Dharmic civilization, which is a much worthier goal than to re-live the comparatively few centuries of oppression.

Let us only note that the missionaries are responsible for associating Hinduism with sati much more prominently than would be fair. The missionary assault on Hinduism dramatized the practice of sati, which had been an 'exceptional act' performed by a minuscule number of Hindu widows over the centuries, of which the occurrence had been 'exaggerated in the nineteenth century by Evangelicals and Baptist missionaries eager to Christianize and Anglicize India'.

KRISHNA

Many Hindus believe that sati is an external contribution, probably triggered by Muslim conquests. In reality, sati is as old as scriptural Hinduism. Already the *Rig Veda* (10:18:7-8, quoted and discussed in p.4–5) describes a funeral where the widow is lying down beside her husband on the pyre, but is led away from it, back to the world of the living. So it already provides a description of a sati about to take place, as well as of the Brahmanical rejection of sati.

Likewise, the *Mahabharata*, the best guide to living Hinduism, features several cases of sati. The most prominent is the self-immolation by Pandu's most beloved wife, Madri. Less well known, perhaps, is that Krishna's father, Vasudeva, is followed on the pyre by four wives, and that Krishna's death triggers the self-immolation (in his absence) of five of his many wives. But unlike Mohammed, Krishna need not be emulated by his followers. By contrast, Rama's influence on the women in his life is not such that they commit sati (on the contrary, his wife Sita comes unscathed out of the flames of her 'trial by fire'), and he counts as the perfect man, the model whose behaviour should serve us as exemplary.

The oldest foreign (viz. Greek) testimony on Indian sati reports on the death of an Indian general in the Persian army. His two wives fought over the honour of climbing his funeral pyre. Both had a case: one was the eldest, the other was not pregnant (whereas the eldest was, and should not deprive the deceased man of his progeny). So the authorities had to intervene, and they ruled in favour of the younger wife. It should be repeated, for the sake of clarity, that 'favour' here really means the honour of committing self-immolation, as emphatically desired by the young widow.

Indeed, a woman wanting to commit sati needed some willpower, for Hindu society did not take this as a matter of course. As per the many testimonies, she usually had to overcome the dissuasion from her family and from worldly or priestly authorities. (But rather than leading her away in chains for her own good, as modern psychiatrists would do, they give her the decisive last word.) That is why the first British report on the practice spoke of 'self-immolation of widows'. Contrary to allegations of 'murderous patriarchy' by modern feminists (who hold the same ignorant prejudices about Hindu culture as the average foreign tourist), women themselves chose this spectacular fate.

Contrary to a common assumption, the practice was not confined to the Rajputs or to the martial castes in general, where passion and bravery were prized. It is traditionally believed that prominent Hindu rulers like Shivaji Bhonsle and Ranjit Singh were followed on their pyres by a handful of wives and concubines. Among the lower castes, like among the Muslims, life usually resumed and a widow soon remarried, not to let any womb go to waste. But nevertheless, a British survey in Bengal found that no less than 51 per cent of sati women belonged to Shudra families. Among the other upper castes, and among the majority of women even in the martial castes, widows would be confined to a life of service and asceticism. But no matter how rare the actual practice of sati, it remained a glamorous affair, honoured among the Hindu masses with commemorative stones (sati-kal) and temples (sati-sthal).

HINDU SATI?

Sati was not confined to the Hindu civilization. It existed elsewhere, both in Indo-European and in other cultures. Rulers in ancient China or Egypt are sometimes found buried with a number of wives, concubines and servants. In pre-Christian Europe, the practice was related (directly, not inversely) to the status of women in society: not at all in Greece, where women were very subordinate, but quite frequently among the more autonomous Celtic women. Among the Germanic people, a famous case is that of Brunhilde and her maidservants following her husband Siegfried into death. Yet, Indian secularists preferentially depict sati as one of the unique 'evils of Hindu society'.

The only shortcoming in this wonderful book is not a mistake but a hiatus, less than a page long. One important point I would have liked to see discussed more thoroughly is the question raised by Alaka Hejib and Katherine Young in their paper "Sati, widowhood and yoga" (p.xv-xvi). They see a 'hidden religious dimension: yoga; though neither the widow nor the sati was conscious of the yogic dimension of her life'. Indeed, 'the psychology of yoga was instilled, albeit inadvertently, in the traditional Hindu woman'. Well, well, yoga as the most consciousness-oriented discipline in the world is imparted unconsciously: 'instilled, albeit inadvertently'. Professor Jain reports this hypothesis but does not comment on it. So I will.

Naïve readers may not have noticed it yet, but here we are dealing with an instance of a widespread phenomenon: the crass manipulation of the term 'Hindu'. Every missionary and every secularist does it all the time: calling a thing 'Hindu' when it is considered bad, but something (really anything) else as soon as it is deemed good. Many Hindus even lap it up: It is 'instilled, albeit inadvertently'.

Thus, whenever Westerners show an interest in yoga, the secularists and their Western allies hurry to assure us: 'Yoga has nothing to do with Hinduism.' (It is like with Islam, but inversely, for whenever Muslims make negative-sounding headlines, we are immediately reassured that these crimes 'have nothing to do with Islam'.) There may be books on 'Jain mathematics', but never about 'Hindu mathematics', for a good thing cannot be Hindu. If the topic cannot be avoided, you call it, say, 'the Kerala school of mathematics' or fashionably opine that it 'must have been borrowed from Buddhism'. So yoga cannot be Hindu when its merits are at issue. However, when it is presented as something funny, with asceticism and other nasty things, then it can be Hindu, and even used as a middle term to equate something else (something nasty, of course, like sati) with Hinduism. So: Sati is Hindu!

In this case, the poor, hapless secularists are even right. Sometimes even a deplorable motive, like their single-minded hatred for Hinduism, makes men speak the truth: *Sati is Hindu*. Sati is not Brahmanical: the *Rig Veda* enjoins continuing life rather than committing sati, and the Shastras either don't mention it or prefer widowhood, for which they lay down demanding rules. Many of the testimonies cited here mention Brahmanical priests trying to dissuade the woman from sati. Not Brahmanical, then, but nonetheless Hindu, a far broader concept. A Hindu means an 'Indian pagan', as per the Muslim invaders who first introduced the term in India. And indeed, sati has existed in many countries but certainly in India, and it is not of Christian or Islamic origin, so it may be called pagan. And so can the rejection of sati. See?

This, then, makes for half a page that I would have done differently. The rest of this book, 500-something pages, is designed to stand the test of time. It will survive the flames that tend to engulf its topic: the brave sati.

Hindus Need Dharmic Awakening? Rather, the BJP needs Dharmic Awakening*

It doesn't happen often, but here I must totally disagree with David Frawley** (read "Hindus Need Long-Term Political Strategy and Dharmic Awakening", *Swarajya*, 20 April 2016). Or should I say, with the Sangh Parivar, for this is the standard argument I have heard from them for more than twenty years. The central refrain is 'unity'. This is code for 'don't criticize us'—as it was in the Soviet Union and other unpleasant regimes.

The choice apparently is: Either take a principled position and end up too fragmented to achieve anything, or practise unity behind the party and still achieve nothing, because the BJP has firmly chosen to do nothing. In that event, I would rather take a principled and honourable stand to end up with nothing, rather than toe the party line against better counsel and still end up with nothing. The first choice may at least point the way for others in the future.

Patience is good advice, in the event that one is trying. If the BJP were working for any Hindu causes, the Hindus could put up with the sight of setbacks and difficulties, for those are honourable reasons not to have results to show yet. But the BJP is not trying.

---

*Published on Hindu Human Rights, 23 April 2016

**David Frawley, 'Hindus Need Long Term Political Strategy and Dharmic Awakening', *Swarajya*, 20 April 2016, accessed 31 January 2019, https://swarajyamag.com/books/hindus-need-long-term-political-strategy-and-dharmic-awakening

If you sow a seed, you need patience before you can see a plant sprouting and growing up. But if you don't sow a seed, no amount of patience will make you ever see that result.

David asserts that the BJP is taking many initiatives for remedying the many discriminations Hindus face. He would have sounded more convincing if he had summed up a few of those initiatives, as well as the incredibly tough resistance that the enemy is putting up against those. Is the enemy alleging many governmental pro-Hindu initiatives too? For as long as I follow this, I have heard the secularists repeating that same refrain.

It was not true back then, and it is not true now. And it is at any rate not a good sign for the BJP to be in the same boat as the secularists: Both serve their own interests by asserting that the BJP has its many tentacles frantically active in promoting Hindu causes, whereas any non-involved party (which includes serious Hindus, who have no say in government policy and don't even get a hearing) can see that nothing is being done.

Ah, but first we need 'development'! No, there is nothing in remedying discriminations that comes in the way of development. Discriminations are harmful for society and therefore, remedying them *is* a form of development. Workload is certainly not the issue: Don't tell me all those hundreds of BJP men in Parliament are involved full time in 'development'. The development wing inside the BJP, in unison with the secularists, claims that development is what brought this government to power.

I wonder if anyone really believes this. Even the BJP leadership tried to keep Narendra Modi with his Hindu image away from the PM seat, and only accepted him when his charisma turned out to arouse the masses. The secularists whipped up his Hindu image to mobilize the minorities against him, but thereby also mobilized the Hindus around him.

They will try that again in 2019, but that time they will have to contend with actions, rather than words. The minorities will still be made to believe that Modi is a militant Hindu, but the Hindus will judge him by his lack of Hindu action. They will simply not show up to militate or vote for the BJP. The 'development' wing will have to do it. Yes, that will be a repeat of 2004, when A.B. Vajpayee unexpectedly lost.

David asks what the Hindus gained by abandoning Vajpayee. Okay, what did Vajpayee gain by abandoning the Hindus, except defeat? What is this government going to gain by abandoning the Hindus, already with dogged persistence for two years? What sign is there that those who took David's advice and exercised 'patience' will be rewarded with any results of a policy that doesn't exist yet?

Hindus need Dharmic awakening? Rather, the BJP needs Dharmic awakening. Hindus need a long-term strategy? Rather, it is the BJP that remains emphatically defective in developing any strategy. Some independent Hindu groups are developing a strategy, but they will make little difference as long as the governing party remains smugly inert.

Book Review of 'Academic Hinduphobia: A Critique of Wendy Doniger's Erotic School of Indology'*

Rajiv Malhotra's new book, Academic Hinduphobia: A Critique of Wendy Doniger's Erotic School of Indology, is a serious commentary on the ineptness of the so-called experts of Hinduism, holding positions of power and prestige in American universities. It is a pleasant read, rich with anecdotes from the author's personal journey.

Malhotra is the belated Hindu answer to decades of the systematic blackening of Hinduism in academe and the media. This is to be distinguished from the negative attitude to Hinduism among ignorant Westerners settling for the 'caste, cows and curry' stereotype, and from the anti-Hindu bias among secularists in India. Against the latter phenomenon, Hindu polemicists have long been up in arms, even though they have also been put at a disadvantage by the monopoly of their enemies in the opinion-making sphere. But for challenging the American India-watching establishment, a combination of skills was necessary, which Malhotra has only gradually developed and which few others can equal.

In the book *Academic Hinduphobia* (Voice of India, Delhi, 2016, 426 pp.), he documents some of his past battles against Hinduphobia in academe, i.e., the ideological enmity against

*Published on Pragyata.com, 5 July 2016

Hinduism. We leave undecided for now whether that anti-Hindu attitude stems from fear towards an intrinsically better competitor (as many Hindus flatter themselves to think), from contempt for the substandard performance of those Hindus they have met in polemical forums, or from hatred against phenomena in their own past which they now think to recognize in Hinduism ('racism = untouchability', 'feudal inborn inequality = caste').

In this war, American academe is linked with foreign policy interests and the Christian missionary apparatus, and they reinforce one another. Hindus have a formidable enemy in front of them, more wily and resourceful than they have ever experienced before. That is why a new knowledge of the specific laws of this particular battlefield is called for.

DEMONIZATION

Malhotra correctly lays his finger on the links between Christian traditions and present-day Leftist techniques to undermine India. Many Hindus think that Western equals Christian, but this is wrong in two ways: Not all Christians are Western, and not all Westerners are Christian. Yet, secular and Leftist Westerners are nonetheless heirs to Christian strategies and modes of thinking. Thus, many of the Christian saints have a narrative of martyrdom and, usually, it is that which made them saints. The early church deliberately spread or concocted martyrdom stories, for it empirically found these successful in swaying people towards accepting the Christian message.

Today, this tradition is being continued in secularized form: 'Western human rights activists and non-Westerners trained and funded by them go around the world creating new categories of "victims" that can be used in divide-and-conquer strategies against other cultures. In India's case, the largest funding of this type goes to middlemen who can deliver narratives about "abused" Dalits and native (especially Hindu) women.' (p.219)

Here, Malhotra prepares the ground for his *Breaking India*

thesis, where different forces unite in a common goal: to deconstruct India's majority culture and fragment the country. At the same time, he sketches the psychology of the Hindu-haters, explaining why they have such a good conscience in lambasting Hinduism and trying to destroy it. They like to see themselves as the oppressed underdogs, or, in this case, as champions of the oppressed, in spite of their privileged social position and their senior position vis-à-vis the born Hindus who come to earn PhDs under their guidance.

Among those confronted here are Sarah Caldwell, David Gordon White, Deepak Sarma, Robert Zydenbos and Shankar Vedantam. Note the names of some Hindu-born sepoys. The term 'sepoy' for Hindus trying to curry favour with their white superiors needs to be nuanced a little bit. In colonial days, it was black and white: Britons trying to perpetuate and legitimize their domination, and Indian underlings trying to prosper as much as possible in the British system. Today, American Indologists are also partly influenced (especially in their furious hatred of *Hindutva*) by Indian secularist opinion, but then this has, in turn, been oriented in an anti-Hindu sense precisely by the earlier cultural anglicization of the elites during colonial times. Anyway, in the present context, it is indeed Americans leading the dance and Indians trying to keep up.

Principally, Malhotra focuses on different episodes in the one controversy that made him a household name in Indology circles: exposing Wendy Doniger's brand of roundabout and candid-sounding anti-Hindu polemic. By his much-publicized example, he has galvanized many Hindus into actively mapping the battlefield and even coming out to do battle themselves against the mighty and intolerant Hindu-watching establishment. There is no longer an excuse for the all-too-common Hindu attitude of smug laziness hiding behind the spiritual-sounding explanation that, instead of our own effort, the law of karma will take care of everything.

The book is a pleasant read, because the described characters are variegated and the events on the ground are swiftly advancing, all while the ideas are being developed. For understanding the entirety of its message, I can only advise you to read it—it is really worth your time. Here I will limit myself to a searchlight on a few passages.

WENDY'S PSYCHOANALYTIC FREE-FOR-ALL

One of the faces of academic 'Hinduphobia' is the flippant eroticizing discourse about Hindu civilization developed by Chicago University's Professor Wendy Doniger, continued by her erstwhile Ph.D. students and eagerly taken over by prominent media establishments like *The Washington Post*. Here, Malhotra, first of all, amply documents the reality and seriousness of the problem. Imagine: A number of professors who are not at all qualified as psycho-analysts and would be punishable if they applied their diagnosis to a living human being, feel entitled to psycho-analyse a guru like Ramakrishna or a god like Ganesha.

Thus, Jeffrey Kripal's thesis about Ramakrishna (*Kali's Child*) is, according to a quoted Bengali critic, marred by 'faulty translations', 'wilful distortion and manipulation of sources', 'remarkable ignorance of Bengali culture', 'misrepresentations' and a simply defective knowledge of both Sanskrit and Bengali. (p.101) He has, like too many academics, the tendency to 'first suspect, then assume, then present as a fact' his own desired scenario, i.e., 'that Ramakrishna was sexually abused as a child'. (p.105) A closer look at his errors could make the reader embarrassed in Kripal's place—e.g., mistranslating 'lap' as 'genitals', 'head' as 'phallus', 'touching softly' as 'sodomy', etc. Kripal's whole scenario of Ramakrishna as a defiler of boys is not only unsubstantiated—and it provides not only a peep into Kripal's own morbid mind—but it is also, in this age of cultural hypersensitivity, a brutal violation of Hindu and Bengali feelings. If it were an unpleasant truth, it had a right to get said in spite of what the concerned communities would think, but even then, a more circumspect mode of expression and more interaction with the community directly affected would have been called for. But when it comes to Hindus, riding roughshod over them is still the done thing.

Similarly, Paul Courtright (in his book *Gane'sa: Lord of Obstacles, Lord of Beginnings*) develops his thesis about Ganesha's broken trunk being a limp phallus, and of Ganesha being the first god with an Oedipus complex, on the basis of what is clearly defective knowledge about the elephant god. The lore surrounding Ganesha is vast, and does not always live up to Courtright's stereotype of a sweets-addicted diabetic. He has some stories in Hindu literature to his credit where his phallus is not exactly limp. Indeed, I myself am the lucky owner of a Ganesha bronze where he is doing it with a dakini (a nymph serving as partner to a tantric yogi or deity).

Doniger herself is now best known for the numerous errors in her book *The Hindus: An Alternative History*, diagnosed in detail by Vishal Agarwal. Known among laymen as a Sanskritist, her shoddy translations of Sanskrit classics have been criticized by colleagues like Michael Witzel, not exactly a friend of the Hindus. In a normal academic setting, with word and counter-word, where the peer review would have included first-hand practitioners of the tradition concerned, Doniger's or Kripal's or Courtright's gross errors would never have passed muster. It is only because the dice have been loaded against Hinduism that these hilarious distortions are possible. It is, therefore, a very necessary and very reasonable struggle that Malhotra has taken up.

THE RISA LIST

When I wrote my book *The Argumentative Hindu* (2012), I seriously wondered whether to include my exchanges with the RISA (Religion In South Asia) list about the dishonourable way listmaster Deepak Sarma and the rest of the gang overruled list rules in order to banish me, and how many prominent Indologists actively or passively supported his tricks. I didn't consider my own story that important, but finally I decided to do it, just for the sake of history. Future as well as present students of the conflicting worldviews in India and among India-watchers in the West are or will be interested in a detailed illustration of how mean and pompous the anti-Hindu crowd can be in defending their power position.

Here we get a detailed report on a much more important RISA debate that took place in 2003, and as it turns out, it was indeed worth making this information available. A lot of anecdotal data become known here, useful one day for the occasional biographer, such as the interesting titbit that Anantanand Rambachan—with whom Malhotra crossed swords in his book *Indra's Net*—was an ally back then (p. 210). More fundamentally, and affecting the whole Hindu-American community, we note Courtright's turn-around to a sudden willingness for dialogue with the Hindus about his erstwhile thesis (p.211). The reason that mattered most in the prevailing *zeitgeist* was that 'American Hinduism is a minority religion in America (...) that deserves the same treatment that is already being given to other American minority religions—such as Native American, Buddhist or Islamic—by the Academe. The subaltern studies depiction of Hinduism as being the dominant religion of India must, therefore, be questioned in the American context.' (p.213)

On the other hand, in all sobriety, I must also note how, in spite of that hopeful event, very little has changed. Recent incidents, some concerning Malhotra himself, confirm that the exclusion of people because of their opinion, the systematic haughtiness because of institutional rank ('Malhotra is not even an academic', a sophomoric attitude unbecoming of anyone experienced with how progress in research is made, and by whom), the intellectually contemptible use of 'guilt by association', are all still in evidence in Western Indologist forums.

Malhotra notes an improvement in the general mood as a result of the debate: 'For the first time in RISA's history, to the best of my knowledge, the diaspora voices are not being branded as saffronists, Hindutva fanatics, fascists, chauvinists, dowry extortionists, Muslim killers, nun rapists, Dalit abusers, etc. One has to wait and see whether this is temporary or permanent.' (p.215)

So far, the impression prevails that the mood has not changed much. We saw this in 2015, when Malhotra was accused of plagiarism.

A detailed look at the case exonerated him and actually made the whole controversy rather ludicrous, yet otherwise moderate voices on the Indology and the Indo-Eurasian Research lists (I can't speak for the RISA list, but it contains the same people) all ganged up against him. They acted very indignant over something that, even if it were true, would only be a trifle, immaterial to the debate at hand. It is this persistence of the same anti-Hindu attitudes that makes this book more than a historical document: It teaches Hindus what to expect today if they challenge the Indological establishment.

In 2003, one factor was perhaps that a BJP government ruled in Delhi and, in spite of its so-called 'saffronization' of history textbooks, refuted in practice all the apprehensions about 'Hindu fascist' rule that the same Indologists had uttered in the 1990s. Remember, they had predicted a 'Muslim holocaust' if ever the BJP would come to power (and have never had to bear the consequences of their grossly wrong prediction in the field of their supposed expertise). Even ivory-tower academics had to be aware of that feedback from reality. Then again, this consideration ought to prevail even now, with Narendra Modi opening many doors internationally and not at all living up to the hate image many India-watchers had sworn by in the preceding years. Yet, 'Hinduphobia' is still with us.

PHOBIA

The major flaw in this book is its title. I object to political terms ending in '*-phobia*', normally a medical term meaning 'irrational fear', as in *arachnophobia*, the 'irrational fear of spiders'. As far as I know, the first term in this category of political terms borrowed from the medical register was '*homophobia*', the 'irrational fear of homosexuals'. First of all, the word was wrongly constructed. Literally, it means 'fear of the same', i.e., 'fear of the same sex', whereas men criticizing homosexuality are not usually afraid of men. In fact, the words target people who *disapprove* of homosexuality, no matter what their rational or emotional motive.

The term or connotation of 'sexuality' is missing (you might try 'homophilophobia') and the targeted 'disapproval' is not the same thing as the stated 'fear', nor as the intended 'hate'. Still, the neologism won through, thanks to the bourgeoisie's sheepish acceptance of it.

Next came '*Islamophobia*', literally 'irrational fear of Islam', intended to mean 'hatred of Islam', and in effect targeting 'disapproval of Islam' or 'Islam criticism'. This term was first launched in the 1990s by the Runnymede Trust, a British quango dedicated to fighting racism. It was taken over by many governments and media, and especially promoted by the Organisation of Islamic Cooperation. It is an intensely mendacious term trying to criminalize the normal exercise of the power of discrimination. The targeted critics of Islam need neither fear nor hate Islam—their attitude may rather be likened to that of a teacher using his red pencil to cross out a mistake in a pupil's homework. But again, a mighty promotion by powerful actors made the word gain household status.

On this model, the term '*Hinduphobia*' was coined. At bottom, we have to reject this term as much as we rejected the use of psychiatry against dissident viewpoints in the Soviet Union.

On the other hand, an irrational anti-Hinduism is a reality. It is precisely through comparison with Islam that this becomes glaring. Whenever a group of people gets killed in the name of Islam, immediately the politicians concerned and the media assure us that this terror 'has nothing to do with Islam'. In the case of Hinduism, it is just the reverse. Of any merit of Hinduism, it is immediately assumed that 'it has nothing to do with Hinduism', whereas every problem in India is automatically blamed on Hinduism, from poverty ('the Hindu rate of growth') to rape.

Thus, it is verifiable that books may be written about 'Jain mathematics', but when Hindus do mathematics, it will be called 'Indian mathematics' or 'the Kerala school of mathematics'. Congress politician Mani Shankar Aiyar once praised India's inherent pluralism, enumerated its well-attested hospitality to refugee groups, and then attributed all this not to Hinduism but to 'something in the air here'. In missionary propaganda and in the secularist media, it is always emphasized that 'tribals are not Hindus'—except when they take revenge on Christians or Muslims, because then the media reports on 'Hindu rioters'.

This obsessive negativity towards Hinduism needs to be named and shamed. Now that the bourgeoisie has interiorized terms like 'homophobia' and 'Islamophobia', it is clear that the neologism 'Hinduphobia' belongs to a language register they will understand. Once heightened scruples prevail and linguistic hygiene is restored, all three terms may be discarded together. But until then, the use of Hinduphobia in counter-attack mode is a wise compromise with the prevailing opinion climate.

The Aurangzeb Debate*

Unfortunately, I have no time for a full review of Audrey Truschke's book, checking primary sources and all that, though if it somehow proves necessary, I will do it anyway. I am concentrating on more complex and more important issues in the history of Hindu thought, while the history of Islam has lost my interest because it is so simple and our conclusions about it are not at all threatened with a need for revision. As a doctrine, Islam is a mistake, and as a historical movement, it has a very negative record vis-à-vis Unbelievers, especially the Hindus. The secularists and their foreign dupes may cry themselves hoarse in their denial of these straightforward and amply proven facts, but they don't stand a chance, though not for want of trying.

Nonetheless, let me offer some general observations. If Hindus are wrong anywhere in their evaluation of Aurangzeb, it is not in misstating his record, which was highly reprehensible even by the standards of his own day. But because of the crimes he undeniably committed against the mass of non-Muslims and against a few unorthodox Muslims, Hindus tend to launch this shrill rhetoric against the person Aurangzeb, as if he were an evil man. He was not.

Unlike Audrey Truschke, I will not have to do a counterfactual whitewash in order to relativize Aurangzeb's guilt. He did destroy the Kashi Vishvanath, the Krishna Janmabhumi and thousands of other temples, and their ruins or the mosques built in their stead remain mute witnesses to his practice of iconoclasm. Yet, he was also verifiably a pious and ascetic man. While we cannot look inside

*The author's letter replying to a review of Audrey Truschke's book *Aurangzeb: The Man and the Myth*, published in *The National Interest* on 22 April 2017

his skull to know what he really thought, all contemporaneous documents confirm that he set himself high standards of conduct. For example, he earned his own livelihood and did hold it against his father that he squandered taxpayers' money on luxuries like building the Taj Mahal.

Among Hindus too, we know of numerous pious and ascetic people, but none of them earned a reputation as an iconoclastic monster. Then what happened in the case of Aurangzeb? The answer is in the contents of the doctrine he came to take ever more seriously: Islam. When people at some point in their lives 'get religion', their freshly upgraded or newfound faith colours the nature of the behavioural changes that ensue. In the case of Islam, the religious enthusiast may take inspiration from the Prophet's life and works, more than the average Muslim brought up with the same ideals but less inclined to put them into practice. He was a better Muslim than most. Thus, he enacted laws harmful to the interests of the ruling class but more in keeping with Islamic jurisprudence. But the same devotion and religious earnestness that made him an ascetic also made him an iconoclast.

Whenever Islamic rulers or warlords feel compelled to provide a justification for their iconoclasm, they point to earlier Islamic leaders' precedents, but most of all to Mohammed's own model behaviour, especially the epochal moment after the city of Mecca's surrender when the Prophet and his son-in-law Ali removed the pagan Kaaba's 360 idols with their own hands. The job completed, they declared that with this, light had triumphed over darkness—truly a defining moment in Islam's genesis (as described in the *Sirat Rasul Allah*, the Prophet's orthodox biography). Not one Islamic theologian will contradict us when we say that an exemplary Muslim is one who emulates the Prophet.

At the end of his life, Aurangzeb privately repented his policy of iconoclasm, even though not deeply enough to reverse it. If no one else can refute gullible apologists like Audrey, let Aurangzeb himself do it. He certainly realized that his policy was too much for his contemporaries to stomach. And again, this change of heart had nothing to do with his personality but with his deeply held faith. He regretted having destroyed temples not because he was suddenly struck with compassion for the accursed Infidels, but because he had provoked them into rebellion and thus endangered Islam's position in India. For almost two centuries, Islam had thrived and enjoyed power, thanks to a compromise with the Hindu majority—these had a subordinate position, but not emphatically so. Not enough to make them rise in revolt. Now, after Shivaji's successful rebellion, it was becoming clear that Indian Islam had entered a period of decline. The romantic ideal of emulating the Prophet in every detail had come in the way of Islam's larger and deeper goal, viz. consolidating and extending its power, ultimately expected (as ordered by the *Quran* itself) to culminate in world conquest.

Let us note, finally, that on this issue, Audrey's book is representative of a wider concern to whitewash Aurangzeb. In their all-out war on Hinduism and specific Hindu ideas, the South Asia scholars tend to practise groupthink—there is rarely anything original, they only outdo each other in how daring they can make their own articulation of ever the same position. In 2014, I participated in an all-day session on Aurangzeb at the biannual conference of the European Association for South Asian Studies in Zürich. One paper after another highlighted some quotes from contemporaneous writers in praise of Aurangzeb. These are easy to find, as he had the last say in their success or marginalization, even over life and death. On Stalin, too, you can easily find many contemporary sources praising him, and then silly academics concluding therefrom that he can't have been so bad.

Thus, one of the sources was Guru Gobind Singh's *Zafar Namah* or 'victory letter'. If you quote it selectively, you might think he was an admirer and ideological comrade of Aurangzeb's. But the Guru was strategically with his back against the wall and had to curry favour with the man holding all the cards. So he wrote a diplomatically worded letter and held his personal opinions to himself (and here is one case where personal relations must have trumped ideology). It is entirely certain, and academics cover themselves with shame if they cleverly try to deny it, that the Guru hated Aurangzeb from the bottom of his heart. Aurangzeb was responsible for the murder of his father and all four sons. Any proletarian can understand that, in private, Guru Gobind Singh must have said the worst things about Aurangzeb. You have to be as silly or as partisan as a South Asia scholar to believe that the Guru meant to praise Aurangzeb.

To sum up, the presently discussed thesis by Truschke comes to add to the numbers of what formally look like studies in history, but effectively are meant as strikes in the ongoing battle against self-respecting Hinduism.

Ayodhya: Meeting Romila Thapar Halfway*

The School of Oriental and African Studies (SOAS), together with the neighbouring British Museum, is a centre of orientalism in its proper sense, viz. the study of 'oriental' civilizations. Exactly one hundred years ago, it came about as the headquarters of what Edward Said notoriously called 'orientalism', meaning the colonial empire's project of pigeonholing every oriental culture in order to better dominate it.

At that same time, on the enemy side in the ongoing First World War, the German scholar Max Weber published one of the most influential studies of the Orient, focusing on the question of the economic views and implications of the world religions, and especially the part about Hinduism and Buddhism. It sought to understand why not they but Protestantism had presided over the technoscientific and economic breakthrough to industrial capitalism and modernity.

Some fifty people gathered in the SOAS's Brunei Gallery Lecture Theatre for the centenary of both SOAS and Max Weber's work. As for SOAS's anniversary, Chairman Peter Flügel quoted viceroy Lord Curzon calling SOAS at its time of conception the 'necessary furniture of the empire', for 'oriental studies are an imperial obligation'. This is a key citation in Said's 'orientalism' thesis, viz. that orientalist scholarship was essentially a strategic

*This impression of a conference in London on Max Weber's Hindu-related work was first published as 'Max Weber's afterglow' on Pragyata.com, 11 September 2016

investment by the colonial establishment.

As for Weber, his view is fairly representative of general Western opinion (partly by having created it) regarding the Hindu-Buddhist counterpart to the role of the Protestant work ethic in the genesis of capitalism. He had concluded that the orientals certainly succeeded in launching a mercantile capitalism but, partly because of their otherworldly religion, failed in creating modern industrial capitalism. However, he had also testified in 1916 how, in the middle of the First World War, he had found his study of the Hindu-Buddhist worldviews invigorating. We were going to recreate some of that spirit.

PROFESSOR ROMILA THAPAR

The keynote lecture was given by the octogenarian historian Professor Romila Thapar. She looked quite good for her age, elegant and dignified in her sari. She thus exemplified Sita Ram Goel's observation that secularists often display a sincere affection for traditional Hindu culture, all the more striking when supposed Hindutva militants go all out for Westernization, from the British-style RSS uniform and brass bands to the present-day BJP-facilitated guzzling down of American economic mores and cultural mannerisms. The secularists of the older generation are culturally still very Indian, and have a traditional pride presenting an unassuming alternative identity to the present idealization of Western examples. (I am reminded of her colleague Professor Irfan Habib's proud old-Marxist rejection of US patronage, contrasting with the complete conceptual as well as outwardly Americanization of the younger generation of secularists and Ambedkarites.)

It transpired that she had a vivid interest in Weber's work regarding India, whom she read some forty years ago. As no Indian scholar of the younger generation showed a similar interest, she had graciously accepted the invitation from SOAS. The institution was familiar ground to her. She earned her Ph.D. degree at SOAS with a dissertation on Ashoka's inscriptions, published as an authoritative book in 1961. (Also present here was retired Oxford Buddhologist Professor Richard Gombrich, who strongly disagrees with her on those inscriptions, which he doesn't consider 'secular' at all, but instead outspokenly promoting the specific Buddhist worldview.) She immediately established a good rapport with the audience, speaking slowly with a clear and authoritative diction, as an experienced professor should.

She started with noticing the obvious: that Max Weber's research on Indian history and society relied heavily on colonial writings available then, and necessarily differed from the present-day theories. Being a prisoner of the colonial view, he did not thematize the implications of colonialism itself (unlike Karl Marx, who wrote about colonialism in Ireland and India). Weber reproduced and refined the colonial theory of 'oriental despotism', which militated against the individual freedom and social mobility needed for the genesis of modern capitalism.

RELIGIONS AND THEIR WORK ETHIC

Weber remains most famous for his thesis that the Protestant work ethic in the United Kingdom, the US and Germany was responsible for the rise of industrial capitalism. Weber argued that capitalism could not have originated in India because of its lack of fraternization between different groups (especially during apprenticeship, where Indian pupils were confined to their caste environment), its lack of social mobility, its cultural depreciation of commerce and its otherworldly religious orientation. He did not give sufficient consideration to the Jains, whose trading activity, moneylending and renunciation of enjoying their profits come closest to the Protestant work ethic, though in passing he admits they had potential. In precolonial times, China and India were the main economies in Eurasia and practised mercantile capitalism. But they missed the shift to industrial capitalism, which took place in Europe.

But then, Weber neglected the specific eighteenth–nineteenth-century history of India and the role of both native and colonial capitalism therein. More generally, he treated Hindu culture as a monolithic whole, insufficiently considering the differences between classes and regions, and not taking the changes between the different periods into account. In a borrowed distortion typical of the orientalists of the colonial period, he based his understanding of Hinduism only on texts, especially the Vedic corpus to whom different groups across regions and centuries paid due lip service, all while exhibiting variations and going through changes. Thus, that is why the scripture-based fourfold Varna ('caste') system figured far more prominently in the Western image of Hindu society than the real-life thousandfold jati ('caste') system.

The corrective that Hindu society was too readily seen as changeless may have been the most important message in her lecture, seemingly trivial but full of consequences for both Hindus and practising orientalists. In this case, the colonial-age orientalists, with Weber in their wake, may have borrowed their extremely static view of Hindu culture from the Hindus themselves. Allow me to furnish an example.

THE 'HINDU CASTE SYSTEM'

When the Ambedkarites and their Western cheerleaders anchor the caste system, complete with untouchability, in the *Rig Veda*'s Purusha Sukta, they are wrong; yet, they are only following a traditionalist Hindu view that prevailed in the past few centuries. The box-type caste apartheid with caste endogamy of the Puranic and early modern era was nowhere to be seen in the *Rig Veda*: The earlier family books don't report any trace of it, and the Purusha Sukta in the late Book 10 only reports the existence of four distinct functions in a complex society.

After that, the caste system gradually hardened with a stage of hereditary caste only in the paternal line (as with the Brahmin Vyasa, son of the Brahmin Parashara and the fisher-girl Matsyagandha; and as with the sons of dasis who were recruited into the Brahmin caste, mentioned here by Professor Thapar), and finally endogamy. Equating Hinduism with the classical caste system, as is the wont of the Christian missionaries, the Ambedkarites and many an orientalist, makes the mistake of disregarding change in Hindu history, but this mistake is based on Hindus having made the same mistake. For some 2,000 years, any trespass against or doubt regarding the fully grown caste system was condemned with an invocation of the *Rig Veda*'s authority, as if the Purusha Sukta had described the kind of caste system with which later Hindus were familiar.

(It deserves mention here that Professor Thapar has contributed to our awareness of change within Hindu social structure. She has edited the book *India: Historical Beginnings and the Concepts of the Aryan* (2006), in which Marxist historian Shereen Ratnagar asserts (p.166): 'If, as in the case of the early Vedic society, land was neither privately owned nor inherited by successive generations, then land rights would have been irrelevant to the formation of kin groups, and there would be nothing preventing younger generations from leaving the parental fold. In such societies, the constituent patrilineages or tribal sections were not strongly corporate. So together with geographic expansion, there would be social flexibility.' It has become fashionable to moralize about the caste system, with evil Brahmins inventing caste and then imposing it on others; but hard-headed Marxists don't fall for this conspiracy theory and see the need for socioeconomic conditions to explain the reigning system of hierarchy or equality. The pastoral early-Vedic society did have the conditions for a more equal relation between individuals than the more complex later Hindu society.)

Other factual inaccuracies in Weber's work include the total disregard for the presence of Islam in India, like for that of Buddhism in China, because their foreignness jeopardizes Weber's explanation of India's economic performance as stemming from the Indian religions. The different religions were treated as self-contained, not porous. The Indian state was described as agricultural, while recent studies corrected this: There was much commerce, including maritime, and this had only increased with urbanization after the year 1000. Weber also exaggerated the power of karma beliefs to reconcile people to social misfortune. The peasantry often responded to crises by migration, and sometimes even by that supposedly un-Indian behaviour—rebellion. They didn't wait for the next birth to better their circumstances.

Trade was not despised, and even Brahmins and ascetics involved themselves in it—e.g., in the horse trade. Labour division between castes was more flexible than used to be thought. In the century before Weber, the static view of caste was conspicuously challenged by the anti-Brahmin movements and by the upper-caste reform movements. Even a non-specialist could have been more aware of these developments.

CONCLUSION

So, let us sum up. Max Weber's world exists no more, and even the terms of the debate have been altered. Are the categories of religion used by Weber (and likewise, by Marx) still valid? They strike us now as context-free and innocent of the changes that took place. Today, this non-change view is regarded as ahistorical. Weber would have been better if he had compared the same period in East and West, rather than comparing apples with pears: timeless societies in the distance with the familiar recent stage of Western society.

We remain stuck with the large question: What prevented Asia from taking the lead in knowledge? Why was the lead grabbed by Europe, after having lagged behind for so long? More was required for this than the Protestant work ethic. And another question, rather trivial but appropriate on this occasion: How would Max Weber have seen the religion of India a hundred years later?

AFTERTHOUGHT

So much for the Weber lecture. People who know something of the Ayodhya controversy may be surprised to learn that afterwards, I had a few friendly interactions with Professor Thapar. Remembering the flak I drew in India from Hindu nationalists when I took my erstwhile Aryan-origins adversary Michael Witzel's side in the controversy that followed the publication of his book on global mythology (2013), I will take the trouble to explain.

Firstly, it is all rather long ago, about a quarter century back. Back then, Professor Thapar took a leadership role in the secularist plea that there was no basis for historians to accept the belief that a Hindu temple had stood at the site of the Babri mosque in Ayodhya. In the dominant political and academic circles, that position suddenly became a consensus, and I stood out by challenging it. But the debate for me has been largely settled with the court-ordered excavations in 2003, which laid bare plenty of signs of a temple. When the war is over, soldiers go home, and let the war psychology that had animated them on the battlefield subside.

I will not mention the names of some Hindu and some anti-Hindu scholars who are still repeating quite exactly what they said decades ago, especially in the Aryan-origins debate. They foam at the mouth when they argue their point, and keep doing so. But for better or for worse, I am not like that. So, the second reason is that I really don't believe in personalizing debates on specific issues. Admittedly, I was not quite immune to that tendency when I was younger. But gradually, you not only know in theory, but also realize in practice that human relations should not, or should as little as possible, be affected by controversies. Even in controversies that I find myself in today, I endeavour to stay on friendly terms with my adversaries.

Number three is the principle I want henceforth to guide all my dealings with adversaries. As Socrates said, the root of everything deemed evil is ignorance. People who objectively do evil, subjectively believe they are doing the right thing, because somewhere they have picked up a mistaken idea of what constitutes right or of what exactly it is that they are doing. There is no need to intensify the impression that they are evil, it is more helpful to make them see reason, and automatically they will correct their position; for it is not in eagerness to do the right thing that they are lacking. It also helps to remain aware that you yourself, with all your good intentions, seem likewise to be on the wrong side from your adversaries' viewpoint. That is no reason to assume all positions are equal, or to drop your own convictions, but it will help you to better understand how anyone could have taken the opposite position to your own.

Meanwhile, on the lawn outside the SOAS gate, I noticed a statue of the Tamil poet Thiruvalluvar. It carries a translated quotation of his, which I would like to reproduce as my parting shot:

> 'Meet with joy, with pleasant thoughts part,
> Such is the learned scholar's art.'

Guha's Golwalkar

It is a rare and healthy thing in Indian intellectual life when a leading thinker promises to devote an analysis to Guru Golwalkar's work, given the latter's influence on the RSS and indirectly on what is now the ruling party, the BJP. But given this analysis' flaws, a comment was also called for.

Part 1*

Ramachandra Guha's column, 'A question of sources: The unholy holy book of the RSS' (*The Telegraph*, 17 September 2016) draws attention to the fiftieth anniversary of a major ideological manifesto of Hindu nationalism: 'Guru' Madhav Sadashiv Golwalkar's book *Bunch of Thoughts*. After the death of Dr Keshav Baliram Hedgewar (1889–1940), who, in 1925, had founded the Rashtriya Swayamsevak Sangh, or the National Volunteer Association, the Benaras Hindu University-trained biologist Golwalkar (1906–1973) was the second sarsanghchalak, or 'the chief guide of the association', until his own death. He is credited with greatly expanding the RSS's presence in Indian society by creating a parivar ('family') of specialized organizations, including a pan-Hindu religious platform, a trade union, a student organization, a network for tribal welfare and a political party.

This party, the Bharatiya Jan Sangh (BJS, 'Indian People's Association'), founded in 1951, was a venture into explicit politics

*Published on Pragyata.com, 25 October 2016

which Golwalkar agreed to against his wishes, after the Hindu Mahasabha ('Hindu Great Council', °1922) had irredeemably fallen from grace with the murder of Mahatma Gandhi by one of its members. Reportedly, Golwalkar gave his consent to the party's creation with the words: 'Alright, then, a house also needs a lavatory.' The party existed until 1977, when it fused with others to form the Janata Party ('People's Party') and was reconstituted in 1980 as the Bharatiya Janata Party (BJP), the ruling party at the time of this writing.

The title of Golwalkar's book was inspired by Jawaharlal Nehru's collection *A Bunch of Old Letters*, effectively a 'bunch' or random collection of disparate writings. This was not the best choice for what was intended to be an ideological guidebook.

THE PLACE OF BOOKS IN HINDU NATIONALISM

Guha misrepresents (probably because he misunderstands) the role of books in the Sangh. His inference that *Bunch of Thoughts* somehow determines today's BJP government's policies is a typical secularist fantasy, if only because the BJP has emancipated itself from the RSS. Most BJP men today are not from the RSS, and even the RSS men inside or outside the BJP have rarely read this Hindutva manifesto. The short attention span of many Hindus (as an outsider, I would not dare to say this, but Hindu intellectuals themselves keep bewailing this tendency) militates against reliance on hefty volumes like *Bunch of Thoughts*. Ploughing through demanding books is only given to few—among ethnicities mainly the Chinese, northern Europeans and Jews, and even there not exactly the majority. Whenever you present a book to an RSS leader, he is bound to say: 'Can't you summarize this volume to a small pamphlet?' (On the bright side, Hindu consciousness-raising is currently getting a tremendous boost by the developments in communication technology: through less-demanding means like Twitter messages, and through the return to oral culture, as in webinars.)

This aversion to reading is especially true of the RSS. This has a historical cause as well as a conscious decision behind it. The historical cause is the circumstances of the RSS's founding: Dr K.B. Hedgewar came from the Bengal revolutionary faction of the freedom movement, and brought its secretive methods along. Like the revolutionaries, wary of feeding written evidence of their designs to police informers, RSS men never communicated in writing but travelled around to pass information orally. Hence the enormous physical locomotion performed by RSS officers. As the wife of an RSS veteran confided to me: 'It is a status symbol for them.'

The (indeed real) influence of *Bunch of Thoughts* in RSS discourse is mainly through oral sermons by bauddhik (intellectual) officers selecting a few nice passages. Most RSS men won't recognize the more difficult passages that Guha draws grim conclusions from. It is like the *Bible* in Roman Catholicism, where the raw passages are kept out of hearing distance: The flock is only fed the elevating passages through selected Sunday readings.

There is a big difference between BJP texts from thirty years ago and those available today, having become more sophisticated but also more secularist and less Hindu. In BJP discourse, pace Guha, the term 'Hindu rashtra' (Hindu state), dear to Golwalkar, is now unthinkable. While the Congress has evolved from secular nationalism to making common cause with the *Breaking India* forces, the BJP has evolved from Hindu nationalism to secular nationalism. (Which, on the bright side, makes it the natural party of government.) This is to a lesser extent true of the RSS, but it is still closer to Golwalkar. However, the person-cult of Golwalkar, still as strong as ever, is unrelated to the influence of *Bunch of Thoughts*. The RSS position regarding Golwalkar's ideas might well evolve, all while the devotion to Golwalkar remains the same. Secularist intellectuals like Guha may find this absurd, but it is the reality.

'WE, OR OUR NATIONHOOD DEFINED'

Guha's critique is certainly not the lowliest kind of anti-Golwalkar polemic. In articles of that category, used unquestioningly as source in the majority of the introductions to Hindu nationalism, the targeted Golwalkar book would not be *Bunch of Thoughts* (1966) but his slim maiden volume, *We, or Our Nationhood Defined* (1939). That attempt at ideological contemplation of the political challenges before Hindu society has earned notoriety because of two overquoted passages. In one, Golwalkar is selectively cited as seemingly supporting Nazi Germany. I have analysed this passage in the context of the book and its time (one chapter each in *The Saffron Swastika*, 2001, and *Return of the Swastika*, 2006, or online at https://www.academia.edu/14793753/Disowning_Golwalkars_We), and found this common allegation, present in every introductory text on Hindutva, totally wanting. Thus, anti-Semitism was the core doctrine of National Socialism, yet the Jewish people were the foremost role models upheld by Golwalkar for the 'Hindu nation'. As for the Nazis' militarism, he contrasts Germany's champions of martial virtues with the sages who form the Hindu role models 'in serene majesty'. This oft-quoted passage is irrelevant for contemporary debates, except to show to what mendaciousness secularists and foreign India-watchers can stoop.

The other passage could have more to do with contemporary politics. It clearly distinguishes Christians and Muslims from the Hindus, as mere guests vis-à-vis the host society, entitled to protection and an honourable life, but to nothing more. Golwalkar proposes that they 're-assimilate', or else accept a protected status as foreign residents 'claiming nothing, not even citizens' rights'. Yet, as the book disappeared from circulation in 1948 and Golwalkar vetoed its reprint for being 'immature', most Sangh members have never even seen that line. It doesn't reflect the current party line of the RSS, let alone the BJP.

The only incriminating fact that still attaches to *We* is its disowning by the RSS. It officially disowned the book in 2006, only confirming half a century of the book's factual non-existence, and with that decision, we have no quarrel. But it also claimed, quite mendaciously, that the book had not been written by Golwalkar and did not reflect his ideas. Nobody got fooled, except the most obedient among the RSS's own volunteers.

'BUNCH OF THOUGHTS'

By contrast, the contents of *Bunch of Thoughts* remain a central part of most Sanghis' ideological formation. The only book to rival it is Deendayal Upadhyaya's *Integral Humanism* (1965), adopted as official ideology by the Bharatiya Jan Sangh and (after some confusion with 'Gandhian socialism', finally agreed to be but another name for the same ideology) its successor body, the BJP. If you would want to honestly criticize the BJP through a book, it would be Upadhyaya's *Integral Humanism*, but even the sheer mention of that book is absent from the immense majority of 'expert' publications about the BJP. *Bunch of Thoughts* only plays a role for the party's old guard that was groomed in the RSS. The party has moved away from its parent body and most members today don't have an RSS past.

While *Bunch of Thoughts* is of limited consequence to our evaluation of the presently governing BJP's policies, it has a historical link to the party and may, of course, form the object of research. Without being fooled by the secularists into thinking that any fault found in it can be applied to the party, we will nonetheless take note of the Hindutva gems that Guha has discovered in it.

Golwalkar does indeed remain 'the chief ideologue of the organization', meaning the RSS, and till today, his 'bearded visage is prominently displayed' at RSS functions. It may also be true that as an RSS veteran, Prime Minister Narendra Modi 'hugely admires Golwalkar'. Yet, in general, it is a big stretch of Guha's to claim that *Bunch of Thoughts* is 'of enormous contemporary relevance' and is for the ruling party what the *Quran* is for Muslims. Firstly, the RSS impact on the BJP is limited and waning. Secondly, Islam is a 'religion of the book' and heavily determined by the contents of the *Quran*, to which it explicitly pays obeisance; but Hinduism is not that book-oriented, even when it pays plenty of lip service to the scriptures.

This counts even more for its Hindutva variety. Indeed, Golwalkar himself was emphatically anti-bookish and berated his volunteers when they were caught 'idling' by reading a book. More than anyone else, he is responsible for the RSS's anti-intellectual orientation, which has been very consequential: (1) a complete absence from the public debate (2) a propensity to make fools of themselves with fantastic claims, e.g., that 'ancient Indians had airplanes', as if India's real contributions to science and technology weren't good enough (3) a complete passivity when Nehruvians and Marxists moved in to monopolize the cultural and educational sphere, and (4) to really drive the negative implications home, an utter inability to give a credible defence of Golwalkar's own books.

NATIONALISM

Golwalkar was a nationalist, and the movement he led is known worldwide as 'Hindu nationalism' even today. Contrary to what the secularists allege these days, the RSS was very much rooted in the freedom movement, in anti-colonial nationalism. It started as a security force to protect a Congress meeting in 1925, and its founder, K.B. Hedgewar, had been trained by the Bengali revolutionary wing of the freedom movement. (This explains a working principle of the RSS, viz. its secretiveness and reliance on direct communication.) Its slightly older sister, the Hindu Mahasabha (1922), was originally a Hindu lobby within the Congress.

This nationalism was a logical choice, at least in the 1920s. The immediate pressures from the anti-colonial struggle and the international after-effect of the national passions of the Great War, made nationalism honourable and obligatory. Even associations for sports or music took the habit of marching in uniform, as if they were armies marching to the battlefield. The RSS followed this pattern.

Emotionally, this nationalist appeal undoubtedly works. Election campaigns fought on national issues tend to unite the citizens around them, transcending and trumping the usual contests between collective self-interests (communal, casteist or regional), which are divisive.

It is another question whether it still is such a wise choice after 1945, when nationalism got a bad name through its identification with the losing side in the Second World War; after 1947 and the decades of independence, when India has other concerns than its relatively assured national freedom; after 1947 again, as the year when many Hindus became citizens of the suddenly separate countries of Pakistan and (what was to become) Bangladesh; after the resettlement of millions of Hindus abroad and their acquisition of a foreign nationality (apart from those already in Nepal, Bhutan, Myanmar, Sri Lanka, Malaysia, Singapore and Afghanistan); and after quite a few non-Indians became Hindu. As I have argued elsewhere, 'nationalism is a misstatement of Hindu concerns'.

Thus, the reason why Muslim invaders destroyed Hindu temples was not that they were 'foreign invaders', as claimed in most RSS pamphlets, for then they would have imposed 'foreign temples' on Hindu sites. No, it was because they were *Muslim*, a word avoided nowadays in RSS parlance, and they imposed *mosques*. In discussions about Ghar Wapasi ('homecoming'), the reconversion of Christian converts to Hinduism, promoted by the RSS, I often hear the justification: 'Christianization also entails Westernization'—as if Christianization without Westernization were alright. But that is not the problem: Hindus themselves are fast Westernizing (without the RSS-BJP doing anything against it), but this does not make them non- or anti-Hindu. And at least the Catholic missionaries are responding to this complaint by 'inculturation', i.e., Christianization without Westernization. So that is alright for the RSS: Indian Christians smashing Hindu 'idols', as long as they duly wear a dhoti? For 'nationalists', blind to the religious dimension, it is.

HINDU RASHTRA

Why was the nation conceived as 'Hindu', rather than 'Indian'? In Hedgewar's analysis, Hindu society constituted the Indian nation, while the minorities were mere guests. In older documents of the RSS and the Jan Sangh, you still find this idea of a 'Hindu nation', as evidenced by the oft-quoted Golwalkar sentence from *We* about minority inhabitants having 'not even citizens' rights'. However, even then the RSS and the BJS adopted terms like 'Bharatiya' (Indian) and 'rashtriya' (national), and thus prepared the ground for a more recent shift away from Hindu identity politics, towards 'secular' or 'inclusive' nationalism. This shift, very outspoken in the BJP but also affecting the RSS, leads to inventive constructions such as that of the Indian Muslims as 'Mohammedi Hindus', a term repeatedly insisted on by L.K. Advani during the Ayodhya campaign of ca. 1990.* Not that Indian Muslims will ever accept this contradictory label, but their honest opinion is not asked. The rationale for this term is the post-Golwalkar doctrine that 'Hindu' is synonymous with 'Indian'.

Earlier, 'Indian' was reduced to 'Hindu' (subtracting any non-Hindu Indians from the 'Indian' category, as in Golwalkar's quotes above), but in the RSS discourse of the last decades, 'Hindu' is being reduced to 'Indian'. This purely geographical and thus 'secular' notion was the meaning of the Persian word 'Hindu' 1,500 years ago. But when the Muslim invaders imported it into India, it immediately had a religious meaning: all Indian pagans in the broadest sense, i.e., all those who were not Jews, Christians or Muslims. This, then, is the original Indian meaning of Hindu: any Indian pagan, whether Brahmin, Shudra, Buddhist, tribal or any other grouping or denomination, but emphatically excluding Muslims and Christians. Since it is the historically foundational meaning, those who insist on giving it a different meaning have the

---

*As reported in e.g. 'Advani wants Muslims to identify with "Hindutva"', *Times of India*, 30 January 1995

burden of justification on them. In this case, it is the RSS that owes us, already for a few decades, a justification for its absurd redefining of 'Hindu' as simply 'Indian', including Christians and Muslims.

Haven't the 'experts' on whom Guha relies, noticed this shift in meaning of the all-important term 'Hindu'? It explains, to name a current and important example, the grim and determined passivity of the Modi government regarding specifically Hindu demands, such as the abolition of the blatantly anti-Hindu (so, communally partisan and hence anti-secular) Right to Education Act, which has forced hundreds of Hindu schools to close down. A Hindu party would be up in arms against anti-Hindu discriminations (and the BJS was, but did not have the power), but in their present state of mind, the Hindu movement simply cannot conceive of 'anti-Hindu' discriminations any more, as this would mean 'anti-Indian'.

A government advisor confided to me that the BJP now, having learnt its lesson from the A.B. Vajpayee government's passivity on Hindu issues, wants to 'keep the pot boiling'. It wants to throw some crumbs to its Hindu constituency, such as a punitive strike against Pakistani terrorist camps, to buy sufficient loyalty from its Hindu support base—but without doing anything substantive on important Hindu demands. The most important of these is not risky projects pregnant with communal violence, such as the common civil code dear to the erstwhile BJS, but the perfectly reasonable and secular abolition of all legal and Constitutional discriminations against Hinduism. (I invite the BJP to prove me wrong, not with denunciations but with legislative *action*.)

This shift also means that both organizations, the BJP formally and the RSS effectively, have renounced one of Golwalkar's core ideas: the *Hindu rashtra*, or the 'Hindu state' (though the RSS used to fussily insist that it means an ill-defined 'Hindu nation' instead). It was an un-Hindu idea to start with: The Gupta or the Chola empire or any other pre-modern Hindu political entity was coronated with Hindu rites and facilitated Vedic and Puranic traditions, but never called itself a 'Hindu rashtra'. Further, Hindu states have always been pluralistic, regardless of the ruler's personal orientation.

In India this is now termed 'secular', an infelicitous term deviant from its original meaning of 'non-religious' or 'not acknowledging as consequential any religious identities', but one that has been accepted by the RSS itself in its 1990 slogan, 'Hindu India, secular India.' By the RSS's own post-Golwalkar logic, Hindu rashtra, when analysed, would only mean 'a (genuinely) secular state'. Why then uphold a Hindu rashtra as a distant goal in contradistinction to the present principle (admittedly imperfect in its realization) of a secular republic? Golwalkar's and the present RSS leadership's positions on this question, and the probable difference between the two, would make an excellent topic for a thorough intra-RSS debate, followed by an authoritative publication explaining the whole question in detail and finally offering clarity. Are they capable of doing this?

INDIA'S UNITY

Unlike Jawaharlal Nehru, Golwalkar didn't see this nationhood as a project, a 'nation in the making', but as an ancient heritage: 'Long before the West had learnt to eat roast meat instead of raw, we were one nation, with one motherland.' Indeed, in many RSS writings, it is claimed that the Vedic expression *matrbhumi*, or 'motherland', meant 'India', in the sense of 'the subcontinent'.

That is not true, but the belief has a long tradition. A close reading of the *Vedas* shows a geographical horizon stretching from roughly Prayag to the Afghan frontier. The only Vedic seer credited with crossing the Vindhya mountains was Agastya, and that was noticed precisely because it was an exceptional adventure, not a visit to a province of his familiar motherland. In the *Mahabharata*, an epic based on a historical war of succession in the Vedic Bharata dynasty ca. 1400 BC, the geographical ambit of the events and persons involved is similarly limited. Yet, by the time of the final editing, around the time of Christ, dynasties from the farthest ends of India had had themselves written into the narrative. They wanted to belong to the expanding Vedic civilization, which is also why they invited Brahmin families and donated land to them, in order to have them confer Vedic legitimacy on their dynasties.

Not since a God-given eternity, but at least for more than 2,000 years, all of the subcontinent has had a sense of unity. This is far more than most countries can say, and it is enough to justify its political unity today. The pilgrimage cycles, the narration of the same epics in village squares all over the country, and the visible presence of the otherwise self-contained Brahmin caste and the monastic orders, created a degree of self-conscious cultural unity. This sometimes approached but never fully reached political unity, which at any rate only concerned the elites: Changing borders made little difference to ordinary life. Clearly, political unity existed at least as an ideal.

The fact is that here, Golwalkar gave utterance to a feeling common among Indians. Whatever the details of the past, Indians believe in national unity. And this is not a nationalism 'in the making'—on the contrary: The Nehruvian elites dish out all kinds of reasons why not Indianness but the separate communal identities are 'real', yet when push comes to shove, Indians stand united. Before the Chinese attacked in 1962, Tamil Nadu was in the grip of separatist fervour, but when the invasion came, the Tamils, all while remaining wedded to the Dravidianist cultural demands, abandoned the separatist camp and threw their lot in with India. Also, history shows that the surest way to win an election lies in having just won an Indo-Pak war. The local and communal identities are real, but so is the 'national' identity.

Hence Guha's Golwalkar quotation: 'Hindu society developed in an all-comprehensive manner, with a bewildering variety of phases and forms, but with one thread of unification running inherently through the multitude of expressions and manifestations.' Here Golwalkar's observation is impeccable, though I would call this unity 'civilizational' rather than 'national'. Guha comments: 'What precisely this unifying thread was is never defined.' Well, it is Hinduism. This is a vague and capacious notion, but adequate enough to explain India's self-conscious unity.

Part 2*

In Part 1, we saw Ramachandra Guha drawing grim conclusions from the supposed influence of M.S. Golwalkar's fifty-year-old book *Bunch of Thoughts* on the ruling party. Here we discuss some more aspects of Golwalkar's vision that, in Guha's understanding, should be cause for worry.

WORLD TEACHER

According to Ramachandra Guha, another 'assumption that Golwalkar works with is that despite their fallen state today, Hindus are destined to lead and guide the world'. He cites Guruji (Golwalkar) as asserting that it 'is the grand world-unifying thought of Hindus alone that can supply the abiding basis for human brotherhood', so that world leadership, no less, 'is a divine trust, we may say, given to the charge of the Hindus by destiny'.

It is not as if other nations are waiting for India's contribution. Then again, what they did take or accept from India was the most precious contribution. China had no mean philosophy sprung out of its own soil, but nonetheless accepted and integrated Buddhism. Among the Greek philosophers, Pythagoras and later the neo-Platonists were but the most explicit in copying Indian concepts and even practices, and they influenced the whole of European philosophy, as well as a bit of Christian theology. A much later revolution in European thought was wrought by Immanuel Kant, who admitted the decisive influence ('awakened from my dogmatic slumber') from David Hume's sudden development of a quasi-Buddhist view. Hume doesn't mention Buddhism, and would perhaps have been laughed out of court if he had, but recently we have discovered that his philosophical awakening had been triggered by his reading two detailed accounts of Buddhist thought by Catholic missionaries posted in Tibet or Thailand. Modern

*Published on Pragyata.com, 4 November 2016

thinkers like A.N. Whitehead, C.G. Jung and Ken Wilber tapped directly into Indian thoughts and practices, even if not always acknowledging it (an attitude discussed by Rajiv Malhotra in his innovative thesis of the 'U-turn').

On the other hand, translating this natural attractiveness of Indian traditions for outsiders into a missionary spirit is not very Hindu either. When real Evangelists meet someone from a different religion, immediately their missionary mechanic sets to work: What buttons are there in him that I can click to make him open to my message? Hindus don't have this at all. When they meet someone from a strange religion, they become naturally curious. They feel no need to destroy that foreign religion and replace it with Hinduism, but assume that there must be a core of wisdom in it, something essentially the same as what makes Hindus tick.

Moreover, this international appeal as a 'world teacher' sits uncomfortably with Golwalkar's nationalism. It is now the need of the hour to stress that Indian contributions are really from India (against, for example, American attempts to obscure the Sanskrit terms and Indian references in yoga), and that in some respects India has indeed been a 'world teacher'. But apart from that, the further propagation of Indian contributions abroad, as of foreign contributions inside India, will go on for some time. In a footnote of their schoolbooks, the brighter among Chinese or European or Latin-American pupils will still learn that yoga originated in India, or that the zero originated in India, but otherwise it will simply be part of their own life, that is their own mathematics. Just like rocket science came from Germany, the train from England, gunpowder from China and mankind from Africa. So many world teachers!

THE BUDDHA'S COSMOPOLITANISM

Like most Hindus, Golwalkar praises the Buddha. The Buddhists, by contrast, he accuses of beginning to 'uproot the age-old national traditions of this land. The great cultural virtues fostered in our society were sought to be demolished.' It could have made sense to accuse the Buddhists of neglecting certain virtues because they emphasized other virtues more. A slightly earlier Hindu nationalist, V.D. Savarkar, had already considered the Buddhist (but not Buddhist alone) value of non-violence harmful for India's defence. But the destructive design of 'seeking to demolish' anything of value is not normally associated with Buddhism. While there is no doubt that foreigners were important in the history of Buddhism, especially the Indo-Greeks (Menander/Milinda) and the Kushanas (Kanishka), Golwalkar surprises us with the information that 'devotion to the nation and its heritage had reached such a low pitch that the Buddhist fanatics invited and helped the foreign aggressors who wore the mask of Buddhism. The Buddhist sect had turned a traitor to the mother society and the mother religion.'

This is bad history, and rather nasty towards Buddhist fellow-Indians. But we can agree that Buddhism never set great store by defending India's borders, which were not threatened in the north or the east, where the Buddha lived and worked. The northwestern frontier was known to the Buddha, and indeed culturally familiar, not felt to be a foreign land at all, for his friends Prasenajit and Bandhula had studied there, at Takshashila University. (Yes, it existed before Buddhism: Contrary to the Nehruvian received wisdom, the university as an institution was not a Buddhist but a Vedic invention.) But he was not in the business of defending it: At that very time it was not threatened either, and he indeed had other priorities anyway. But neither he nor his followers ever shot anyone in the back who felt called upon to fight aggressors.

Something similar counts for other Indian sects. The *Vedas* and the epics report a number of wars, but never a defence against foreign aggression. Once there was real aggression, by Mohammed Ghori, defender Prithviraj Chauhan was betrayed by Jayachandra, the latter as much a Hindu as the former. They were aware of some cultural unity stretching from Attock to Cuttack, but politically they were attached to their own part of the subcontinent—and to hell with the neighbours. The RSS notion of a deshbhakt (a 'patriot', 'devotee of the country', meaning a devotee of the whole subcontinent) did not exist in pre-modern Hinduism.

Sects with any kind of spiritual goal had another purpose than nationalism: liberation, self-realization, knowledge, isolation (of consciousness from nature), awakening, or anything the different sects chose to call the ultimate state of consciousness. None of the classical manuals for the seekers of the ultimate mention India. If, in recent centuries, it does come up by way of geographical detail, it is still not invested with value pertaining to their goal. The Motherland is where you come from, a natural given; not where you go to, not the norm you aspire to reach. It is just there.

Then again, you do get the notion of India as a 'punyabhumi', a territory fit for earning merit, which you have to purify yourself to re-enter after a stay abroad. Here you get the bridge between Hindu spirituality and Hindu nationalism. In my opinion, like in that of cosmopolitan secularists, this was a degenerative trend, but as an outsider, I don't want to tell Hindus what to do or believe. So here we do have to admit that Golwalkar had a traditional basis for his assertion of India's uniqueness.

CASTE

Buddhism had come into the limelight in 1956, shortly before the book was written: with Dr B.R. Ambedkar's adoption of, or (in Guha's borrowed Christian construction of the event) 'conversion' to Buddhism. Ambedkar had wanted to show a fist to caste Hinduism, yet that did not make him a 'traitor to the mother society and the mother religion'. On the contrary: He said that conversion to a foreign religion would harm the nation, which he did not want, hence his embracing of a sect born in India. As Savarkar had commented, Ambedkar's 'refuge' in Bauddha dharma was 'a sure jump into the Hindu fold'. That is why the RSS, thanks to advancing insight, has gradually included Ambedkar in its pantheon. But that development was not on the horizon yet under Guruji. Guha correctly notes that Golwalkar 'does not so much as mention the great emancipator of the Dalits'.

For people involved in a crusade against Hinduism, like the Nehruvian secularists, it was a foregone conclusion that whatever a Hindu leader ever wrote, he would most of all be judged for his position on caste. That this will always be a negative judgement is an equally foregone conclusion. Hinduism, for them, is 'caste, wholly caste, and nothing but caste'. This implies that a nominal Hindu is deemed to have turned against his religion if he takes an approvedly egalitarian position—only then is he the good guy. If he spits on his mother, bravo! But if he chooses to defend Hinduism, as Golwalkar does, every possible position he takes will always be deemed an intolerable discrimination on caste lines. Even if he pronounces himself in favour of full equality, he is still lambasted for being patronizing and exercising his 'Brahmin privilege'.

According to Guha, 'Golwalkar vigorously defends the caste system, saying that it kept Hindus united and organized down the centuries'. Yet, what follows is something else than a 'vigorous defence'—it is a nuanced historical understanding that a social system at variance with modern homogenizing nationalism may yet have had its historical advantages: 'On the one hand, the so-called "caste-ridden" Hindu society has remained undying and unconquerable... after facing for over 2,000 years the depredations of Greeks, Shakas, Hunas, Muslims and even Europeans, by one shock of which, on the other hand, the so-called casteless societies crumbled to dust, never to rise again.' Whether a causal relationship can be established between caste and the survival of Hinduism should be investigated, but it is a reasonable hypothesis that deserves better than Guha's blanket condemnation.

'*Bunch of Thoughts* altogether ignores the suppression of Dalits and women in Hindu society.' Look at these double standards. Pray, Mr Guha, show me a book written in defence of Islam that expounds on the mistreatment of women in Islam. After you have done that, you may ask this very similar question of Hinduism. As a prolific writer, have you published anything about the oppression of women in Christianity, a critique developed by the very originators of feminism in the world? Why do you single out Hinduism here?

We have never seen you ask feminist authors why they haven't contributed anything to the struggle for Hinduism's self-respect against its many enemies, so why the reverse? Further, we may speculate that the women's viewpoint just didn't occur to Golwalkar, as a confirmed bachelor leading an all-male organization; and that in the India of the 1960s, women's issues were not as high-profile as today.

By contrast, caste inequality has continuously been on the agenda in the Indian republic. Golwalkar was not silent about it, but gave much less prominence to caste than anti-Hindu authors do, who assume that 'Hinduism is caste, wholly caste, and nothing but caste'. RSS veterans who still knew Golwalkar in person told me he took a nationalist and non-conflictual view of the issue: As a nationalist, he believed in the minimization of all divisive factors and in a large measure of equality for all members of the Hindu nation, but not in social engineering, much less in quota or reparative discrimination ('affirmative action'). Thus, when a Brahmin neophyte at first refused to eat together with the other castes, he allowed him to eat separately, until he was familiar enough with the RSS attitude that he himself came around to eating with the others. That way, his acceptance of inter-caste commensality was much better anchored than if imposed on him. The RSS boasts of being the only caste-free civil organization in India. By contrast, the political parties that for historical reasons call themselves 'anti-caste' practise naked caste advocacy. They typically are informal or even self-designated interest groups of a particular group of castes.

COMMUNALISM

Guha accuses Golwalkar of paranoia vis-à-vis Indian Muslims and Indian Christians, and quotes him: 'What is the attitude of those people who have been converted to Islam and Christianity? They are born in this land, no doubt. (...) Do they feel it a duty to serve her? No! Together with the change in their faith, gone are the spirit of love and devotion to the nation.'

The memory of the Partition was still fresh, and of the fact that a vast majority of the Muslim electorate had voted for it. The missionaries, too, had considered it likely that with Independence, India would lapse into chaos, so that some Christian-dominated areas in Kerala and the Northeast could declare their independence. It had also been noticed in the Northeast that non-Christianized tribals gave 'Indian' as nationality to census officers, while Christians gave their tribal identity. So Golwalkar's suspicion of the minority, while not to be accepted like that, still had a core of truth to it.

Then Guha goes in for the kill: 'There is a striking affinity between the questions Golwalkar asks here and those asked by European anti-Semites in the nineteenth and early-twentieth centuries. French, German and British nationalists all suspected the Jews in their country of not being loyal enough to the motherland.' Aha! So Golwalkar was a Nazi, after all!

Well, not exactly. First of all, before the Jews became the object of world conspiracy suspicions, the allegation of a foreign or international loyalty originally concerned not the Jews but the Catholics, with the Jesuit order as their main weapon of aggression. The Protestants, somewhat like the Orthodox Christians, were organized nationally and accepted doctrinal differences, at least within the confines laid down by the *Bible*; by contrast, the Catholic church was a global monolith with aspirations for world domination. My own country, Belgium, was a Catholic frontline state, with institutions for Irish, English and Dutch Catholics to support them and eventually allow them to topple the Protestant domination of their countries. There were also real-life incidents that nurtured the suspicion of a Popish Plot, most famously the 'gunpowder plot' by Jesuit agent Guy Fawkes to blow up the British Parliament. So, there was a core of truth to those suspicions. Even in demography, these suspicions were not baseless. As late as the 1950s, Dutch Protestants used to warn: 'Be careful with those Catholics; with their large families, they may overtake our country.' And, indeed, today the percentage of Catholics is larger than that of Protestants—only, between them, they are not even the majority any more, and the

Protestant-Catholic dichotomy has become irrelevant. Also, the Catholic birth rate has plummeted to the national average.

The suspicion of a Jewish world conspiracy was mainly based on a forgery, *The Protocols of the Elders of Zion*, originally fabricated by the Czarist secret police, though disapproved of by the czar himself. When Islam critics in the West point out that Islam has ambitions for world domination, the Guhas in our midst try to be funny and allege that we fantasize, after the same model, a 'Protocols of Mecca'. No: The *Zion Protocols* were a forgery, but the so-called 'Mecca Protocols' for world domination are real. The *Quran* itself, authoritative for every single Muslim (though ignored by many, fortunately but un-Islamically), says, 'War and hatred will reign between us until ye believe in Allah alone (Q.60:4)', or 'Make war on them until idolatory does not exist any longer and Allah's religion reigns universally (Q. 2:139 and again Q. 8:39)'. The *Jewish Bible* has a doctrine of domination too, but only of the Promised Land, while the *Quran* speaks of world domination.

So, the difference between the anti-Jewish and the anti-Islamic suspicions is one between falsity and reality. I am aware that for propagandists, reality doesn't count, only perception does. With the studied superficiality typical of Nehruvian secularism, the seemingly similar perception of the anti-Jewish versus the anti-Islamic suspicion is enough. They can throw that around as a grave allegation, as here in Guha's article, and be confident that no one will step in to correct them.

The endless mendaciousness of the secularists would have been remedied to a large extent if there had been a counter-party capable of responding to them and diagnosing their errors. But the only counter-party to be reckoned with was the Hindu nationalists, and they had been fixed in argumentative impotence by Golwalkar himself.

Christians have a similar doctrine of world conquest, though less confrontational. In its formative first centuries, Christianity lived as a minority in the vast Roman Empire, and unlike Islam, it had to accommodate national laws not of its own making. This fitted Saint

Paul's repudiation of the biblical law: It is the spirit (viz. of charity) that counts, not the letter of the law. This means that Christianity became naturally secular: It separated the religious sphere, thoroughly Christian, from the worldly and political sphere, dominated by non-Christian forces. During the heyday of Christian power, Christianity impinged ever more on the political sphere, but in the modern era, it did not have too much difficulty returning to its original 'secularist' position of accepting the separate identity of the political sphere. A telling criterion: Comparatively few people were killed in the struggle to wrest worldly power from the Churches, compared, for example, to the struggle between secular ideologies in the twentieth century. And in this struggle, the secular forces were more violent than the Christian forces, witness the French Revolutionary genocide in the Vendée or the persecution of Christianity in the Soviet Union.

However, in a more moderate and sophisticated way, Christianity does have an ambition of world domination too. Like in Islam, all non-believers are deemed to go to hell, though few Christians now take this seriously any more. Jesus's injunction to 'go and teach all nations' means that India, too, is on Christianity's conversion programme. When the Pope came to India in 1999, he said openly and in so many words that his church wanted to 'reap a great harvest of faith' in Asia, which implies destroying Hinduism the way the native religions of Europe and the Americas were destroyed. He, thereby, badly let his secularist allies down, for they had always ridiculed the Hindu nationalist suspicion that Christianity only meant destruction for Hinduism. Yet, after being put in the wrong so bluntly, here is the secularist Guha again shamelessly ridiculing Golwalkar's suspicion of Christianity.

On one point, though, Golwalkar is blatantly wrong: It is not India that the Christians want to destroy, but Hinduism. Here again, *nationalism is a misstatement of Hindu concerns*. Not the nation, but the religion is their target. Christians were loyal to the Roman Empire (of which the fifth-century Germanic enemies were already Christian too), but when the empire fell, they adapted: After all, their main loyalty was not a political structure but a religion. And then they became loyal citizens of Visigothic Spain, Ostrogothic Italy and Frankish France, a political loyalty that was inevitably secondary. They were not deshbhakts, they were Yesubhakts. And similarly, they sing the Indian anthem with as much conviction as their Indian compatriots. And they will do so even more when they come to live in a 'post-Hindu India' (of which Christian convert Kancha Ilaiah dreams). But if a different political structure comes to replace the Indian republic, they will effortlessly adapt to that too. Defending the nation against a Christian onslaught leaves their real target undefended: the Hindu religion.

GANDHI

Guha quotes Golwalkar as asserting that 'the foremost duty laid upon every Hindu is to build up such a holy, benevolent and unconquerable might of our Hindu people in support of the age-old truth of our Hindu nationhood'. This was never said in the *Upanishads*—it is not part of the fabled Hindu spirituality. But then, Hinduism has survived because of other factors than spirituality. At times, it is simply right to emphasize the martial virtues. Proof *a contrario*: Buddhism was purely about spirituality and didn't practise self-defence, so when it was really attacked, during the Muslim invasions, it was wiped away from Central Asia and India in one go. In spite of Golwalkar's unhistorical view of 'Hindu nationhood', he was right to extol the project of 'unconquerable might'.

Guha compares this 'supremacist point of view' with what M.K. Gandhi regarded as the duty of Hindus— to 'abolish untouchability and to end the suppression of women' and to 'promote inter-religious harmony'. Indeed, Mr Guha, 'there could not be two visions of what it takes to be a Hindu, or an Indian, that are as radically opposed as those offered by Golwalkar and Gandhi respectively'.

There are several things wrong with this picture. Factually, it is not true that the Mahatma opposed 'suppression of women'; on the contrary, he notoriously practised it. Perhaps his wife Kasturba accommodated the arrangements Gandhi imposed on her, but there cannot possibly be an illusion that their relationship was one of equality. Towards his wife, as well as his children, he was an unmitigated family tyrant. And as shown by Radha Rajan in her book *Eclipse of the Hindu Nation: Gandhi and His Freedom Struggle*, his relations with the young women with whom he carried out his 'experiments with chastity' was also perversely exploitative.

As for untouchability, Gandhi made it his priority, and at that junction of history, it was indeed a necessity; but to make it a defining trait of Hinduism is simply wrong. For thousands of years, Hindu society didn't know of hereditary untouchability, which is not mentioned in the *Rig Veda* (and no, you shrill screamers out there, not even in the Purusha Sukta). Later it did, and was comfortable with it. For opposite reasons, Hindus in those periods were not preoccupied with abolishing untouchability: First because it wasn't there, then because they thought it was alright. One can be a Hindu without practising untouchability, but also without being fired up to abolish untouchability. Today's Hindu communities I know in Holland (Bhojpuri-speaking Rama worshippers from Surinam) have only the faintest notion of caste and none of untouchability, but are very much Hindu. In the same spirit, the RSS ranks were not tainted with untouchability either. In that respect, Golwalkar's vision was different from but by no means 'radically opposed' to Gandhiji's.

Abolishing untouchability is a good thing, but it is not the essence of Hinduism, nor of anti-Hinduism. Hinduism is a lot more and a lot bigger than caste. It is only the ignorant Nehruvians who can't pronounce the word 'Hindu' without manoeuvring the word 'caste' into the same sentence. If Gandhi put an unusual stress on this, it may have been a necessity of the times, and that is not what I want to hold against him. What was wrong with him, however, was that, regardless of caste, he had a very warped view of Hinduism.

Thus, Gandhi was wrong to equate Hinduism with non-violence, which is extolled as a virtue on the spiritual path, but not a virtue for the warrior. No matter how the warrior class is recruited, at any rate it is deemed necessary in the real world. Hinduism is a complete system: It accounts for society's needs as much as for the requirements of the spiritual path. Gandhi's version of Hinduism was very unbalanced and morbidly moralistic. It ought to be a warning sign for Hindus that the secularists are so insistently dangling Gandhi as a role model before them.

Likewise, 'inter-religious harmony' was a natural practice between the many sects within Hinduism, and partly even towards Christianity and Islam. When Muslims pass a mosque, they greet it, but not a temple or a church. It is only Hindus who greet any building or object that is deemed sacred to anyone. This was the practice long before Gandhi. But these Hindus, or certainly their intellectual vanguard, had the power of discrimination, sharpened by their many debates between the different sects. Being nice to Muslims and sympathizing with the piety that finds its expression in prayer or fasting, is different from assenting to the illusory Islamic doctrine, starting with the funny belief that Mohammed was God's exclusive spokesman.

In Gandhi's days, this critical role vis-à-vis Christianity and (at the cost of a number of murders) Islam was taken by the Arya Samaj, which Gandhi lambasted. His role in this regard was entirely negative, abolishing the power of discrimination in the Hindu worldview. He thus prepared the ground for the wilful superficiality characteristic of the Nehruvians. He also, through his wider influence on all Hindus, prepared the ground for the complete ideological illiteracy among RSS men, along with Golwalkar.

The differences between Gandhi and Golwalkar are dwarfed by one overriding influence on their Hindu contemporaries that they had in common. It is that both of them sold a voguish Western import as quintessentially Hindu. Gandhi's view of non-violence came from some quietist Christian sects. Remaining unmoved and without fighting back when thugs manhandle you is typical of the Amish and similar Christian pacifist sects. Through Tolstoy and other exalted Christians, Gandhi inserted a lot of Christian influence into Hinduism. Similarly, Golwalkar's nationalism was a belated import of a nineteenth-century influence, particularly through the Italian nationalist Giuseppe Mazzini, whose political manifesto had been translated by V.D. Savarkar. Today in the West, nationalism has gone out of fashion; but in India, nothing ever dies, and so nationalism keeps working its distortive influence on the movement for Hindu self-defence.

What Hindus should urgently do is to forget both Gandhi and Golwalkar. (That means two idols less on Narendra Modi's house altar.) Gandhi is now only artificially kept alive by the secularists and some sentimental Hindus, purely for Hindu consumption. (Nobody is telling the Muslims that Gandhiji was there for them too, and that they should emulate his very Christian message of turning the other cheek.) The problem is not that what they imported came from abroad. As the late Bal Thackeray said, 'You cannot take this Swadeshi (own produce, economic nationalism) thing too far, for then you would have to do without the light bulb.' So, if Gandhi's moralistic sentimentalism or deliberate lack of discrimination had something positive to offer, we shouldn't mind it being of Christian origin. If Golwalkar's nationalism helped in properly diagnosing the problems facing Hindu society, we should not complain of its Italian origin. But the thing is that they are not beneficial at all; or if they ever were, they definitely have outlived their utility.

Another very important thing they had in common was their emphasis on emotions, as opposed to thought. As RSS activists are wont to say, 'Do you need to read a book to love your mother?' Working on the emotions quickly creates a popular appeal: Both Gandhi and Golwalkar were hugely successful at getting crowds marching. The Marxists were never equally popular, but more successful in determining actual policies. They worked on people's minds instead, and that had a more penetrative and lasting effect.

Instead of following false prophets like Gandhi and Golwalkar, Hindus had better return to their real role models: to Dirghatamas and Vasishtha, to Rama and Krishna, to Canakya and Thiruvalluvar, to Vishnu Sharma and Abhinavagupta, to Ramdas and Shivaji. Their contribution in ideology and the art of living should be made relevant to the present—they had everything in them that we need. Hindus should not follow Western categories, like 'national' vs 'anti-national', or 'Left' vs 'Right', not because they have been imported, but because by now they have been sufficiently put to the test and found wanting.

VANGUARD OF HINDU SOCIETY

According to Guha, the RSS fancies itself the vanguard of Hindu society: 'Golwalkar further assumes that if Hindus are destined to lead the world, the RSS is destined to lead the Hindus.'

In better days, and even recently, the rest of the world has eagerly drunk from Mother India's nipples. In spite of all her defects, she has a lot to offer, and this has been proven already from the distant past onwards. This much is indisputable. By contrast, the RSS's claim to leadership over the Hindus (or more recently, over the Indians) is a tall claim that deserves to be put to the test.

Certainly, the RSS does a lot of good work at the basic level. Best known in India, though passed over in silence by the world media in emulation of the English media in India, is its disaster relief work. This, indeed, cannot be praised too much, if only to compensate for the culpable silence about it in every anti-Hindutva article, including this one by Guha. Whenever a flood or an earthquake strikes, RSS men immediately come on the scene and do the thankless jobs that secularists feel themselves too precious for.

It is all the more tragic that all these constructive energies of millions of ordinary Hindu volunteers are not channelled towards a higher goal. The RSS at one time wanted to serve Hindu society; today it is only busy perpetuating itself. The RSS leadership has failed to set useful and attainable goals for Hindu society. It has failed to map the Kurukshetra or do a SWOT (strengths, weaknesses, opportunities and threats) analysis of the different forces in the field. According to the ancient Chinese strategist Sunzi, knowing both your enemy and yourself yields constant victory, knowing only one of the two sometimes yields victory and sometimes defeat, and not knowing either will end in assured and ignominious defeat. By this criterion, the RSS, in spite of its size, is headed for complete defeat.

And effectively, for advertising itself as the 'vanguard' of Hindu society, the RSS has little to show. Is India more Hindu today than in 1925? Several parameters show a definite decline—demographic percentage of Hindus; percentage of Hindu-controlled schools (not to speak of the hard-to-quantify degree of Hinduness of those schools); percentage of subcontinental territory where Hindus can live with honour; percentage of soil and other assets controlled by Hindu temples; percentage of men who wear dhotis or of women who wear saris; and the proportion of conversions to the different religions relative to their demographic weight.

Ah, the RSS will say with a triumphant smile, at least we managed to bring our political party to power! Yes, they did, and that is precisely where you can see their failure. Just compare the programme with which the BJS started in 1951 and the actual policies of the BJP in power. Rather than Hinduizing secularist India, the Hindu party has been secularized. In 1947, the Hindu forces deplored the inclusion of the green colour in the Indian flag, but by 1980, they themselves put green into their party flag. This is a visual symbol of how they now wholeheartedly support what they originally condemned as 'minority appeasement'.

Let me state at this point what has made me write this article. A BJP worker of RSS background asked me to write a reply to this article by Guha. In response, I pooh-poohed *Bunch of Thoughts*: While not endorsing Guha's critique, I still expressed my scepticism of Golwalkar's worldview. He got angry with me, a case of 'turning a good man into an angry man' by banking too much on his goodwill and understanding. I owed this man a lot, and it was rude and inconsiderate of me to belittle his guru like that. I sincerely apologize for it, and I hope to repair it a little bit by writing this counter-critique.

Yet, at the same time, I cannot help noticing that this incident at the personal level is a very small part of the very large tragedy wilfully wrought for decades on end by the RSS leadership, including Golwalkar. There cannot be two opinions about the idealism and loyalty of numerous RSS men; but the leadership has channelled this enormous reservoir of constructive energies towards nothing better than the RSS itself. What their own rank and file had assumed to be a service to Hindu civilization is diverted away from that goal. If the RSS had not existed, many of those activists would not have found an outlet for their dedication to the Hindu cause. Yet, many others would have set up their own initiatives, and the net result is that the Hindu cause could have advanced much further than where it has landed under RSS tutelage.

INDIA'S UNITARY STRUCTURE

Guha raises the issue of the Constitution's place in the Hindu nationalist scheme of things: 'Narendra Modi may swear that the Indian Constitution is his only holy book, but his guruji, Golwalkar, believed that document to be deeply flawed and that it must be rejected or at least redrafted.' The logical conclusion would be that after fifty years, Golwalkar's ideas would have given way to new ideas. That Modi, in spite of his personal veneration for his guruji, would have evolved away from Golwalkar's opinions. But instead, the same way committed Muslims always go back to the *Quran* and live as if in seventh-century Arabia, Guha expects Modi to live by the old book, without any changes.

Guha quotes *Bunch of Thoughts*: 'The framers of our present Constitution also were not firmly rooted in the conviction of our single homogeneous nationhood.' He thinks Golwalkar 'was angry that India was constituted as a Union of States, for in his view, the federal structure would sow "the seeds of national disintegration and defeat".'

The framers did indeed sow the seeds of divisive politics steered by sectional interests, though not with their purely symbolic definition of India. On the other hand, their responsibility should not be exaggerated: A good political structure is not all-powerful and cannot indefinitely prevent the eruption of divisive tendencies. Golwalkar's obsession with this 'single homogeneous nationhood' is historically incorrect, but so is the Constitution's claim that 'India is a Union of States'. An example of a union of states is the European Union, where separately existing countries threw in their lot together. Or the budding United States, where thirteen separate British colonies, upon their gaining independence, formed a union. In India, even the nominally independent princely states were effectively part of British India, so the Indian republic was but a continuation of an existing unitary political entity.

According to Guha, 'Golwalkar wanted the Centre to be all-powerful. Modi may now speak of the virtues of cooperative federalism, but his *guru*, Golwalkar, wrote of the need "to bury deep for good all talk of a federal structure of our country's Constitution".' Here again, we see that Modi simply, and quite normally, doesn't follow the book written by Golwalkar. In this respect, though, Modi does stand in a Hindu tradition and even a BJP tradition, from which Golwalkar was deviating. Ancient Hindu empires had to respect each vassal-state's swadharma: It had its own ways, and even the inclusion in a larger political structure should not interrupt that vassal-state's attachment to its distinctive ways.

As for modern India and the BJP, the A.B. Vajpayee government split the states of Bihar, Madhya Pradesh and Uttar Pradesh to give political expression to the relative distinctiveness of the Jharkhand, Chhattisgarh and Uttarakhand areas. It also extended recognition as official language to several 'tribal' languages. Like in some other respects, Golwalkar's and the RSS's view deviates from the wise Hindu attitude encapsulating the wisdom of millennia. Modi sets an example for all RSS followers by abandoning the pro-monolithic Golwalkar view and re-embracing the Hindu tradition of pluralism and differentiation.

An unexpected positive side to Golwalkar's stand is that it is more democratic in spirit than Modi's or anyone else's veneration for the Constitution: 'Let the Constitution,' he insisted, 'be re-examined and re-drafted, so as to establish (a) unitary form of government.' Regardless of his doubtful concern for the unitary form of government, he very correctly refused to worship the Constitution. In a democracy, laws are a human product, which we can choose to keep unchanged or to amend. They are not above us; we ourselves make them. Modi had better stop treating the Constitution as holy writ and give it a critical look to see for himself that some articles in there are undesirable and in need of being amended.

CONCLUSION

Guha concludes thus: 'No one who reads *Bunch of Thoughts* can reach a conclusion other than the one the (entirely representative) quotes offered above suggest—namely, that its author was a reactionary bigot, whose ideas and prejudices have no place in a modern, liberal democracy. If ever the prime minister has the courage to give an unscripted, no-holds-barred press conference, the first question an honest journalist should ask him would be, "Sir, how do you reconcile your (long-standing) admiration for Golwalkar on the one hand with your (new-found) respect and regard for Ambedkar and Gandhi on the other?"'

Guha's passing assurance of representativeness is false. Just as has happened in the usual references to Golwalkar's book *We*, here, too, passages have been cherry-picked to make him look bad. *Bunch of Thoughts* is a repetitive and mediocre book, but is on the whole rather harmless. It rarely raises the reader's indignation. If it were not like that, i.e., if things in the book were as bad as Guha claims, then this indictment of the book would at once be a serious indictment of its faithful readers. And not just of its actual readers, a minority of RSS activists, but of everyone alleged by Guha to be an obedient reader, including Narendra Modi.

Now to the contents of Guha's advice to Modi. It is a doubtful trait of Hinduism that in can reconcile contrasting entities. At best, this means finding common ground underneath a seeming opposition. But, often, it means untruthfully papering over real conflicts of interest. Hence Guha's suspicion that Modi juxtaposes these three characters on his home altar and yet is unable to reconcile their worldviews. To reconcile Golwalkar with Gandhi is not so bizarre—they actually have fundamental traits in common, as argued above. To reconcile Ambedkar with Gandhi is already harder, though this is a couple whose like-mindedness Guha seems to take for granted; in fact, they had a sharp conflict between them, which neither of them had with Golwalkar. Not only was their outlook on both religion and modernization very different (rationalist versus crassly sentimental), but they actually clashed on what to Guha is clearly the most important topic in the universe: caste. However, the real challenge here is to reconcile Ambedkar with Golwalkar.

Well, first off, they were both ardent nationalists. Even when Ambedkar collaborated with the foreign occupiers of his country by serving on the Viceroy's Council, he did so because, in his judgment, British rule was best for his country and, in particular, for his own Depressed Castes constituency. It is to Jawaharlal Nehru's credit that he took Ambedkar, who had been his opponent during the freedom struggle, into his first national cabinet so that the country could avail of his service. Ambedkar's rejection of the Christian missionary seduction in favour of Swadeshi Buddhism was nationalist par excellence. It did not endear him to Golwalkar in so far as we know, but it won him the sympathy of the later RSS, including Narendra Modi. To some, this element of nationalism is less essential, but to RSS men, it is all-important.

Secondly, while Ambedkar was more emphatically egalitarian than Golwalkar, the latter's nationalism equally had egalitarian implications. In the feudal system, the nobility was not tied to a nation. Till today, the remaining royal dynasties in Europe are biologically the most pan-European families. By contrast, the commoners were mostly tied to a particular nation and easily rallied around the banner of the modern nation-states. Moreover, nationalism allowed those commoners to feel equal to their upper-class compatriots. And historically, it is nationalism, first through the initiative of Otto van Bismarck, which created a social security system and its consequent strong bond of self-interest between the commoners and their nation. Likewise, even if Golwalkar were a Brahmin (and already for that reason fated to be forever hated by the Ambedkarites and the foreign India-watchers in their pocket), he advocated a common identification of everyone with the nation, regardless of caste.

Contrary to the secularists' hazy assumption, Hindu nationalism is distinct from Hindu traditionalism, and the central point of contrast is precisely caste. Genealogically, in the 1920s, Hindu nationalism sprang from Hindu reformism as incarnated in the Arya Samaj, intended as a stalwart Hindu movement ('back to the *Vedas*!') but emphatically anti-caste. The foundational insight of this Vedic egalitarianism was that Vedic society had no castes—which is accurate at least for the age of the Rig Vedic family books. Several leading early Hindu nationalists had been Arya Samajis. The main self-imposed task of the Hindu Mahasabha and the RSS was Hindu 'self-organization', or *sangathan*. This was the practical application of Swami Shraddhananda's book *Hindu Sangathan, Saviour of the Dying Race* (1924). If one book can make you understand modern Hindu activism in general, of which Hindu nationalism and a fortiori the RSS is only one current, it is that one, far more than *Bunch of Thoughts*. But Swami Shraddhananda, murdered by a Muslim in 1926 (as related, for example, in B.R. Ambedkar's *Thoughts on Pakistan*), had been a radically anti-caste Arya Samaji.

Undoubtedly, Guha's comment has the merit of drawing attention to Guru Golwalkar's main political manifesto. However, to a moderate extent, it suffers from the main flaws of the Nehruvian depiction of Hindu nationalism. Based on a very hazy knowledge of the facts on the ground within the Hindu movement, it cultivates a stereotypical enemy image. It also conflates very distinct strands, such as Hindu traditionalism versus Hindu reformism, and anachronistically takes past states of affairs to be still in force. It further imagines the Hindu movement to be a powerhouse and fails to realize its weaknesses.

The RSS in Western Media*

On Friday 3 November, the Flemish broadcaster VRT Canvas, in its programme *Terzake* ('To the point'), presented a Dutch documentary from the series *De Westerlingen* ('The Westerners'), in which young Dutchmen meet youngsters in countries across the world to explore the differences in culture. In the past, the impression was that all cultural differences were on the way out because the non-Westerners were simply Westernizing. Now, it has become clear that some differences are here to stay, and that even in non-Muslim countries, there is a tough resistance against too much Westernization.

This time around, we were taken to India where a Dutch youngster called Nicolaas was meeting young Hindu nationalists. According to the announcement on the TV station's website: 'In India extremist associations acquire ever more influence. Nicolaas Veul meets activist young Hindu nationalists in the holy city of Allahabad. He goes around with Divya, Ritesh and Vikrant. They fight for a Hindu India, and against influences from outside.'

HINDU FASCISM?

At the outset, in the car on the way to an event of the RSS, he was quickly briefed by an Indian secularist on the Hindu nationalists. These were said to be 'increasingly powerful', to be issuing for use in schools 'textbooks rewritten in a pro-Hindu sense' and to be 'openly linked with the Nazis'.

This was a nice summary of the power equation in the reporting

*Published on Pragyata.com, 15 November 2017

on India worldwide and in all the different segments of the media: All press correspondents in and 'experts' on India look at Indian society, especially the communal conflict, through the glasses that a handful of secularists have put on their noses, reproducing the latter's anti-Hindu bias and disinformation. For the average viewer, every topic in the ensuing meetings came under the cloud of these initial 'revelations', even though nothing in the RSS performance effectively filmed confirmed or illustrated any of them.

Since the 1980s, I have never heard the term 'Hindu nationalists' without the addition that they are 'emerging' or 'increasingly powerful'. They should have been all-powerful by now. The only (partial) exception was the few years after the 2009 elections, when the BJP had been defeated even worse than in 2004, so that supporters of the socialist-casteist parties, including partisan experts like Christophe Jaffrelot, concluded that Hindu nationalism was on the way out. However, instead of building on the existing power equation to push Hindutva deeper into oblivion, the secularist Congress wasted its chance because it got too wrapped up in driving corruption to unprecedented levels, too much for the electorate to stomach. Once the next electoral campaign got under way, even the secularists soon conceded that a BJP victory was becoming inevitable.

However, contrary to what the observers all think or say, the present BJP government under Narendra Modi, while numerically strong, is ideologically extremely weak. It is not in any way Hinduizing or 'saffronizing' the polity or the education system. It is continuing the Congressite-Leftist anti-Hindu policies mandated by the Constitution, or at best looking the other way but not changing the Constitution to put a definitive stop to such policies. Thus, subsidized schools can be Christian or Muslim, but not Hindu: In the latter case, either they get taken over by the state and secularized, or at best, have to do without subsidies. Temples are nationalized and their income channelled to non-Hindu purposes, a treatment against which the law protects churches and mosques. And this is no less the case in BJP-ruled states, where the government could have chosen not to avail of the opportunities given to it by the Constitution.

Nowhere in this documentary would you pick up any hint to the main communal reality in India: the anti-majority discrimination. It is admittedly hard to explain to outsiders, and therefore easy to conceal or deny, but Hindus are indeed second-class citizens in their native country. I am aware that right now, many non-Indian readers will refuse to believe me, but it is really like that. Anywhere in the world you can download the text of the Indian Constitution, so please verify for yourself, starting with Article 25-30.

So, what did you get to see? Many people in the city were on the streets converging on an open ground where a meeting of a local RSS unit (shakha, or 'branch') with physical and ideological training was about to take place. They were wearing (or in the case of newcomers, buying) the RSS outfit—white shirt and black cap and trousers. It was the new uniform, for till recently, the black trousers would have been brown knickers, even more colonial-style. Their military style was highlighted, though everyone could see for themselves that all the 'weapons training' they did was with sticks, rather harmless in the age of the Kalashnikov. Naturally, there was no hint that an endless series of murders of RSS men has been committed by Kerala communists, Khalistanis in Punjab and others. The RSS youngsters also did not bring it up, or if they did, that part was not shown. The persistent suggestion was that they were the perpetrators of violence, not its victims, though no such violence was actually shown.

When interviewing these RSS activists, Nicolaas repeatedly remarked that this or that guy was actually impeccably friendly and quite nice. Not at all how we would picture the fascists announced initially by the secularist. Then what was wrong with them?

VALENTINE'S DAY

The real topic of this documentary series was the culture clash and the native resistance against Westernization. And indeed, these young people refused to absorb the flood of Westernizing influences. One example of a pernicious influence was Valentine, taken straight from the existing Western commercial pop culture. More ideologized people denounce it also as a 'Christian' holiday. Valentine was a Roman priest who performed tabooed weddings, and when martyred and sainted, the church gave him a day in the saints' calendar, 14 February, coinciding with the pre-Christian fertility feast presided over by the goddess Juno Februa ('clean, purifying') of 13–15 February. It took a thousand years, to the age of the troubadours and courtly love, before he graduated to becoming the patron saint of romanticism.

As such, commerce catapulted him to the fore, and made the saint's day into an occasion pious Christians would frown upon: the feast of sentimentalism and getting carried away with infatuation. Since the late eighteenth century, there is a whole literature, and later movies, about youngsters following their hearts and overcoming the resistance of their unfeeling, narrow-minded parents. This is now re-enacted in India, where commerce and the secularist-promoted fondness of all things Western is spreading the highly artificial celebration of Valentine's Day. This has become the symbol of Western decadence, in which the pursuit of emotional kicks takes precedence over long-term institution-building, marriage and the resulting children's well-being. Nicolaas's Indian interlocutor wants to spare his country the breakdown of family life that has come to characterize the modern West.

But in the documentary, in the interview with the RSS activist, we only see a humourless spoilsport's jaundiced rant against a day of innocent fun. The Dutch lad just doesn't see that there is another side to it, and that the Hindu critique of Valentine has its legitimacy. This RSS fellow was voicing a very positive viewpoint, one in favour of the precious fabric of traditional social values, of the time-tested *mos maiorum* ('ancestral custom'), which is being undermined by modernist influences symbolized by Valentine's Day. Possibly it is not good enough to overrule modernization, but that remains to be seen, and the traditionalist view deserves a proper hearing.

In the streets, the Dutch newcomer to India saw Westernization all over the place. Western fashion, neon lights, shopping malls, Kentucky Fried Chicken, young couples kissing in public. Even an RSS spokesman admitted he sometimes went to McDonald's. So, the final impression that the viewers will take home is that, in India at least, Westernization is unstoppable. It is not uncontested, true, but the nativists, though not convincingly put down as 'fascists' any more, are not very competent and are at any rate unable to stop it.

COMMUNICATION

But then, come to think of it, the RSS fellow didn't have the required communication skills to overturn an anti-Hindu bias instilled in the Western public since decades. And by 'anti-Hindu', I do not mean the kind of grim animus seen in the missionaries or the secularists, but a background conditioning: Nicolaas has no quarrel with the Hindus as such, and he is probably not even aware of his implicit anti-Hindu bias, but like most Westerners with an interest in India, he has innocently absorbed the partisan view of India fostered by the really hostile people.

It is unrealistic to expect this one fleeting television conversation to change a bias built up over decades. Still, the RSS spokesman could have defended his position better. On the other hand, his peaceful and civilized but weak argumentation was a logical illustration of a deliberate policy pursued since the 1920s. It was in line with the old RSS's boy-scout mentality of disdain for all communication ('do well and don't look back'). Founder K.B. Hedgewar, who had started out as a member of the revolutionary wing of the freedom movement, with secretive and purely oral communication to avoid discovery by the police, installed in his new organization a hostility to any concern for outside approval, and to the media and its narrative. A consequence today is that RSS spokesmen are gravely lacking in communication skills. On average, they have a far better case than their clumsy performance in interviews and TV debates would suggest.

Twice the RSS refused a media presence. I was somewhat surprised to see this. In the early Nineties, when I went around to RSS/BJP centres to interview Hindu nationalist leaders, there was still plenty of distrust for outsiders, and communication was largely excluded. I knew then that I was exceptionally privileged to be allowed access, as a result of my lone pro-Hindu conclusions in my book on the Ayodhya temple/mosque conflict. But then private TV stations conquered India, gaining entry into the remotest villages, and finally the Internet made communication unavoidable, even for the RSS. I had thought that this seclusion had by now become a thing of the past, but the RSS appears to have retained some of it.

The result is that RSS spokesmen, while not at all the 'fascists' of secularist mythology, come across as village bumpkins. In this case, an interviewed RSS man suffered from a lack of serious historical knowledge, or of a chauvinist type of gullibility. He explained that India has invented plastic surgery and, as proven by the *Ramayana*, the airplane. This story has two related drawbacks: As far as evidence can tell, it is not true; and it is bad publicity, for while it may make a handful of gullible folk admire Hindu culture, it turns Hinduism into a superstitious laughing stock for many more. When the Dutchman brought up homosexuality, the RSS man said: 'That doesn't exist in our country.' Just like it didn't exist in the Soviet Union ('a symptom of bourgeois decadence'), nor in Africa, according to Robert Mugabe ('they may be gay in America, but they will be sad people in Zimbabwe'). Again, even those Westerners who condemn odd sexual behaviour will laugh at these clumsy attempts to make it stop at your country's border. This way, the RSS tendency is particularly weak in the prime precondition for communication, viz. seeing things also through the eyes of your interlocutor.

GRIM

Today, the image of Hinduism is less grim than when Hindu nationalism realistically coveted power, or for the first time came to power (1990s). One reason is reality: All the grim Doomsday predictions of Hindu nationalists 'throwing all Muslims into the Indian Ocean' and 'turning the clock back regarding Dalit emancipation' failed to come true. Recently, Narendra Modi conducted a very successful foreign policy, and the Western powers can only dream of the economic growth figures India takes for granted. Less importantly but tellingly, the Hindu parents are making progress in the California textbook affair (i.e. the proposed reform of insensitive passages in school textbooks concerned with Hinduism), where some negative portrayals of Hindu culture will be amended, contrasting with the total defeat inflicted on the Hindus in 2006. The anti-Hindu lobby in American academe, largely consisting of NRIs and Indologists, has lost considerable steam.

(The same impression could be had from Sona Datta's documentary on Hindu art and temple architecture, a few days later. Overall quite informative as well as full of awe for Hindu brilliance, it nonetheless started out with familiar secularist lies about pluralist Moghuls who 'built their magnificent mosques next to Hindu temples' and presided over a peaceful and tolerant empire 'when Europe was savaged by wars of religion'. But unlike in the recent past, this propaganda was not that obtrusive.)

And so, this Dutch young man approached the RSS men with an open mind, in spite of the hateful briefing he had initially received from a secularist. He had good things to say about the nativists he met. But he also carried his prejudices with him, less against the 'Hindu' than against the 'nationalist' element, and less intense than ten or twenty-five years ago, but still palpable. Conclusion: The power equation on the publicity front is still favourable to the secularists but not unfathomably desperate for the Hindus any more.

In Favour of Freedom of Expression*

Many people—Hindus, Westerners and the rest—pay lip service to freedom of expression, but then add that this freedom is not absolute, that it should be hemmed in and supervised. I disagree, and have argued it out in this article.

In the lifetime of the older ones among us, freedom of expression in India first became a hot item with the Salman Rushdie affair, when, in 1988, his novel *The Satanic Verses* was banned. This was done by Rajiv Gandhi's Congress government at the request of Muslim leader Syed Shahabuddin, in exchange for the latter's calling off of a Muslim march on Ayodhya (then a hotspot because of the temple/mosque controversy), expected to cause bloodshed (see my afterword to Daniel Pipes' *The Rushdie Affair*).

For the younger generation, the main events were the withdrawal of A.K. Ramanujan's essay *Three Hundred Ramayanas* from Delhi University's syllabus in 2011 under Hindu pressure (see e.g. 'Ramanujan & the Ramayana', *Sunday Guardian*, 30 October 2011); and the publisher Penguin's withdrawal of Wendy Doniger's book *The Hindus: An Alternative History* in 2014, likewise under Hindu pressure. It was propagandistic hyperbole to speak of 'censorship' in these cases, but there is simply no comparison with the Rushdie case, where the book was not just legally banned but the writer was threatened with the death penalty and several

*Published in Astha Bharati's periodical, *Dialogue*, in 2016

of its translators (Norwegian, Japanese) were effectively killed. Yet the media and the academics have done their best to whip up indignation over these affairs, so that they now pass as grim examples of censorship.

Neither document was judicially banned, but the Hindu plaintiffs wielded an article of law as threatening argument, and this could not be ignored: Section 295A of the Indian Penal Code. Why is this article there, and what role does it play in India's public life?

LOOKING IN FROM OUTSIDE: THE DONIGER AFFAIR

In November 2014, at its annual conference, the AAR held a panel discussion on censorship in India under Section 295A of the Indian Penal Code, itself occasioned by the Penguin publisher's withdrawal under Hindu pressure of Doniger's book. This translated into a section of the July 2016 issue of the *Journal of the AAR* (*JAAR*) with four contributors and a response from Doniger. It addresses 'the true source of the conflict, section 295A of the Indian Penal Code'. (Pennington 2016:323)

This article 295A criminalizes 'outraging the religious feelings of any class of Indian citizens'. Dina Nath Batra, former national director of the Hindu nationalist organization Vidya Bharati, had entered a lawsuit against the publisher under Section 295A. The latter recognized that the case had a solid legal footing and decided to avoid defeat by settling out of court. He agreed to withdraw the book from circulation and pulp all remaining copies. Not that any book actually got pulped: Before they could be physically withdrawn, 'all extant copies were quickly bought up from the bookstores' (Doniger 2016:364) because of the sudden free publicity.

While many academics accused Penguin of cowardice, Doniger understood that they had acted under threat of law, and emphatically denounced Section 295A: 'The true villain was the Indian law that makes it a criminal rather than a civil offence to publish a book that offends any Hindu, a law that jeopardizes the physical safety of any publisher, no matter how ludicrous the accusation brought against a book.' (Doniger 2014, quoted by Pennington 2016:330)

This statement is entirely correct, except for one word. Doniger is being brazenly partisan and incorrect where she claims that the law prohibits every book that 'offends any *Hindu*'. Formally, it does not discriminate, and applies to all Indians regardless of religion. Historically, as we shall see, the law was enacted to prohibit books that offended Muslims, and to silence Hindus. Her insinuation that this law has a pro-Hindu bias, giving Hindus a privileged protection that it withholds from others, is simply false in both respects. It fits in with the common narrative that India is a crypto-'Hindu rashtra' oppressing the minorities, when, in fact, the minorities are often privileged by law vis-à-vis the Hindus.

Likewise, in Pennington's paraphrase (2016:329), Martha Nussbaum claims that in India, such defamation laws 'are used primarily by majority groups to bludgeon minorities'. This is wildly untrue (though it is true in the other successor-state of British India, viz. Pakistan), as will become clear when we see how Section 295A came into being.

REACTIONS AGAINST BOOK WITHDRAWALS AND CENSORSHIP

But first a word about the significant reactions to this famous case of book-burning. The recent changes in syllabi and the objections to books by pro-Hindu activists, both phenomena being summed up in the single name of Dina Nath Batra (who is also editor of some schoolbooks), have met with plenty of vocal reprimands and petitions in protest, signed by leading scholars in India and abroad.

Thus, at the European Conference for South Asia Studies in Zürich, in July 2014, we were all given a petition to sign in support of Doniger's book, against the publisher's withdrawal under Batra's judicial challenge. (Full disclosure: I signed, with heartfelt conviction.) The general opinion among educated people, widely expressed, was to condemn all attempts at book-banning. Unlike other petitions, this one did focus on the negative role of Section 295A.

To be sure, most intellectuals' indignation was selective. There have indeed been cases where they have failed to come out in defence of besieged authors. No such storms of protest were raised when Muslims or Christians had books banned, or even when they assaulted the writers. Thus, several such assaults happened on the authors and publisher of the Danish Mohammed cartoons of 2006, yet at its subsequent annual conference, the prestigious and agenda-setting AAR hosted a panel about the cartoons, where every single participant supported the Muslim objections to the cartoons, though to different degrees, and none of them fully defended freedom of expression. (Another panel there was devoted to lambasting the Jihadwatch.org website by Robert Spencer and Pamela Geller, both targets of death threats and at least one effective but failed attempt on their lives, but not defended at the AAR panel by anyone.)

In their own internal functioning too, the AAR scholars and Indologists don't put a premium on the freedom to express dissident opinions. Here I speak from experience, having been banned from several forums where Doniger and some of her prominent supporters were present and gave their tacit consent. (Elst 2012:350-385) The most high-profile target of this policy has probably been Malhotra, a sharp critic of Indologist mores and anti-Hindu bias, some of whose experiences in this regard have been fully documented. (Malhotra: *Hinduphobia*, 2016)

It is entirely reasonable for India-watchers, like for freedom-loving Indians, to deplore this law and the cases of book-banning it has justified; but less so for people who chose not to speak out on the occasion of earlier conspicuous incidents of book-banning. Where was Doniger when Rushdie's book was banned? At any rate, many Indian secularists, who mostly enjoy the support and sympathy of those American academics, upheld the ban, which was decreed by a self-declared secularist prime minister (Rajiv Gandhi*), and ruling party (Congress). Where were they when demands were made to

*See e.g. Arun Shourie, *Indian Controversies*, Roli 1989, p.395

ban Ram Swarup's *Hindu View of Christianity and Islam*, or when the Church had Dan Brown's *The Da Vinci Code* banned?

American Indologists including Doniger have always condoned religious discrimination on the condition that Hindus are at the receiving end; they only protest when Hindus show initiative. And much as I deplore Batra's initiative, it meant at least that Hindus were not taking Doniger's insults lying down. Briefly: While everything pleads against this act of book-burning, the American India-watchers are not very entitled to their much-publicized indignation.

The point is that the intellectuals' selective indignation shows very well where real authority lies. Threats of violence are, of course, highly respected by them. The day Hindus start assaulting writers they don't like, you will see eminent historians turning silent about Hindu censorship, or even taking up its defence—for that is what actually happens in the case of Islamic threats and censorship. Even more pervasive is the effect of threats to their careers. You will be in trouble if you utter any 'Islamophobic' criticism of Islamic censorship, but you will earn praise if you challenge even proper judicial action against any anti-Hindu publication. This, then, safely predicts the differential behaviour of most intellectuals vis-à-vis free speech.

THE DONIGER AFFAIR: WHAT IS IN IT FOR THE HINDUS?

For the Hindus, the book withdrawal was a pyrrhic victory. The publicity they gained worldwide was entirely negative, and it corroborated their recently manufactured image as authoritarian and intolerant. The decision was also ineffectual, for, in the days of the Internet, it remained easy to access a soft copy of the book. The Hindus concerned also kind of admitted that they were unable to fight back with arguments.

Yet, they did have the arguments. A list of the numerous factual errors in Doniger's book has been compiled by Vishal Agarwal, an Indo-American medical engineer and Sanskritist (2014, but already online since 2010). Most of all, he has shown how her book's treatment of Hinduism is unconscientious and flippant to a degree that would can never be acceptable from a professor of her rank (Mircea Eliade Distinguished Service Professor at Chicago University, top of the world) for more established religions. In the reprint of her book through another publisher (Speaking Tiger, Delhi, 2015), she didn't deign to acknowledge this work, nor make any correction.

This is a serious aspect of the case that Western academics and their Indian cheerleaders have strictly kept the lid on. On the contrary, Pennington (2016:330) claims that the book was lambasted 'even when a scholar is demonstrating what is manifestly true based on her research'.

We can vaguely get an idea of Hindu opinion in India about Doniger's book through the sparse comments by the Hindi-language press. S. Shankar in *Dainik Jagran* 'charged Doniger with a familiar set of shortcomings: overlooking standard classical works, exoticizing the Hindu tradition, writing history in league with India's Marxist historians and relying largely on foreign rather than Indian scholarship' (Pennington 2016:331). In Shankar' own words, she shows a 'negligent and arrogant mindset...born of colonial and racist thinking'. Vivek Gumaste at Rediff.com asserts that 'this is not a pure battle for free speech', but 'a parochial ideological ambush masquerading as one' (Pennington 2016:331). He calls it 'subtle authoritarianism' out to 'suppress the Hindu viewpoint' (Pennington 2016:331).

To an extent, this is true—there is no level playing field, and the American academics, including Doniger herself, have done their best never to give the Hindus a fair hearing. On the other hand, this power equation is the Hindus' own doing. They have never invested in scholarship, and so they had to take umbrage behind a threatened judicial verdict now that they had the chance. Here, Hindus only pay the price for their self-proclaimed vanguard's intellectual non-performance over the last decades.

Building a scholarly challenge to the present academic consensus is a long-term project that admits of no shortcuts. By going to court and twisting Penguin's arm, Hindus think they have scored a clever victory, but in fact, they have only demeaned Hinduism. Prominent Hindus from the past would not be proud of Hinduism suppressing freedom of expression: great debaters like Yajñavalkya, the Buddha, Badarayana, Shankara or Kumarila Bhatta.

Ancient Indian thought was never divided in box-type orthodoxies on the pattern of Christians versus Muslims, or Catholics versus Protestants. This is only a Western projection, borrowed as somehow more prestigious by the Indian 'secularists', who impose this categorization on the Indian landscape of ideas. At any rate, the vibrant interaction of ancient India's intellectual landscape, where free debate flourished, was nothing like the modern situation where Doniger's own school has locked out the Hindu voice and the latter has reactively demonized her and thrown up hurdles against expressions of her viewpoint.

But the taste of victory had become so unusual for Hindus that even many people who should have known better have cheered the book's withdrawal (see Elst 2015:74-87). It was not the best response, but at least it was a response. And of course, Article 295A may be a bad thing, but as long as it is on the statute books, it should count for Hindus as much as for Muslims and Christians.

HISTORY OF SECTION 295A

Section 295A was not instituted by Hindu society, but against it. It was imposed by the British on the Hindus in order to shield Islam from criticism. Thus, it is truthfully said on the Digplanet.com/wiki website, consulted on 5 August 2016, under the entry Rangila Rasul: 'In 1927, under pressure from the Muslim community, the administration of the *British Raj* enacted *Hate Speech Law Section 295(A)*.'

The reason for its enactment was a string of murders of Arya Samaj leaders who polemicized against Islam. This started with the murder of Pandit Lekhram in 1897 by a Muslim, because Lekhram had written a book criticizing Islam. A particularly well-publicized murder took place in December 1926, eliminating an important leader, Swami Shraddhananda, writer of *Hindu Sangathan: Saviour of the Dying Race* (1924), next to V.D. Savarkar's *Hindutva* (1924), the principal ideological statement of Hindu revivalism. (However, the trigger to the murder lay elsewhere, viz. the protection he personally gave to a family of converts from Islam to Hinduism.) Moreover, there was commotion at the time concerning another very provocative subject: Mohammed's private life, discussed by Mahashay Rajpal in his (ghost-written) book *Rangila Rasul*, a response to a Muslim pamphlet disparaging Sita. Rajpal would be murdered in 1929 (the series of murders was discussed e.g. in Ambedkar 1940; for Shraddhananda's story, see Jordens 1981).

Doniger and the four authors who wrote about the origin and meaning of Section 295A for *JAAR* strictly keep the lid on this crucial fact. None of the contributors has let on that the trigger for this legislation was repeated unidirectional communal murder, viz. of Arya Samaj leaders by Muslims, nor that it was meant to appease the Muslim community. None of them so much as hints at this. Anantanand Rambachan (2016:367) even alleges that 'the aggressive party was the Arya Samaj'. No, the Arya Samaj criticized Islam, an attitude which psychologists might call 'aggression' in a metaphorical sense. But aggression in the sense of inflicting violence on the other party was one-sidedly Muslim.

And even verbally, the Arya Samaj was not really the 'aggressive' party. In Shraddhananda's authoritative biography, not by a Hindu, we read that 'some of his writings about the Muslims expressed harsh and provocative judgments. But (...) they were invariably written in response to writings or pronouncements of Muslims which either vehemently attacked Hinduism, the Arya Samaj, and the Swami himself, or which supported methods such as (...) the killing of apostates, and the use of devious and unfair means of propaganda.' He himself 'never advocated unfair, underhand or violent methods' (Jordens 1981: 174-175).

C.S. Adcock (2016:341) comes closest to the truth by writing that 'polemics continued to cause resentment and, increasingly, it seemed, serious violence'. For an academic writer on the origins of Section 295A, it is bizarre that he has so little grasp of the basic data and doesn't know the nature of the 'seeming' violence. And even he falsely insinuates that this violence was symmetrical, avoids mentioning the deliberate murders (as opposed to mere emotional riots) and hides the Muslim identity of the culprits. When Hindus allege that Indology today is systematically anti-Hindu, they can cite this as an example.

The British finally resolved to curb this form of unrest. While their justice system duly sentenced the murderers, they also decided to make an end to the religious polemics that had 'provoked' them. After the Mutiny of 1857, Queen Victoria had solemnly committed the British administration to avoiding and weeding out insults to the native religions. However, the right to religious criticism had been taken for granted, on a par with the right of Western missionaries to criticize native religions in a bid to convince their adherents that they would be better off joining Christianity.

For example, in 1862, the magistrate sitting in judgement upon a case against a reformist who had criticized the caste-conscious Vallabhacharya Vaishnava community upheld this right: 'It is the function and the duty of the press to intervene, honestly endeavouring by all the powers of argument, denunciation and ridicule, to change and purify the public opinion.' (Adcock 2016:345) He 'upheld the importance of religious critique, and held public opinion in religious matters to be susceptible to reasoned argument.' (Adcock 2016:345)

In Britain, reasoned debates between worldviews flourished, for public opinion was held to be 'susceptible to reasoned argument'. Initially, the colonial authorities treated Indians the same way. But this assessment was reversed by Section 295A, and quite deliberately.

This process had started a bit earlier, in a case against Arya Samaj preacher Dharm Bir in 1915. Ten Muslims were sentenced for rioting, but Dharm Bir was also charged and 'a judge was brought in who could assure conviction' (Adcock 2016:346). Dharam Bir was duly found guilty, then under Section 298 for 'using offensive phrases and gestures (...) with the deliberate intention of wounding the religious feelings' of another community; and under Section 153, for 'wantonly provoking the riot which subsequently occurred' (Adcock 2016:345).

As described by Adcock (2016:346), the British twisted the existing laws into prohibiting any religious polemic: 'Because religion is "rooted in sentiments", the judge concluded, religion is likely to provoke a riot, and that is all it can do. Religious debate is pointless and therefore unjustifiable; the right publicly to controvert arguments, therefore, does not properly extend to religion. To enter into religious debate is nothing but a provocation, an act calculated to arouse hatred. Therefore, it is intolerable.'

Note that the British public would never have stood for such a reasoning. But what was unacceptable to them, and not even countenanced for the Indian subjects fifty years earlier, was imposed on the colonial underlings during the last phase of the British Raj. And has remained with us since.

The murder of Shraddhanada finally made the British rulers turn this attitude into law: 'In 1927, Section 295A was enacted to extend the ease with which "wounding religious feelings'" by verbal acts could be prosecuted.' (Adcock 2016:345) Apart from punishing the murderer, they sought to punish Shraddhanada as well, retro-actively and posthumously.

COUNTERPRODUCTIVE

The British were not so much interested in justice, they merely wanted peace and quiet so the economy could flourish. The Arya Samaj was not doing anything that the Christian missionaries had not been doing (and are still doing today) to the populations they wanted to convert, viz. trying to convince them that their native religion was unwholesome and wrong. This implied saying negative things about that religion, or as the emotion-centric phrase now goes, 'insulting' it.

But if the Arya Samaj's *words* provoked unwanted Muslim *deeds*, they were part of the problem and had to be remedied. However, in spite of this intention to prevent riots, the new law did not end the recurring Muslim murders of Arya Samaj leaders until the Second World War, nor the concomitant riots, as discussed by Dr Ambedkar (1940:156). It was the Partition that broke the Arya Samaj's back, driving it from its power centre in West Panjab with the Dayanand Anglo-Vedic College in Lahore. After Independence, anti-Islamic polemics were widely blackened as 'communal' by an increasingly powerful 'secularism', and thus abandoned by the Arya Samaj. But Section 295A had little to do with this.

More fundamentally, this law put a premium on violence by making it the best proof that the statements prosecuted had indeed 'provoked' violence. It 'extended the strategic value of demonstrating that passions had been aroused that threatened the public peace, in order to induce the government to take legal action against one's opponents. Section 295A thus gave a fillip to the politics of religious sentiment.' (Adcock 2016:345)

And so, 'when coordinated acts of violence are justified as the inevitable result of hurt feelings, legal precautions against violent displays of religious passion may be said to have backfired' (Adcock 2016:347). This present-day effect of Section 295A could easily convince the scholars to sign a petition against this undeniably despotic and un-secular law. Still, it is odd that with their widespread anti-Hindu and pro-minority bias, they object to a law originally enacted to shield a minority from criticism and to punish Hindu words for Muslim murders.

Though initially and for a long time serving to shield Islam, Hindus gradually discovered that they, too, could use the religiously neutral language of this section to their seeming advantage. Christians as well have invoked it, for example to ban Dan Brown's novel *The Da Vinci Code*. This creates a sickening atmosphere of a pervasive touch-me-not-ism, with every community outdoing the other in being more susceptible to having its sentiments hurt.

RATIONALE BEHIND SECTION 295A

When Batra and other Hindus put publishers under pressure to withdraw Doniger's book, or earlier, Ramanujan's *Three Hundred Ramayanas*, the publishers buckled under the fear of having to face trial under Article 295A, as well as under their regard for the Hindu public's purchasing power. Apart from ideological factors, entrepreneurs also take into account the purely commercial aspect of a controversy. In this case, they reckoned with the only power that Hindus have: their numbers.

But the Hindu instigators did not inspire 'fear', and definitely did not have the backing of political authority. This all happened when the Congress party was in power. It is not entirely unheard of that Indian judges are on the take, but in most cases, the Indian judiciary is independent, so a government sometimes has to suffer verdicts not to its liking. Thus, Narendra Modi was repeatedly cleared by the courts from alleged guilt in the post-Godhra riots of 2002 while the Congress, which invested heavily in anti-Modi propaganda, was in power.

It is strange how fast people can forget. Modi's BJP has only very recently come to power—in May 2014, after ten years in the opposition. At the time of the Ramanujan and Doniger controversies, the Congress was safely at the helm. If the publishers were in awe of any powers-that-be, it must have been of the Congress 'secularists'. So, regardless of the prevailing regime, Section 295A by itself exercises a pro-censorship influence.

Now that the BJP is safely in power, we find it is not making any move to abolish Section 295A. This is partly because it has apparently resolved not to touch any communally sensitive issue with a barge pole, committing itself instead to safely secular 'development'—partly for a deeper reason.

The colonial view, ultimately crystallized in Section 295A, came to the fore after the Mutiny of 1857, which had formally erupted over seemingly irrational religious sensitivities: objections to the use of cow or pig fat, taboo to Hindus and Muslims respectively. India was reorganized as an empire ruled by the Queen of Britain, henceforth also the Empress of India. She made a solemn declaration to win over the Indians: 'Queen Victoria's declaration of religious neutrality (...) explicitly promised to refrain from interference in the religious beliefs and practices of Indian natives. (...) What provoked Victoria's declaration was the assumption that religion in India was the source of volatile passions that were a threat to peace.' (Vishwanath 2016:353)

This position was colonial par excellence, contrasting Britons capable of reasoned debate with natives who were prisoners of emotions and superstitions. Yet, it had a kernel of truth: not that Indians were more emotional or superstitious than Britons, but they seemed to have an aversion to religious debate. Nineteenth-century Europeans were keen to know the world, and everywhere the conquerors of foreign lands were followed by students of the new-found languages and cultures. They prided themselves on this curiosity and thought it typical of the indolent natives that they did not have it. Thus, the early Indian pioneers of linguistics were greatly admired and accepted as inspiration for the budding science of linguistics in Europe, yet it was also noticed that they had not shown any interest in foreign languages. Though the ancient Sanskrit grammarian Panini lived close to the Iranian- and Burushaski-speaking peoples, he is not known to have used their languages in his linguistic theories.

So, it was only a logical extension to apply this to religion. Consider the native welcome given to the Syrian Christians in Kerala, the Zoroastrians in Gujarat and other refugees: No questions were asked about the contents of their faith. They were perfectly allowed to practise their traditions (within the bounds of 'morality', as the Constitution still says, for example, the prevailing taboo on cow slaughter, which they had not known in Syria or Iran), to honour any prophets or gurus or scriptures they wanted, to build any churches or temples they chose, yet no interest was paid to what exactly their religion was about. This was simply not the business of the natives, who were satisfied with practising their own traditions. Not even purely for scholarly sake did Hindus or Muslims show any interest in other religions; Al Biruni and Dara Shikoh being the exceptions that prove the rule.

Colonial prejudices are not always incorrect, yet this one really does injustice to the average Hindu, who is more interested in other religions than was the case among Christians until recently. But perhaps they show less of a tendency to criticize. From experience, I tend to think that their natural tolerance as shown towards the refugees is not due to indifference and smugness but to open-mindedness.

For Western religious converts like Saint Paul (Judaism to Christianity), Saint Augustine (Manicheism to Catholicism) or John Newman (Anglicanism to Catholicism), it would be an insult to deny the role of reason in their religious development, or to say that 'to enter into religious debate is nothing but a provocation, an act calculated to arouse hatred', as the British judge had told the Arya Samaj in 1915. But the colonial view crystallized in Section 295A did hold the Indians to be a different race, less rational and not to be trusted with debate, but fortunately also disinclined to such debate. So, it would only be a slight exaggeration of a tendency already present in Indian culture to outlaw religious debate.

That, indeed, is how many Indian secularists and their allies in Western academe now justify this continued muzzling of debate: 'In India, the notion that to be truly tolerant in religion is to refrain from criticism of religion is a widespread secularist ideal.' (Pennington 2016:346)

SECULARISM

To assert that refraining from religious criticism is a 'secularist ideal' brings in the S-word. This would trigger a far longer discussion than we are prepared for here, but because it now serves as the new justification for the colonial Section 295A, at least this.

For a scholar, it is very poor to use this word as if it hadn't acquired a meaning in India (since Jawaharlal Nehru, ca. 1951) totally at variance with its original Western meaning. This should be obvious to whoever studies the types of Indians calling themselves secularist, and those lambasted as anti-secular: 'The concept of secularism as known to the modern West is dreaded, derided and denounced in the strongest terms by the foundational doctrines of Christianity and Islam. (...) It is, therefore, intriguing that the most fanatical and fundamentalist adherents of Christianity and Islam in India—Christian missionaries and Muslim mullahs—cry themselves hoarse in defence of Indian secularism, the same way as the votaries of communist totalitarianism coming out vociferously in defence of democracy.' (S.R. Goel 1998:vii)

Thus, in the West, secularism means that all citizens are equal before the law, regardless of their religion; or what Indians call a common civil code. In India, by contrast, all secularists swear by the preservation of the present system of separate religion-based personal laws, though they prefer to avoid the subject, hopefully from embarrassment at the contradiction. And all Indian secularists swear by the preservation of constitutional, legal and factual discriminations against the Hindu majority. (In case you have recently been living on another planet and don't believe that there are such discriminations, one example: The Right to Education Act 2006, which imposes some costly duties on schools *except minority schools*, has led to the closure of hundreds of Hindu schools.)

Likewise, in the West, the enactment of secularism went hand in hand with deepening criticism of religion, which was pushed from its pedestal and recognized as just another fallible human construct, open to questioning and criticism. In India, by contrast, secularists cheer for the application, formally or in spirit, of Section 295A to outlaw religious criticism—except when it is Hinduism that gets criticized. And that is why the AAR scholars, in solidarity with their Indian secularist friends, have never moved a finger about minority-enforced censorship but made a mountain out of the Doniger molehill. Here, they vehemently denounced the clumsy

Hindu attempt at banning an otherwise poor book that, to them, has the cardinal virtue of riding roughshod over Hindu self-perception.

CONCLUSION

All the Hindu justifications of the 'withdrawal' of Doniger's book amount to: 'Freedom of speech does not mean freedom to insult.' This just shows the speakers' thoughtlessness and illiteracy. All debates about book-banning, or at least one of the contending parties in them, will at some point come up with George Orwell's famous observation: 'If liberty means anything at all, it means the right to tell people what they do not want to hear.' Freedom of speech doesn't mean much if it doesn't imply the freedom to offend. If the freedom to insult were forbidden, then anything meaningful would be found to displease at least someone somewhere and thus be forbidden.

Moreover, many lambasters (including Doniger) honestly feel that they have done a fair job and not 'insulted' anyone. So, even the term 'insult' is merely subjective: 'Insulting is everything that anyone feels insulted by.' This would make the worst touch-me-not the arbiter of whether books are allowed to be published.

So, down with censorship or any procedure amounting to the same, including forcing publishers to withdraw their publications with the threat of Section 295A. Down with censorship laws. Freedom of expression is a fundamental element of democracy, a precondition for making it possible at all. Equal participation in decision-making implies equal access to information and opinions, rather than one group deciding what another group is allowed to read and write.

As for the stated fear that if 'insults' are not curbed by law, soon the atmosphere will be filled with unbearable swearing in the guise of 'criticism': India has done without such censorship laws for thousands of years, and the amount of insults in the religious field was not appreciably worse than in the colonial period or today. Such exaggerated fears can be laid to rest by civil society without state interference. People will give each other feedback and they themselves will keep criticism and 'insults' within reasonable bounds.

Finally, the possibility has to be faced that the fanaticism potentially emanating from certain worldviews has something to do with the contents of these worldviews themselves. Not every religion is equally prone to getting provoked to violence by criticism. I make bold to say that, through a felicitous coincidence, the religions originating in India are quite capable of solving ideological differences of opinion peacefully.

BIBLIOGRAPHY

Adcock, C.S., 'Violence, passion, and the law: A brief history of section 295A and its antecedents', *Journal of the American Academy of Religion*, June 2016, Vol. 84, 337–351

Agarwal, Vishal, *The New Stereotypes of Hindus in Western Indology*, Hinduworld Publishers, Wilmington DE, 2014

Ambedkar, Bhimrao Ramji, *Thoughts on Pakistan*, 1940, republished as Vol. 8 of Ambedkar's *Writings and Speeches*, published by the Government of Maharashtra, 1986–90

Doniger, Wendy, *The Hindus: An Alternative History*, Penguin, Delhi, 2009

——, 'Public Statement from Wendy Doniger following withdrawal of her book by the publisher', South Asia Citizens Web, 11 February 2014

——, 'Roundtable on outrage, scholarship, and the law in India: A response', *Journal of the American Academy of Religion*, June 2016, Vol.84, pp. 364–366

Elst, Koenraad, *The Argumentative Hindu*, Voice of India, Delhi, 2012

——, *On Modi Time*, Voice of India, Delhi, 2015

Goel, Sita Ram, ed., *Freedom of Expression*, Voice of India, Delhi, 1998

Jordens, J.T.F., *Swami Shraddhananda: His Life and Causes*, Oxford

University Press, Oxford/Delhi, 1981

Malhotra, Rajiv, *Academic Hinduphobia*, Voice of India, Delhi, 2016

Pennington, Brian K., 'The unseen hand of an underappreciated law: The Doniger affair and its aftermath', *Journal of the American Academy of Religion*, June 2016, Vol. 84, pp. 323–336

Ramachan, Anantanand, 'Academy and community: Overcoming suspicion and building trust', *Journal of the American Academy of Religion*, June 2016, Vol. 84, pp. 367–372

Swarup, Ram, *Hindu View of Christianity and Islam*, Voice of India, Delhi, 1993

Viswanath, Rupa, 'Economies of offense: hatred, speech, and violence in India', *Journal of the American Academy of Religion*, June 2016, Vol. 84, pp. 352–363

Academic Bullies*

This is an intervention in the debates about historical accuracy and about freedom of expression.

Audrey Truschke is a professor of Religious Studies in Stanford, California, and has gained some fame with her work on the patronage of Sanskrit by the Moghuls. In order to get that far, she had to toe the ideologically mandatory line: Neither in America nor in India does the Hindu-baiting establishment allow a dissident to get seriously established in the academic world. Predictably, we see her elaborating the same positions already taken by an earlier generation of academics, such as whitewashing Aurangzeb. Not that this was a hard job for her: One gets the impression that she is a true believer and really means what she says. Then again, she may have done an excellent job of creating the desired impression, all while secretly knowing better.

BULLYING

Her position in the article "The Right's problem with history" (*DNA*, 26 October 2016) is summed up as: 'Unable to defend a fabricated history of India on scholarly grounds, many foot soldiers of the Hindu Right have turned to another response: bullying.' It would be normal to compare secularist historians and their Western dupes with people of the same rank, namely different-minded historians,

---

*Published on Pragyata.com, 30 November 2016

in this case belonging to the 'Hindu Right'. These are not exactly numerous, having been blocked systematically from academe by the single permitted opinion in both India and America, but they exist. Yet, they and their output are absent from her paper. From a street bully, I would expect a denunciation of street bullies, and from an academic a polemic against her own peers.

The photograph accompanying the article tells it all. If it had been about her own school of history, the picture would have shown established historians involved in this debate, such as Wendy Doniger or Sheldon Pollock. But now that the opposition is at issue, it shows a group of non-historians, not in an air-conditioned college hall but in a street demonstration exercising their freedom of expression. The reader is expected to recognize them as representatives of the 'Hindu Right' and as 'bullies'.

She testifies to verbal attacks she herself has endured 'from members of the Hindu Right', and which she evaluates as 'vicious personal attacks on the basis of my perceived religion, gender and race'. Correction: She could have maintained the very same religion, gender and race and yet never be attacked by those same Hindus (indeed, most Jewish female whites have never experienced such attacks), if she had not belonged to the 'scholars who work on South Asia' and who have earned a reputation as Hindu-baiters. She has been attacked on the basis of what she has written, nothing else.

But it is true, and deplorable, that an uncouth but vocal class of people clothe their denunciations of an ideological position in foul personal attacks. It so happens that I know her plight very well, for I, too, receive my share of what some would call 'hate mail' when I express scepticism of beliefs dear to Hindu traditionalists (e.g. the eternity of Sanskrit, the supernatural origins of the *Vedas*, the Rama Setu or the Krishna Bhakti verses in the *Gita*). And also when going against the dogmas of her own school, such as that Muslim rule in India was benign, or that Sanskrit has an origin of white invaders oppressing black natives. Nothing dangerous, though, and I doubt her claim of 'physical attacks' on Indologists, unless she means the egg thrown at Doniger in London.

From the start, Truschke tries to capture the moral high ground by citing one of her lambasters as tweeting: 'Gas this Jew.' In America, such reference to the Holocaust is absolutely not done, and Indian secularist circles adopt the same sensitivities once they see these as valid for the trend-setting West. To the Hindu mainstream, this hyperfocus on anything associated with the Second World War Second World War is not there, and they had no history with anti-Semitism; but still this quote would be unacceptable there, for regardless of what Jews exactly believe, Hindus tend to respect other faiths.

However, her claim might be correct (not sure there), for there are indeed some Hindu hotheads who have adopted this kind of rhetoric. In pre-Internet days, they would brew their own conspiracy theories, but now the access to websites carrying elaborate Western conspiracy theories, starring the Zionist world conspiracy, entices them into using this kind of language. Certainly deplorable, but not at all representative of the 'Hindu Right': hardly even for its bullies, not for its leaders (both V.D. Savarkar and M.S. Golwalkar described the Jews as role models for loyalty to one's own roots) and not at all for the 'Hindu Right' scholars whom she is carefully ignoring.

ACADEMIC BULLYING

This 'bullying' had best been compared to the 'bullying' on the other side. Like, for instance, the two attempts by Leftist students to silence me, as a twice scheduled speaker, at the Madison, Wisconsin, South Asia Conference in 1996 and a private event preceding it, hosted by Professor Andrew Sihler. Or the successful protests against the Dharma Civilization Foundation's offer to fund a chair at University of California Irvine?, when so many US chairs are comfortably being funded by the Saudi Arabians.

But on Truschke's own side, the dividing line between bullies and academics is not so neat. Why stoop to street bullying if you have tenure? It is far more effective, then, to resort to academic bullying. Thus, in their intervention in the California textbook affair, where Hindu parents had sought to edit blatantly anti-Hindu passages, the explicitly partisan intervening professors even managed to get themselves recognized as arbiters in the matter. This would have been unthinkable if those bullies had not been established academics. (And this I can say even though my criticism of the Hindu parents' positions exists in cold print.) Her focus on street bullies has the effect of misdirecting the reader's attention, away from the more consequential phenomenon of academic bullying.

I myself have been barred from several Indologist forums by active intervention or passive complicity of the same professors who otherwise clamour 'censorship!' when anything at all happens to a book they favour. Thus, they are so very sensitive that they dramatically talked of 'threats to freedom of speech' when ... *Three Hundred Ramayanas*, a book belittling a Hindu scripture, was not selected as required reading in Delhi University, though otherwise it remained freely available. They claimed to champion 'freedom of speech' when Doniger's error-ridden book *The Hindus: An Alternative History* was withdrawn from circulation, though it was never legally banned but was left available for another publisher; who did indeed come forward, so that the book is again lawfully omnipresent. But when I appealed to them to intervene for annulling my banning from the Religion in South Asia (RISA) list, which had been done in violation of its own charter, they all looked the other way.

A recent example. In 2014, I read a paper on the Rig Vedic seer Vasishtha and his relative divinization in a panel on 'divinization' at the European Conference for South Asia Studies in Zürich. My paper was enthusiastically received, also by the panel's organizers when I sent in the final version for publication. First they accepted it, but then, I received an embarrassed e-mail from the organizers stating that they could not include my paper, without any reason given. Upon my enquiring, the half-line reply said that it did not fit their project. In all its insignificance, this still managed to be a blatant lie, and their earlier acceptance confirmed that this could not have been the reason. But some higher-up had warned them that I am to be treated as excluded, just like on many other occasions.

Far more seriously, both in America and in India, scholars suspected of pro-Hindu sympathies are blocked in their access to academe, and their work gets studiously ignored. For India, a tip of the blanket over this hushed-up phenomenon was lifted by Dr A. Devahuti in *Bias in Indian Historiography* (1980). It is seriously in need of an update, but I am given to understand that one is forthcoming. For America, a start was made by Rajiv Malhotra with his books *Invading the Sacred* (2007) and *Academic Hinduphobia* (2016).

HINDUPHOBIA

Coming to contents, Truschke accuses 'Hindu Right-wingers' of attacks on 'academics'. I would have expected them to attack 'anti-Hindu Left-wingers', and, indeed, I learn that this is exactly how they see it—and how they see her. If she doesn't like being characterized this way, she is herewith invited to stop calling her adversaries similar names. The binary Left/Right is at least problematic here, yet for a quarter century I have seen this scheme used to explain matters. Except that the Left doesn't call itself Left: It treats itself as the natural centre, and anything to its right is deemed politically coloured: 'Right' or very easily 'extreme Right'.

Anyway, she calls 'alleged Hinduphobia' nothing more than 'a strawman stand-in for any idea that undercuts Hindutva ideology'. The term was made popular by Malhotra, whom I have never known to swear by 'Hindutva', a specific term literally translated as 'Hindu-ness' but now effectively meaning 'the RSS tradition of Hindu nationalism'. At any rate, one does not have to follow Hindutva, or even be a Hindu or an Indian, to observe that American India-watchers utter a strong anti-Hindu prejudice in their publications. Not to look too far, I can find an example in myself: I have written a number of publications criticizing both Hindutva as an ideology and the Hindutva organizations, yet I can off-hand enumerate dozens of illustrations of Hindu-baiting by supposed India experts in the West, as well as by their Indian counterparts.

At most, one can criticize the term 'Hinduphobia' for being etymologically less than exact. Words ending in '*-phobia*' normally indicate an irrational fear, and fear is not the attitude in which Hinduism is approached. The term was coined on the model of 'Islamophobia', a weaponized word meant to provoke hatred, yet now a thoroughly accepted and integrated term among progressive academics. A '*-phobia*' is normally a psychiatric term and its use to denote political adversaries is of a kind with the Soviet custom of locking up dissidents in mental hospitals. And indeed, people shielding Islam from proper enquiry do treat their opponents as mentally warped marginals. But the core of truth in the reprehensible term 'Islamophobia' is at least that it points to 'fear of Islam', a religion which its critics do indeed diagnose as fearsome. Hinduism, by contrast, has been criticized as cruel, evil, superstitious, ridiculous, but not as a threat. It is only Hindus who flatter themselves that the 'Abrahamics' want to destroy Hinduism because they *fear* it as being superior and more attractive.

The use of the term 'Hinduphobia' is predicated upon the already existing acceptance and use of the term 'Islamophobia'. If the United Nations, the governments of the United States and the European Union, etc., and the pan-Islamic pressure group Organisation of Islamic Cooperation, were to give up this ugly and vicious term, then the 'Hinduphobia' term so disliked by Truschke would lapse with it and get replaced again by the older and more accurate term, 'Hindu-baiting'. But until then, it throws the Islamophile and Hindu-baiting scholars of Truschke's persuasion back on the bare fact that they themselves have and display the kind of prejudice against Hinduism of which they accuse the Islam critics.

HISTORY

According to Truschke, 'a toxic combination of two realities fuel the Hindu Right's onslaught against scholars of South Asia: Hindu nationalist ideology rests heavily on a specific vision of Indian history, and that version of history is transparently false.'

Now it gets interesting, with two competing views of Indian history, one true and one false: 'Hindu nationalists claim that India's past featured the glorious flourishing of a narrowly defined Hinduism that was savagely interrupted by anybody non-Hindu, especially Muslims. However, the real story of Indian history is much more complicated and interesting.'

A 'narrowly defined Hinduism' is only projected into the Hindu past by semi-literate non-historians who do indeed man the middle ranks of the uniformed RSS. No serious Hindu historian, not the lamented Jadunath Sarkar, R.C. Majumdar, Harsh Narain or K.S. Lal, nor contemporary scholars like Bharat Gupt or Meenakshi Jain, would be foolish enough to simply deny the 'diversity and syncretism' that Truschke sees in India's past. But here again, we see how Truschke has chosen not to address the scholars of a competing persuasion, but the village bumpkins.

In one sense, however, even the most sophisticated historians will affirm that India's past was indeed 'glorious'. And it was not at all 'complicated': India was simply *independent*. Yes, ancient India had its problems too—it had local wars, it was not paradise on earth—but in one decisive respect, Indians under Muslim or British occupation correctly remembered it as 'glorious': It ruled itself. When the British told Mahatma Gandhi that his hoped-for independence would only throw India back into its headaches of casteism, communalism and the rest, he answered that India would, of course, have its problems, 'but they will be our own'. Compared to being under foreign tutelage, such self-rule is nothing less than glorious.

This brings us to Truschke's own field of research: 'Especially problematic for Hindu nationalists is current scholarship on Indo-Islamic rule, a fertile period for cross-cultural contacts and interreligious exchanges. This vibrant past is rightly a source of pride and inspiration for many Indians, but the Hindu Right sees only an inconvenient challenge to their monolithic narrative of

Hindu civilization under Islamic siege.'

Note how two issues are artfully mixed up here: the questionable monolithic view of Hinduism and the very correct view of a Hindu civilization besieged by Islam. It is true that non-historian 'Hindu nationalists' are rather inaccurate in their 'monolithic narrative of Hindu civilization'; but it is not true that the period of 'Indo-Islamic rule' is a 'source of pride and inspiration', nor that it is contested only by 'Hindu nationalists'. Her notion of 'current scholarship' is, of course, limited to her own school of thought, heavily overrepresented in academe, partly due to its aggressive policy of exclusion vis-à-vis others.

There are admittedly those who identify with foreign colonizers: Many Indian Muslims identify with Mohammed bin Qasim and with the Moghuls (whom Pakistan considers as the real founders of their Indo-Islamic state), and many Nehruvian secularists share and continue the British opinions about India and Hinduism. But those who identify with India, even if they admit some good aspects of these colonizations, do not take any pride at all in having been subjugated. Yes, there were instances of collaboration with the colonizers, such as the hundreds of thousands of Indians whose sweat made the 'British' railway network possible, or the Rajputs whose daughters filled the Moghul harems in exchange for their fathers' careers in the Moghul army. But those instances are at most understandable, a lesser evil in difficult circumstances, but not a source of 'pride and inspiration'.

A few episodes of Muslim occupation were indeed 'vibrant', viz. after Akbar's realistic appreciations of the existing power equations persuaded him to rule with rather than against his Hindu subjects. Then, as everybody already knew, Hindus did indeed give their cultural best, rebuilding the temples which the Sultanate had demolished (and which would again be demolished by Aurangzeb)—a tribute to the vitality of Hindu civilization even under adverse circumstances. And some Muslims did indeed engage in 'inter-religious exchanges', such as Dara Shikoh translating the *Upanishads* into Persian; later, he was beheaded for apostasy.

But even then, academics had better use their critical sense when interpreting these episodes, rather than piously taking them at face value. In the Zürich conference already mentioned, I heard an 'academic' describe how contemporary Hindi writers praised Aurangzeb, the dispenser of their destinies. Well, many eulogies of Stalin can also be cited, including by comrades fallen from grace and praising Stalin even during their acceptance speeches of the death penalty; but it would be a very bad historian, even if sporting academic titles, who would flatly deduce therefrom that Stalin was a benign ruler.

Guru Gobind Singh's 'victory letter' to Emperor Aurangzeb was, in all seriousness, included among the sources of praise, leaving unmentioned that Aurangzeb had murdered his father and four sons. Every village bumpkin can deduce that Guru Gobind Singh hated Aurangzeb more than any other person in the world, and that he was only being diplomatic in his writing because of the power equation. Academics laugh at kooks who believe in aliens, but it took an academic, no less, to discover an alien who actually admired the murderer of his father and sons.

According to Truschke's admission, a lot of Hindus are 'happy to underscore the violence and bloodshed unleashed by many Indo-Islamic rulers', but she wrongly identifies them as the 'Hindu Right'. It doesn't require a specific ideological commitment or even any religious identity to observe well-documented historical facts. Mostly documented by the Muslim perpetrators themselves, that is. Thus, like Truschke herself, I am neither Hindu nor Indian, yet I can read for myself with what explicit glee the Muslim chroniclers described temple destructions and massacres of Unbelievers.

THE MISTAKE OF PLAGIARISM

'In contrast to the detailed work of academics, the Hindu nationalist vision of India's past stands on precarious to non-existent historical evidence. As a result, the Hindu Right cannot engage with Indologists on scholarly grounds. Indeed, the few Hindutva ideologues who have attempted to produce scholarship are typically tripped up by rookie mistakes—such as misusing evidence, plagiarism, and overly broad arguments—and so find themselves ignored by the academic community.'

The inclusion of 'plagiarism' among her list of 'rookie mistakes' gives away that she is fulminating specifically against the work of Malhotra, whom she is careful not to mention by name. For his book *Indra's Net*, he was famously accused of plagiarism (by a Christian mission mentor), for he quotes the American scholar Andrew Nicholson's book *Unifying Hinduism*, in which he concurs with the same position that Hinduism had elaborated its common doctrinal backbone long before the Orientalists 'invented Hinduism'. In fact, he only used Nicholson as a source to prove that Westerners, too, could acquire this insight, there was nothing 'Hindu nationalist' about it. And he amply quoted him in so many words, though a few times, for the flow of the narrative, he merely rephrased the theses of this much-quoted author. By that standard, most papers contain plagiarism; but what passes unnoticed elsewhere becomes a scandal when done by a self-identifying Hindu.

Yet, numerous Indologists started a holier-than-thou tirade against the 'plagiarism', a comical drama to watch. Malhotra then walked the extra mile, writing Nicholson out of his narrative and quoting original sources instead (thereby incidentally suggesting that Nicholson himself had committed plagiarism, though no Indologist ever remarked on that). But this inconvenient development was given the silent treatment, and Truschke still presupposes that there ever was a substantive 'plagiarism' case against Malhotra, and by extension against the whole 'Hindu Right'.

Malhotra has indeed been 'ignored by the academic community'—until he found a way to make his critique non-ignorable. That indeed shows a lot of skill in dealing with the way of the world, for until then, Hindus had only painstakingly proven themselves right and the 'academics' wrong, but had had no impact at all. By contrast, Malhotra, by personalizing his argument into specific dissections of the work of leading scholars such as Doniger, Pollock or Anantanand Rambachan, has earned a session at the annual conference of the trend-setting AAR. On Indological discussion forums, his input is frequently mentioned, though the academics mostly keep up their airs of pooh-poohing that interloper, in a bid to justify their ignoring his actual critique of their own work.

By the way, notice my term: a 'self-identifying Hindu'. As the case of Malhotra has amply exemplified, it suffices to stand up as a Hindu, or to own up Hinduism, in order to be dubbed 'Hindu Rightist', 'Hindutva ideologue', as well as 'fanatic', 'rookie' and all the fair names Hindus have been called by Professor Truschke's august school of thought. To them, the acceptable Hindu, or what Malhotra calls a 'sepoy', is one who never identifies as a Hindu, but rather as an 'Indian' (or better, 'Bengali', 'Malayali', etc.), 'low-caste', and ideologically 'secularist'. The exception is when countering criticism from self-identified Hindus, for then, he is expected to say: 'But me too, I am a Hindu!' That way, he can fulfil his main task: As long as there are Hindus, he must deny them the right to speak on behalf of Hinduism and give it a presence at the conversation between worldviews.

HISTORY DEBATES

Most Hindu scholars have not found a way to impose their viewpoint on the sphere of discourse yet. In the case of objective scholars among non-Hindus, this would not have mattered. It is, after all, their own job to trace any material relevant to their field of research, including obscure works by other scholars, even adversaries. But in this case, there are some cornerstones of the Indological worldview which tolerate no criticism nor alternative, so these are to be carefully ignored.

Thus, Shrikant Talageri's case against the Aryan invasion theory, the bedrock of the 'academic' view of ancient Hindu history, is painstaking, detailed, voluminous, factual and well formulated—yet Truschke's own entire tribe of 'academics' simply goes on ignoring his case without bothering to refute it. (Well, there are two articles talking down to him, but we mean actual refutations, not mere denials.) If academics were to live up to the reputation they have among laymen, they would have set aside their current business to deal with this fundamental challenge to their worldview.

Or take *A Secular Agenda* by Arun Shourie, Ph.D. from Syracuse, New York, and stunningly successful disinvestment minister in the A.B. Vajpayee government, when India scored its highest economic growth figures. It was a very important book, and it left no stone standing of the common assumption among so-called experts that India (with its religion-based civil codes and its discriminatory laws against Hinduism) is a secular state, i.e., a state in which all citizens are equal before the law, regardless of their religion. Though the book deconstructs the bedrock on which the 'experts' have built their view of modern India, they have never formulated a refutation. Instead, they just keep repeating their own deluded assumption, as in: 'The BJP threatens India's structure as a secular state.' (Actually, the BJP does not, and India is not.) They can do so because they are secure in the knowledge that, among the audiences that matter, their camp controls the sphere of discourse. Concerning the interface between religion and modern politics, the established 'academic' view is not just defective, it is an outrageous failure.

Or consider historian Professor K.S. Lal's works on caste and religion, refuting with primary data the seeming truism, launched by the Communist Party of India ideologue M.N. Roy and now omnipresent in the textbooks, that the lowest castes converted *en masse* to Islam because of its claimed message of equality. Islam mainly won over the urban middle castes (and not because of equality, a value rejected as ingratitude towards the dispenser of destinies in the *Quran*, but because of the privileges vis-à-vis non-Muslims), not the Untouchables. Again, the silent treatment has been the only response the 'experts' could muster.

ICONOCLASM

The Ayodhya controversy was part of a larger issue, viz. Islamic iconoclasm, which victimized many thousands of places of worship in India and abroad, starting with Arabia. Or at least that is how historians like Sita Ram Goel and professors Harsh Narain, K.S. Lal or Saradindu Mukherji saw it: Turn this one controversy into an occasion for educating the public about the ideological causes of the iconoclasm that hit Hindu society so hard and so consistently for over a millennium. But the RSS-BJP preferred to put the entire focus on their one toy in Ayodhya, and obscure or even deny the Islamic motive behind it. (The ideological impotence and non-interest on their part provide yet another contrast with the academics' imaginary construction of a wily, resourceful and highly motivated Hindu movement.)

As part of his effort, Goel published a two-volume book giving a list of 2,000 temples demolished on purpose, mostly replaced by mosques. The part on the theology of iconoclasm proved irrefutable and has never even been gainsaid on any of its specifics. The list of 2,000 temples equally stands entirely unshaken, as so many challenges to the reigning school that tries to downplay the tradition of iconoclasm pioneered by the Prophet. Ever since, the dominant policy has been to disregard Goel's work and carry on whitewashing the record of Islam regardless.

Since stray new proofs of Muslim temple destruction keep popping up, that school has developed an alternative discursive strategy to prevent such cases from suggesting their own logical conclusion. It now preaches that a few temple destructions have indeed taken place, but channels this admission towards a counter-intuitive explanation: that Hinduism is to be blamed for these, not Islam. The core of truth is that a handful of cases have been documented of ancient Hindu kings abducting prestigious idols from their adversaries' main temples, just as happened in Mesopotamia and other pagan cultures. These are then presented as the source of inspiration for Aurangzeb's wholesale destruction (documented in his own court chronicles) of thousands of temples and many more idols.

Not that any of the many Muslim iconoclasts ever testified that such was his inspiration. Their motivation, whenever explicitly stated, and whether inside or outside of India, is invariably purely Islamic. Since the negationist school is unable to document its thesis, let me show them by example how to do it.

Kashinath Pandit's book *A Muslim Missionary in Mediaeval Kashmir* (Delhi, 2009) contains a translation of the *Tohfatu'l Ahbab*, the biography of the fifteenth-century Islamic missionary Shamsu'd-Din Araki by his younger contemporary Muhammad Ali Kashmiri. After describing the many temple demolitions Araki wrought or triggered in thinly populated Kashmir (many more than the 'eighty' which the secularists are willing to concede on Richard Eaton's authority for all of India during the whole Muslim period), the biographer gives Araki's motivation in practising all this iconoclasm.

Does he say 'Araki then recalled the story how a Hindu king ran off with an idol and thereby felt an urge to do something entirely different: destroy all the idols and their idol-houses with it'? No. He recounts the standard Islamic narrative of the Kaaba: It was built by Adam and rebuilt by Abraham for monotheistic worship (thus yielding a far more authoritative precedent than idol theft by an Infidel king), until unbelievers made it 'a place for the idols and a house for the statues. Some Quraish chieftains (...) turned this House of God into the abode of devilish and satanic people. For innumerable years, this house of divine light and bliss became the worshiping place for sorcerers and depraved people and the centre of worshippers of idols (made of stones).'

Fortunately, this injustice didn't last, neither in Mecca, nor in Kashmir. 'When the last of the prophets (Muhammad) saw this situation, he lifted Imam Ali Murtaza on his shoulders so that defiled and impure idols and images were struck down in the House of God. (...) In the same manner, Kashmir was a den of wicked people, the source of infidelity and a mine of corruption and aberration.' (p.258)

And then the enumeration of Hindu sacred places levelled and mosques built in their stead resumes. An extra detail of interest for all those who idealize Sufis is that the text lists many occasions when 'Sufis' and 'dervishes' participated in massacres and temple demolitions.

At any rate, that is what a Muslim testimony of the motive for temple destructions looks like. At least in the real world, not in the make-believe world of our 'academics'. I had already challenged Richard Eaton (the originator of this thesis, a self-described Marxist) and his followers to come up with such evidence in 1999, but nothing ever materialized. Come on, Professor Truschke, you can make an excellent career move by producing this proof.

To sum up: On the one hand, we have Islamic iconoclasts and their contemporary supporters saying in so many words that Islam made them do it. Moderns who highlight this evidence are, in Truschke's estimation, 'bullies'. On the other hand, we have no evidence at all for the claim that the Islamic iconoclasts, intent on destroying Hinduism itself through its icons, took inspiration from Hindu icon-stealers, who installed the icon in their own temple for continued worship (as if abduction, wanting to *have* something close to you, were the same thing as murder, i.e., wanting something to disappear from this world). This claim is nothing more than special pleading. Yet, people who propagate it are, in Truschke's description, 'academics'.

CONCLUSION

The bourgeoisie sets great store by status. Scholars go by a different criterion: knowledge. They know, through learning or personal experience, that for some of the great insights and discoveries, we are indebted to outsiders and amateurs; and that quite a few of their colleagues have big titles and positions not corresponding to their actual knowledge. They also know that holding (or at least uttering) the required opinions can make or break an academic career—either formally, as when a non-Anglican could not get admission to Oxford University, or informally, as under the reign of progressivist conformism today.

To think highly of the academic world presupposes a link between scientific achievement and academic rank, and this largely makes sense in the exact sciences. In the humanities, especially in the social 'science' and literature departments, this link is also deduced, but only as a parasitical extension of the conventions in the exact sciences. Much of what passes for scholarship these days is only ideology wrapped in jargon. Some sophomores take it seriously: Having just gained entry into the academic world, they idealize it and are proud of their belonging to a higher world distinct from lay society. And most laymen believe it: Over-awed by status, they assume that academic status presupposes both knowledge and objectivity, the basis of academic authority.

There exists a test for objective knowledge: A good theory predicts. Physicists who know the relevant parameters of an object in motion can predict its location at future times. Well, how about the predictions by the academic India-watchers? In the mid-1990s, when the BJP's imminent coming to power was a much-discussed probability, top academics predicted that a BJP government would turn India into a Vedic dictatorship, whatever that may be. They were put in the wrong even swifter than expected: In 1996, BJP leader A.B. Vajpayee was prime minister for thirteen days, then lost the vote of confidence, and instead of seizing power for good, he meekly stepped down. Academics predicted the victimization of Dalits and women, gas chambers, 'all the Indian Muslims thrown into the Indian Ocean', and what not. Well, the BJP has been in power from 1998 till 2004, and since 2014: Where are those gas chambers?

Scholars of modern India, as well as historians of fields relevant for contemporary political debates, have a lot to be modest about. They may have academic positions, but their record is not such that they are in a position to talk down to outsiders, the way Truschke now does.

Macaulay's Life and Times*

There are a lot of things wrong with many Indians' unquestioning trust in and use of the thesis put forward by Edward Said in his unjustly famous book *Orientalism* (1978). This work is full of factual errors, leaves unconsidered the German-language mainstay of orientalism (to which its main proposition linking orientalism with colonialism happens not to apply) and essentially appears to be a conspiracy theory, turning all scholars concerned into colonial agents. But with regard to Indians specifically, it uses orientalism in a sense different from the original application related to India, which, in turn, is distinct from its academic use as the name for a philological discipline. 'Orientalist' originally referred to those British administrators of India who, around 1800, opined that the native languages were more suited as mediums of education and modernization than English. Whereas 'orientalism' has become a dirty word among Hindu nationalists as much as among 'postcolonial' Marxists, the historical orientalists actually pursued nativist education policies still advocated by the same Hindu nationalists.

Now a book has appeared which presents the man who put the orientalists out of business by pushing through an anglicist education policy: Thomas Babington Macaulay (1800–1859), considered the godfather of India's anglicized ruling class and hated by Hindu nationalists. Finally, we have an up-to-date biography of this person extremely influential in Indian history. As Zareer Masani says on the

---

*This review of Zareer Masani's biography, *Macaulay: Pioneer of India's Modernization* (Random House, Noida, 2012), was published in *Oriëntalistische Literaturzeitung* in December 2016 (p.528)

cover of his book *Macaulay: Pioneer of India's Modernization*, 'If you're an Indian reading this book in English, it's probably because of Thomas Macaulay.' His last biography was one by his nephew George Otto Trevelyan, still in the nineteenth century.

The present book is a pleasant enough read, giving all the relevant data. It is marred by only one factor, which may even garner the author sympathy among some of his readers, namely his all-too-conspicuous sympathy for his subject, not to say his unconcealed admiration.

By birth and upbringing, Macaulay was part of a British circle of elite people who were both liberal and Christian. The best-known example of this movement was William Wilberforce (1759–1833), who successfully campaigned both for the abolition of slavery and for allowing missionary activity in India. We see Macaulay going to India not to fulfil a historical mission, but as the only way seemingly open to him to boost his finances. He worked as an assistant to Governor-General William Bentinck, most famous for prohibiting the self-immolation of widows on their husbands' funeral pyres (satī). It was formally in a written advice to him that he formulated his famous "Minute on Education" in 1835. Apart from determining education policy for centuries to come (we still have an education system sensibly called Macaulayan), he also made his mark in other areas, e.g., he drafted the Indian Penal Code. Then he returned to stay in England for twenty more years as a scholar and a famous poet, to die at age 59.

It will not endear the man to Indian nationalists that he used his spare time in Calcutta (now Kolkata) to pursue his interest in the Graeco-Roman classics while spurning the native ones. His contempt for Sanskrit writings is well known and comes through in his "Minute", where he equates the whole of Sanskrit literature in terms of knowledge content with a single shelf of a popular library in Britain. Or, according to the approving author: 'Macaulay was notoriously dismissive, if not downright hostile and contemptuous, about native Indian, and particularly Hindu, customs and religious superstitions.' (p.xiii)

Hindu nationalists tend to use his name when they mean the anglicized elite. However, he did not spin a conspiracy that made the influence of the British long outlast their presence in India, as nationalist narrative implies. Instead, Indians themselves have opted for his and against nativist policies regarding language and education. Maybe they have chosen to pursue a wrong course (or maybe not, as this book affirms), but it is, at any rate, their own doing, not that of a Western conspiracy.

Was Macaulay's education policy good for the former untouchables, here called 'Dalits' (the choice of words in this case being very sensitive)? As Dharampal has shown in his book *The Beautiful Tree: Indigenous Indian Education in the Eighteenth Century* (1983), basing himself on contemporaneous British surveys carried out in preparation of the implementation of Macaulay's policies, Indian schools were by no means backward, and the school system was definitely more democratic than the contemporaneous one in England. It did not serve many untouchables, but they were represented, contradicting the usual assumption that low-castes were forbidden from learning to read and write. Moreover, positing a causal relationship between the introduction of the English medium and the emancipation of the low-castes is factually incorrect. China pursued a radical policy of equalization and achieved near-general literacy without using one word of English. Many Chinese engineers of whatever social background work high-tech jobs without knowing English.

Macaulay also did not have the egalitarian reforms in mind which his present-day Dalit fans ascribe to him. Britain at that time had steep class differences, which helps explain why, as administrators in India, the British could so easily accommodate the caste system. As we learn in this book, Macaulay was not in favour of universal franchise, preferring to keep it restricted to people owning property or diplomas. The Indian Leftists and subalterns, the very circles that celebrate his memory, opposed the latest Gulf War, in which a superpower bludgeoned a backward country in the name of human rights (and probably in the service of private capital). Exactly the same conditions prevailed in the First Opium War, which Macaulay passionately and prominently supported. In this case, the author is more even-handed, observing that today, 'Macaulay's ideas about an imperial mission to inform and educate still underpin the way the West exports its values to the rest of the world, especially through "soft" power and the subtle transfer of cultural and economic norms' (p. xv).

Did Macaulay provide the glue that still holds independent India together, as his fans, including the author, believe? The Constituent Assembly envisaged two alternatives to English as the official language: Hindi, taken to be more or less spoken as a mother tongue by some 40 per cent of the population, which was chosen and badly failed (partly but not wholly by sabotage from the English-speaking elite); and Sanskrit, which had a history as an official language and was highly respected both in India and abroad. Sanskrit was little spoken (as was English), but learning it as a common second language would have proved easier than making Hebrew the first language for Jews migrating to Israel, also because of the many vocabulary links between Sanskrit and the vernaculars. If Sanskrit was a difficult language, it was difficult for everyone, and it did not seriously favour one region over another the way Hindi did. Even Bhimrao Ambedkar, law minister and venerated ideological light of most low-caste Macaulay fans, strongly supported Sanskrit. India might have been united under its own classical language. However, after a 50-50 vote, assembly president Rajendra Prasad cast the fateful deciding vote in favour of Hindi, thus aborting the possibly successful Sanskrit experiment and indirectly making English the only viable alternative. Macaulay might have been history by now, but he is back with a vengeance. And if Masani has his way, Macaulay is here to stay.

Indraprastha vs Dînpanah: Nothing Communal about 'Indraprastha'*

Indraprastha was the town founded by the Pandava brothers of the *Mahabharata* fame as their capital. Here, the eldest among them, Yudhishthira, became the 'ruler of righteousness' (dharma-râja). More than 3,000 years later, on 22-23 November 2016, the Draupadi Dream Trust held the first Indraprastha Conference in the National Museum, Delhi. This was part of a larger initiative on Indraprastha, with an exhibition in the Purana Qila (Old Fort). This fort had been built over the ancient site of Indraprastha, now partly made visible by archaeological excavations.

Among secularists, there is predictably an attempt to sow doubt about this. In his 2015 book *Where Stones Speak: Historical Trails in Mehrauli, the First City of Delhi*, Rana Safvi argues that the finds under the Purana Qila have not been established to be the Pandavas' city, which was but 'mythological'. In particular, they are claimed not to contain the characteristic Painted Grey Ware (PGW), as per the 1954 excavations by India's top archaeologist, B.B. Lal. However, sixty-two years later, the nonagenarian Lal edited the brochure of the present exhibition and, taking into account several excavations since then (which Safvi feigns to ignore), asserts that PGW was indeed found there, and that it was certainly the city of the Pandavas. Mehrauli was not the oldest part of Delhi, Indraprastha was.

*Published in *Swarajya*, 3 December 2016

LIGHTNING

A 'prastha' is an open space, a clearing in the forest where you go and settle, a 'colony'. Thus, a vanaprastha, an elderly person who withdraws from society, is 'one who goes and settles in the forest' or 'one who has the forest as his colony'.

The new town was dedicated to Indra. He was the god of the thunderstorm that puts an end to the oppressive summer heat and opens the rainy season. That is why among the twelve Vedic solar months or half-seasons, he rules the first month of the rainy season. As the Rig Vedic seer Vasishtha says in his celebrated *Hymn of the Frogs,* both the priests and the frogs croak with joy when the first rainstorm breaks: the frogs because of the advent of water, the priests because of the manifestation of their god, Indra. Implicitly, the priests' recitation is humorously likened to the frogs' croaking.

He was also the slayer of the dragon Vrtra, a model for all the dragon-slayers in the world, such as Zeus killing Typhon, or Saint George, or Siegfried, or Beowulf. In Iran, he was transformed into a demon, but his nickname Verethragna (Vedic *Vrtrahan,* 'Vrtra-slayer') then became a popular god in its own right. There, we have an Indra on the side of both good and evil.

Less poetically and more philosophically, the *Atharva Veda* puts him at the centre of the sophisticated concept of Indrajâla, 'Indra's net'. In this net, a diamond in every knot reflects every other diamond knot, and thus the whole. The West needed another 4,000 years to develop the similar concept of the 'holographic paradigm'.

In India, Indra's cult gradually declined after the *Mahabharata* age. Originally an embodiment of masculine strength, he becomes the subject of poetic variations extolling his (and his wife Shachi's) sexual prowess. Like his Greek counterpart Zeus, he gets involved in flings on the side, such as with sage Gautama's wife Ahilya. While becoming a character of fun, he further gets disavowed by the *Mahabharata* hero Krishna. In the famous Govardhan episode, Krishna lifts a mountain and holds it like an umbrella over the common people to protect them from the storm, embodiment of Indra's wrath. This spurs on the further decline of the Vedic gods and their replacement with the now-familiar Hindu pantheon. By the time Hindus start building temples in the last centuries BCE, Indra is no longer worshipped.

However, the Buddha arrived just in time for Indra to play a role in his career. It was Indra himself who persuaded the freshly awakened Shakyamuni to start preaching his new-found path. Buddhist monks then spread the cult of Indra to foreign lands as far as Japan. Indra's weapon, the lightning or vajra, became the emblem of instant Enlightenment. The sought-after 'self-nature' (Chinese *zixing*) is present all the time, deep in all of us; but when we embark on the path of meditation and finally awaken to it, it strikes like lightning.

DÎNPANAH AND THE RELIGION

When the Muslim conquerors incorporated the area into their capital and built the Old Fort there, it was apparently not a case of 'a Hindu sacred site destroyed to make way for a showpiece of Muslim power'. Indraprastha had largely fallen into disuse centuries before the conquests, leaving pride of place to other parts of Delhi. Still, the conquerors were aware of the site's past as Indraprastha, for in his *Ain-i-Akbari*, Moghul chronicler Abu'l Fazl writes that it had been built on the site of 'Indrapat'. There was probably no explicitly communal angle to it when the Muslim rulers chose the Indraprastha site.

That changed when the second Moghul emperor, Humayun, decided to reorganize the area as his own glimpse of paradise, calling it Dînpanah, 'refuge of Islam'. *Dîn* is the general Semitic word for 'justice, righteousness', even 'religion' (roughly, dharma). It was in this sense that the syncretistic emperor Akbar was to use it when he founded the Dîn-i-Ilâhî, the 'divine religion'. This new religion was meant as a confluence between Hinduism and Islam, symbolized by Akbar's newly founded city of Ilâh-âbâd ('divine city', wrongly transcribed by the British as Allahabad) on the Ganga-Yamuna confluence. But this religion did not exist yet in Humayun's time.

Akbar's usage of *Dîn* accorded with its original Semitic meaning once used by the Arab pagans. But it deviated from the meaning that Mohammed had conferred on the term during his rulership in Arabia: specifically the religion of Islam. It is in this more limited sense that the word came to be used in names like Saifu'd-dîn, 'the sword of Islam', and likewise in Humayun's Dînpanah, 'refuge of Islam'. Humayun's rulership of Delhi was short-lived, and when he finally recovered it, he found his Dînpanah in disarray. He did not get a chance to rebuild it, for he died soon after. So, it only had a very fleeting existence and made no mark at all in Delhi's long history. By contrast, the earlier town of Indraprastha had existed for many centuries.

Recently, some well-meaning but illiterate bureaucrat came up with the idea that Lutyens' Delhi should be renamed Dînpanah. However, naming a central neighbourhood of Delhi after a particular religion might not go down well with the preponderantly secular-minded population. Probably the bureaucrats who considered naming the area's development project Dînpanah had not considered this, because they had not realized the meaning of *Dîn*. At any rate, the plan was shelved when they learnt of the far better credentials of Indraprastha.

THE GOD

Now, some usual suspects will object upon hearing anything with the Vedic god Indra in it: 'Communal!' They are mistaken. There is nothing communal about the holographic paradigm. There is nothing communal about sudden Awakening. He is the same storm god we find the world over: Zeus among the Greeks, Jupiter among the Romans, Thor among the Vikings (whence 'Thursday'), Marduk in Babylon and Ba'al in the Levant. Note how Indra is likened to a bull, how Zeus seduced princess Europa in the shape of a bull, and how Ba'al was famously worshipped as a bull in the biblical episode of the golden calf.

In fact, in the golden-calf events, two faces of the storm god were in confrontation: Not just Ba'al but even Moses' god Yahweh are evolutes of essentially the same god. A lesser-known face of the storm god was indeed Yahweh among the Midianite Beduins in northwestern Arabia. Among them, then led by chieftain Jethro, the fugitive Egyptian prince Moses found asylum. That is when he acquired both a wife and a new religion. Yes, Yahweh was originally an Arab storm god, whose name was misinterpreted by the *Bible* authors as 'He who is'. His name, as shown by Julius Wellhausen, stems from a verbal root 'h-w-h', also attested in the *Quran*, and meaning 'to move in the sky'. This is both in the sense of the storm wind's blowing (an image of the palpable though subtle power of heaven) and of an eagle swooping in to catch its prey (an image of the sudden whims of destiny).

This Yahweh, this choleric storm god, was then taken to Egypt, apparently in the age when some of Pharaoh Akhnaton's monotheistic reform was in the air. Next, he led Moses and the Israelites in the legendary Exodus through the desert. He remained powerful, sovereign and choleric, but was theologically transformed into the biblical 'jealous god', who tolerates no second god beside him. This Yahweh, the sender of prophets, was later to be embraced by Mohammed under the name Allah, from *al-Ilâh*, 'the god'.

LONG LIVE INDRAPRASTHA!

So, everybody can feel happy with the name Indraprastha. No Muslim invader ever destroyed a temple to Indra, for he had been worshipped before the Hindus even used idols housed in temples. Indra throwing the lightning (elsewhere 'Thor's hammer') is an apt image of heavenly intervention in earthly affairs. Everybody naturally considers thunder and lightning to be the prime symbol of heaven's unchained might over us. Thus, there is nothing communal about this name—on the contrary. Indra's thunderstorms are a pan-religious symbol, an embodiment of the basic unity underlying the plurality of religions.

Indraprastha was founded as the capital of the Pandavas' small-time kingdom but the area was destined by fate to become the capital of the Delhi Sultanate, partly the Moghul Empire, Samrat Hemachandra's short-lived empire, the later British Indian Empire spanning the whole subcontinent, and now the Indian republic. It is a source of pride, and worth celebrating, that here, the 'righteous ruler' once chose to highlight the great universal ideas personified in Indra. Therefore, the open-minded Delhiites all agree: *Indraprastha amar rahe!*

A Diversity of 'White Saviours'*

Mythologist Devdutt Pattanaik wonders: 'Why do many Indians need white saviours?'** The article is a bit chaotic and overstresses the element of 'mythology', but that may be an occupational hazard with a writer on the *Mahabharata* and *Purana* stories. At any rate, it seems to have been written without malice, and it deserves an answer. I will give some observations on the stance of 'whites' in general and then explain my own position.

ENGLISH MEDIUM

The first white person to figure in his list of 'saviours' is Thomas Babington Macaulay. In the 1830s, he pioneered English education in India, at least for the elites, whom he then expected to translate the modern values for the common people. In keeping with the spirit of the times, his reform was explicitly elitist. But with that limitation, it was nonetheless not malicious, contrary to the enemy-image he has acquired. He actually perceived anglicization as a necessary phase of modernization, in preparation of India's independence. Nearly a century before the British loyalist Mahatma Gandhi converted to the 'total independence' ideal, Macaulay already thought in terms of Indians being independent equals with Britons.

Nonetheless, his policies would lead to the biggest hurdle

---

*Published on Pragyata.com, 16 February 2017

**Pattanaik, Devdutt, 'From Macaulay to Frawley, from Doniger to Elst: Why do many Indians need White saviours?', Scroll.in, 24 December 2016, accessed 31 January 2019, https://scroll.in/article/824732/from-macaulay-to-frawley-from-doniger-to-elst-why-do-many-indians-need-white-saviours for India's decolonization. The maintenance and expansion of his English education (and administration) by Jawaharlal Nehru is ultimately responsible for the major colonial remnant in contemporary India: the dominant position of English. Whatever Macaulay's good intentions, which counted for the colonial period, they have had a deeply antidemocratic effect on the Indian republic. As Madhu Kishwar has written: The major determinant of your career chances in India is not your caste or religion, but whether you are fluent in English.

However, only by way of historical reference can this situation be called 'colonial'. According to the Constitution, English should have been phased out by 1965; no outside power was involved when the Indian elite (using the Dravidianist misgivings as pretext) sabotaged this switch. The elite profited too much from the disenfranchisement of the Indian commoners by the dominance of English. Without saying it out loud, they thanked Macaulay for their linguistic privileges. (Ambedkarites in the Christian sphere of influence also laud Macaulay for bringing, through English, Western humanitarian and egalitarian values into India.) 'Decolonization' implies the belated phasing out of English, but this will involve the defeat not of some foreign colonizer but of the indigenous elite.

Something analogous applies to the entire cultural sphere. Certain colonial injections have been embraced by the indigenous elite, which then imposes them on a war footing on the general population. Case in point is 'secularism', originally a phase of late-Christian society, internalized though heavily distorted by India's elite, and then imposed on the entire Indian polity. Another example is the teaching of Western thought models in each of the Humanities, to the detriment of indigenous models. This counts in particular for Pattanaik's own field of mythography, where the ancient indigenous tradition is being subjected to deconstruction by recent Western models.

DECOLONIZATION

In some respects, talk of 'the colonial' and of 'decolonization' is embarrassingly obsolete, because the battle lines have fundamentally changed since 1947. Thus, some Hindu nationalists fulminate against 'white' interference and accuse 'sepoys' (Indians collaborating with the colonizers) of 'kissing the white a**', as if there were some 'white' conspiracy against today's India. When 'whites' (to borrow Pattanaik's racial terminology) care about the rest of the world, it is mostly about the Islamic world as a source of trouble, and about China as a rival. About India, I can testify that very few outsiders care one way or the other. Indians only flatter themselves by imagining India to be the target of a hostile conspiracy. And they are badly living in the past if they imagine that some Westerners are saying to each other: 'For whiteness' sake, we have to thwart those damn Indians.'

To the extent that race has any importance at all, the world has really changed, and 'anti-racism' has now effectively become the state religion of most Western countries. People of other races take the same positions vis-à-vis India as whites used to do, for these turn out to follow from certain geopolitical constraints, not racial concerns. In fact, both under a black secretary of state (Condoleezza Rice) and a black president (Barack Obama), America's South Asia policy has been as tilted towards Pakistan and against India as under, say, Richard Nixon. But admittedly, things become easy when you can divide mankind simply by skin colour, so this racial approach is attractive to lazy minds.

The situation that Pattanaik puts up for discussion has little to do with race. That Indian polemicists nonetheless like to speak in terms of race, as if it were 1940, is not so much morally reprehensible for being 'racist'. Rest assured, for 'whites', being considered the culprit of every wrong in the world only evokes a yawn, we've heard it so many times. The problem with it is that it shows mental laziness among Indians, both in the form of anachronism, as if on a battlefield you can afford the luxury of anything less than cool realism, and of vicarious self-flattery, as if you are carrying the mantle of genuine fighters against racial discrimination like Martin Luther King or Nelson Mandela.

Apparently, it feels great to re-enact the moral equation of colonial times, with the colonizer rightly in the dock and you on the moral high ground. It also sounds safely secular, which is why you can always get the whole audience to applaud when you claim aloud that 'the British imposed the Partition on India'. This is a blatant lie, but one promoted by the secularist establishment, because it exculpates the Muslim League and its accomplices Mahatma Gandhi and Jawaharlal Nehru. The British firmly opposed the Partition plan, until in March 1947, the newly appointed last viceroy, Louis Mountbatten, gave in to the increasingly violent pressure from the Muslim League natives.

That is why I don't like the use of the term 'decolonization' (as opposed to the act of decolonization, wherever needed), even though I myself have prominently used it in the past. It is a term of adolescent rebellion against the colonizer as a father figure, who, in reality, has long left the scene. In the land of proud civilization-builders, not just philosophers like Kapila or Yajñavalkya but also scientists like Lagadha and Panini and resourceful strategists like Chanakya and Bajirao, this adolescent behaviour is unbecoming. It is high time for Indians to shed their acquired inferiority complex as colonial underlings and reconnect with their glorious, or, at any rate, independent, past.

'Decolonization' is also a term of cowardice, because it misdirects your combative energies towards a long-dead enemy, thus hiding your fearful appeasement of more immediate enemies. Whoever speaks of 'decolonization' thereby shows his own use of colonial categories, with your own destiny still having to be wrested from some foreign authority. In reality, your destiny is yours, and foreign powers only have as much power in India as the Indian authorities themselves give them. Indians are responsible, not colonizers or other foreigners.

DO-GOODERS

Nonetheless, it does almost look like the situation of a colonized nation when you consider the enormous cultural power wielded in India by Western, now mostly American-based, NGOs, think tanks and institutions of higher learning. They have rarely been set up to serve some imperial goal, yet they still embody a very colonial psychology. They still think that India has to be lifted out of its own barbarism. They give themselves a civilizing mission, constantly nurtured with atrocity literature to justify the treatment of Indians as backward, in need of tutelage. But today, this 'native barbarism' has been redefined in terms of human rights. American India-watchers and India-meddlers analyse Hinduism as a litany of human rights violations, and present themselves as the saviours whom India's many oppressed categories have been waiting for.

Pattanaik makes a good observation when he writes that high-profile India-watching academics 'need to indulge America's saviour complex if they need a share of the shrinking funding. The objective of the research needs to alleviate the misery of some victim and challenge a villain. And so, (Wendy) Doniger will provide evidence of how Puranic tales reinforce Brahmin hegemony, while (Sheldon) Pollock will begin his essays on *Ramayana* with reference to the Babri Masjid demolition, reminding readers that his paper has a political, not merely a theoretical, purpose.' Exactly.

He also is on to something when he guesses that 'European and American academicians have been on the defensive to ensure they do not "other" the East. So now, there is a need to universalize the "othering" process—and show that it happens even in the East, and is not just a Western disease. And so their writings are at pains to constantly point how privileged Hindus have been "othering" the Dalits, Muslims and women, using Sanskrit, *Ramayana*, Mimamsa, Dharmashastras and *Manusmriti*.'

That doesn't explain everything, but it must be welcomed as a true observation on the 'social justice warrior' nature of current orientalist scholarship. It is scholarly in the sense of coming with lots of footnotes, but not in the sense of being impartisan and objective. Here you should realize its continuity with the colonialist endeavour at its starkest. When Hernán Cortéz conquered Mexico, he used social and ethnic grievances to mobilize the local 'lower castes' as cat's paw against the ruling Aztecs. In both cases, the goal is to dispossess the dominant group among the 'savages' and thus bludgeon it into opening up to 'civilizing' influences, and the means to achieve this is often an alliance with the groups with grievances against it.

This is where Doniger and Pollock come into the picture. They are representative of the enormous ideological clout Westerners still wield in India. The colonial-age orientalists only conditioned the minds of a small intellectual upper class; today, the Western view of India and Hinduism, through mass education and the media, influences everyone and co-determines policymaking. Because Indians have invited the Donigers and Pollocks in.

From her writings, it appears that Doniger does not consciously position herself as anti-Hindu. To be sure, she is partisan—for example, Pattanaik notices that in the dedication to her 'banned' book, 'Doniger refers to a "good fight" against Hindutva'. But she thinks those who have been identified with the struggle for the Hindu cause have misunderstood their own religion, while she is, in fact, restoring the 'real' Hinduism. She genuinely believes that her Freudian interpretative model of Indian mythology somehow reveals true underlying meanings, the hidden logic of Hinduism.

In fact, it is to a large extent the same approach that Pattanaik has also used to build a career of explaining Hindu stories in a manner acceptable to secularists and poorly rooted anglicized Hindus. In that sense, it is to be welcomed that he is now shifting towards a stance critical of Doniger, apparently under the influence of Rajiv Malhotra's criticism of his own Donigeresque approach to Indian stories.

Doniger's conception of Hinduism deserves a more thorough treatment, much of which has already been pioneered by Malhotra. But one general observation, which counts for the whole current of psychoanalytical 'deconstruction' of Hinduism, is that the clumsy Freudian concepts she uses are simply not sufficient to understand Hindu explorations of consciousness and human nature. I once heard an Indian psychologist who had guzzled down big doses of this psychoanalytical framework pontificate that a guru is followed because he is a 'father figure'. You could see him savour this expression, as if he considered what he had said very profound. Well, there are many types of father figure, but only few have the specific qualities needed to be a guru; and psychoanalysis has never been able to turn anyone into a guru in the Hindu sense. The smaller cannot contain the greater.

There is something comical about the psychologist's attempt to fit the hoary Hindu ideas about the psyche into the modern attempts by his own newfangled discipline, still groping in the dark. But because Doniger's flippant approach serves the purpose of belittling and ridiculing Hinduism well, it is welcomed and highlighted by the Indian elite with its many-pronged attack on Hinduism. And she is not even a psychologist: Elsewhere, her 'alternative' (actually quite conformist, only a bit more titillating) deconstruction of a religion would have been criticized as not based on any competence.

POLITICIZED PHILOLOGY

Pollock, a very good Sanskritist, at least in a purely linguistic sense, is more explicitly involved with the anti-Hindu discourse promoted in India by the missionaries and the Ambedkarites, and their first line of attack, the 'secularists'. He has pioneered some valid insights into the Sanskrit 'cosmopolis', which did not oppress vernacular languages from Gandhari to Javanese but fruitfully coexisted with them to their mutual benefit. But at the same time, he has helped greatly in belittling and politicizing the *Ramayana* and in promoting the 'Hinduism bad, Buddhism good' thesis.

This is not very original—in fact, it is only a sophisticated formulation of widely held views. Thus, Pattanaik attributes the same viewpoint to another big name we just met: 'Doniger's essays on the *Puranas* make you see Hinduism as a violent authoritarian force challenged by non-violent egalitarian Buddhism.' But in this discourse of hate, which instrumentalizes Buddhism as a bludgeon to beat Hinduism with, Pollock has gone farther than all others. In 1993, he published a paper, 'Deep Orientalism?', arguing that Hinduism (particularly the Mimansa school, Brahmanical par excellence) sits at the centre of the Nazi doctrine. Yes, it is long ago, and partly explainable from the war psychology emanating from the Ayodhya controversy, in which he explicitly sided with the negationist school denying Islam's well-documented destructive role in Hindu history, but he has never retracted this position.

In this case, as in some other matters (such as the exact place of Christianity in European civilization, often exaggerated in India—for example, Doniger and Pollock are *not* motivated by Christian concerns, a secularist position which Pattanaik here acknowledges to be 'the hallmark of objectivity in educational circles'), my own role has been to help Indians better understand European history wherever it is relevant to Indian debates. The case Pollock has built is untenable for anyone familiar with the concerned part of European history. What few Indomanic racists have existed in Germany during the century before 1945, were not exactly poles apart from Pollock and the secularists: On the contrary, they shared the latter's own anti-Brahmanism and pro-Buddhism. They considered Brahmins agents of the 'dark indigenous' people mired in superstition and puerile ritualism, who contaminated the pure 'Aryan invader' culture, while they held the Buddha to have been a real Aryan trying to restore the genuine and superior Aryan traditions. Hitler was not only an anti-Semite but in passing also a votary of India's equivalent, anti-Brahminism. That is why Pollock fails to quote from the 'National-Socialist Indologists' a single line in praise of Jaimini or Kumarila Bhatta or any other Mimansaka, but has to quote the Buddha's name several times.

This little excursus into the nadir of Pollock's scholarship should, however, not obscure the fact that with his erroneous anti-Brahmin spin on the history of German Indology, he is serving an Indian rather than a Western cause. Today, anti-Brahminism comes in as a helpful tool for US-based missionaries to pit Hindus against one another along lines of caste and ethnicity ('Dravidians' and 'Adivasis' against 'Aryan invaders'), and in the nineteenth century, it has indeed been launched by missionaries; but it has now mainly become an Indian ideology animating much of Indian culture (Bollywood) and politics. More than some CIA conspiracy, it is this Indian current that Western scholars seek to align with.

SKIN COLOUR

'But who does Hindutva turn to for establishing the greatness of Hinduism, and Sanskrit, and the *Vedas*? A European, Koenraad Elst. And an American, David Frawley. So much for "decolonizing" the Hindu/Indian mind. So much for Swadeshi. Does this reveal our deference to white scholarship? Does this reveal Indians are beyond racism? One wonders if African-American Indologists or Chinese American Indologists would ever evoke similar passions.'

The colour obsession, while not entirely absent among the Indian public, does not go very far in explaining our role in Indian politico-cultural discourse. It so happens that 'Oriental Philology and History' (one of my diplomas), the proper name of 'orientalism', was developed in Europe, and some of those roots are still in force, all while it now largely conditions the dominant Indian discourse on India itself. The 'white' presence in this line of scholarship was almost a 100 per cent till recently, as the upcoming non-white presence in Western universities (as Indians know all too well) was mostly in Engineering and Medicine, shortcuts to status and wealth, not in the Humanities and certainly not in its more esoteric departments. It is only recently that the children of Asian immigrants have started entering the 'orientalist' sections. But I am sure that the day a Chinese-American, not to mention an Indian-American, starts putting out theses as provocative as Doniger's or Pollock's, and from equally prestigious positions, he will evoke similar passions among the affected Hindu public.

The use of Westerners, the reason they can serve as argument of authority in India, is firstly that in controversies, they count as outsiders, hence more objective; and secondly, that modern culture does indeed count as intrinsically more scientific. The first argument is very weak: Those who get close enough to Indian culture to have anything to say about it have usually befriended one of the warring camps inside India, and hence have become just as partisan as their Indian sources. Thus, practically, all the Western press correspondents in Delhi are safely in the pocket of the secularists and cherish a vicarious hatred of assertive Hinduism. This yields what I have called the 'circular argument of authority': Indian secularists feed their Western contacts their own view of the Indian religio-political landscape, and when their Western dupes then go public with these same views, the secularists hold them up as independent confirmation of their views by the scientific West.

STRATEGY

Pattanaik is oh so even-handed: 'If we attribute strategy to the works of Doniger and Pollock, the same needs to be done to the works of Elst and Frawley.' I don't know about David's, but in the case of my own work, I am surprised to learn of its 'strategic' dimension. I don't know of any policy that was inspired by my work.

It seems that we 'are catering to a vast latent need of privileged Hindus to feel good about themselves'. I leave it to David to explain his motive (which I think is simply a love of Hindu dharma, but I admit Pattanaik may consider this naïve), but mine is as follows.

Part of it is again given by Pattanaik himself: 'After having been at the receiving end of orientalist and Marxist criticism since the nineteenth century, privileged Hindus have not developed requisite skills in the field of Humanities to launch a worthwhile defence.'

That much is certainly true: Both in India and in the diaspora, talented Indian youngsters have rushed to the Medical and Engineering departments, leaving the Humanities for their not-so-bright brothers and sisters. Hindu activist organizations have never invested in scholarship, and their very few recent attempts to gain a toehold in this little-understood world have been clumsy and unsuccessful. Add to this that in these departments, the Left has built a power position and enforces its vetoes against anyone showing any sign of loyalty to the Hindu cause. So, to say that 'Hindus have not developed requisite skills in the field of Humanities' is not far off the mark. With my limited means, I used to assume I had something to contribute there, viz. a more accurate picture of Indian history compared to the facile or plainly mischievous assumptions that the Left has tried to instil in the next generations.

Then there is the reason Sir Edmund Hillary gave for climbing the Everest: 'Because it was there.' When I noticed the big power-wielders in the Indian landscape with their rope tricks fooling people on the Ayodhya temple or the Aryan debate, the adventurous white man in me was awakened to go 'hunting tigers out in Indiah'. That is, at least, if you try to think up a subconscious personal reason. My conscious reason was that so much bluff as was spread by the Indian intellectual establishment simply had to be answered and defeated.

CONVERSION

'Outsourcing the job to white men is an easy alternative. Particularly those who manage to establish credibility. Frawley does that brilliantly by declaring himself a Hindu, with an evocative title of Pandit Vamadeva Shastri, which makes him a "Brahmin" in Hindu eyes, justified on grounds of his vast knowledge of the Vedic scriptures, and his long practice of Ayurveda and Jyotisha. His wife is Indian, and has the title of "Yogini". Elst, by contrast, insists that he is not a Hindu, for he is well aware that no one can be "converted" to Hinduism—that it is linked to birth, and that Hinduism is deeply linked to geography.'

Secularists are fond of saying (and of quoting Westerners to the effect) that 'there is no conversion to Hinduism': To them it means that Hindus are condemned to keeping mum when the missionaries convert to Christianity. By contrast, I do think conversion to Hinduism is possible. Firstly, communities as a whole have done it throughout history; it is between communities that conversion is rare. (If you are a Jat or a Rajput and you convert to Islam, you will still get identified with your caste for generations. Indian Muslims have been tutored to hide this, to uphold the anti-Hindu fiction of an 'egalitarian Islam', but Pakistanis candidly tell you: 'I am a Rajput Muslim.') Secondly, in borderline situations, such as a mixed marriage, someone can join a particular Hindu community, on condition that its legitimate members accept you as one of theirs.

And then there are the present circumstances, where Hindus are forced to compete with predators and hence modestly organize Ghar Wâpasi ('return home'), the reconversion of people once estranged from Hinduism. I fully support that policy. It mostly works among villagers, with whom bookish me has little rapport; but if my writing about Islamic scripture can help a Muslim free himself from his religious conditioning so that he wants to 'return home', I will be most happy.

In spite of all that, I myself have never converted to Hinduism, though I have received initiations from several acknowledged gurus. I do not sport a Sanskrit name. But that is not at all meant as a tacit criticism of the course David Frawley has chosen.

'Frawley overcomes this bottleneck easily by insisting Vedic civilization is universal and open to all humanity, and by defining what it means to be a true Brahmin. It is significant, however, that no white convert to Hinduism ever identifies themselves as Vaishya or Shudra. It is either Brahmin or Kshatriya— intellectual or combative—and always superior. So much for the "division of labour" thesis of varna.'

The Brahmin name 'Shastri' was given to David, it is not he who claimed Brahminhood. As for myself, by traditional definitions of varna, I would, of course, be a Shudra, and there is nothing wrong with that. A Swiss friend of mine (and of 'Vedic socialist' Swami

Agnivesh), who lived in an ashram in Rishikesh for years, calls himself Shûdrânanda: Shudra and happy to be one! Among great Hindu figures I particularly like, is Sant Ravidas, who was a cobbler on the outskirts of Varanasi. Well, the outskirts of Hinduism, that is where you might situate me.

POLEMICS

I feel flattered by Pattanaik's accurate assessment of the history debates I have participated in: 'Elst has done a lot of research on Ayodhya and endeavours to provide evidence to prove the Babri Masjid was indeed built on a site that once housed a Hindu temple. He has strongly challenged views of scholars like Richard Eaton who seek to secularize the iconoclasm of Muslim rulers. The standard trope in modern historical studies seems to be that Hindu temples were destroyed not only by Muslim rulers but also by Hindu rulers as part of establishing their authority. It disregards all Hindu memory and Islamic writing that shows motivation of Muslim rulers at its core was religious, designed to replace the Hindu faith with Islam. This is aligned with Western academic anxiety at being seen as Islamophobic—no points lost if one is Hinduphobic. Elst provides the fodder to challenge this view.'

But here I break rank with many history-rewriters: 'Both Elst and Frawley provide strong arguments to support the "Out of India" theory that seeks to establish India as the true homeland of the Aryan race or the Sanskrit language, claiming it gave civilization to the world.'

'Despite their deep knowledge of Hinduism, neither Elst nor Frawley, neither Doniger nor Pollock, believe in letting go and moving on, which is the hallmark of Hindu thought, often deemed a feminine trait. Instead, Elst and Frawley keep drawing attention to injustice done by colonizers, goading Indians to rise up and fight, a violent tendency that is the hallmark of Western thought, often deemed a masculine trait. Likewise, Doniger and Pollock keep reminding their readers that Hinduism's seductive "spirituality" must at no point distract one from its communal and casteist truths.'

Wow, psychoanalysing people from a distance—that must be tough. Look, I don't understand all this jargon dividing civilizations into 'feminine' and stuff. I merely see a debate (about the invasion theory) that has not been satisfactorily concluded yet, so I keep working. That is not an idiosyncratic refusal to let go. After the pre-existence of a temple at the site of the Babri Masjid has been largely accepted, I have left that debate behind. I let go of it.

By contrast, the injustice done by the Muslim colonizers remains a fact with consequences in the present day, and continuous with some presently existing injustices (violent oppression of Hindus in Muslim-majority states, anti-Hindu discriminations in the Constitution). Letting go of those concerns would be too early. That is just a matter-of-fact view. Myth cannot really throw new light upon it.

Likewise, I assume that Doniger and Pollock take the causes they fight for seriously. In that case, they must realize that those causes are large and not exactly ephemeral: They will still be with us on our dying day. So, people are free to change course in life, but abandoning a project you have worked for before seeing it through is not particularly virtuous. I don't think sons of the Indian soil, like B.R. Ambedkar and S.R. Goel, abandoned the causes they worked for halfway. It is not always time to 'let go'.

PARTING SHOTS

So far so good. But *in cauda venenum*, the venom is in the tail. I strongly object to Pattanaik's parting shots: 'So both parties keep the Hindu wound festering. Both also offer the balm of "justice", a Western approach that is politically volatile for India, and commercially lucrative for them.'

The people who created doubts about the temple in Ayodhya and inflicted the whole controversy on India (and on Hindu communities in Bangladesh and the UK) did unnecessarily revive an old wound and then kept it festering. Those who sought the exact historical scenario and its doctrinal background did just the opposite. And as for the bystanders who ignore the factual results that the latter have achieved, they, too, seem to want the controversy to 'fester'.

As for 'lucrative', for those familiar with the vetoes and exclusions inflicted on dissenters by the Humanities establishment in the West and the secularist establishment in India, such a thought is beneath contempt. If 'lucre' had been my motive, I would, of course, have joined the opposite camp.

And here he is really mistaken: 'Neither privileges the Indian idea of diversity, that rejects homogeneity and allows for multiple paradoxical, even hierarchical, structures to coexist.' At least when speaking for myself, I can confidently state that on the contrary, my criticism has always been directed precisely at the religions and ideologies that are out to suppress diversity.

The mythographer speaks: 'Doniger and Pollock follow the Greek mythic pattern that establishes them as heroes who are in the "good fight" against "fascist" monsters. Elst and Frawley follow the Abrahamic mythic pattern that establishes them as "prophets" leading the enslaved—colonized—Indians back to the "Vedic Promised Land".'

I don't know how Greek a 'good fight' is, but that is indeed how they see their work—and so do we. As for prophets, I don't really believe in divine spokesmen, so let that sobriquet pass. Perhaps David, who is more of a visionary, could be described in those terms, though he himself, as far as I know, never did. Me, I only see specific errors being made, and I am simply the much-needed schoolteacher wielding his red pencil. If that can lead anyone to his Promised Land, fine, but I don't even look that far, I just want those errors out of the way. Perhaps Bhangi (sweeper) would be a good caste for me.

But then: 'Being placed on a high pedestal is central to both strategies. Criticism also evokes a similar reaction on both sides—they quickly declare themselves misunderstood heroes and martyrs, and stir up their legion of followers. Doniger and Pollock have inspired an army of activist-academicians who sign petitions to keep "dangerous" Indian leaders and intellectuals out of American universities and even American soil': Subramanian Swamy, Narendra Modi, and in similar controversies, Rajiv Malhotra, the Dharma Civilization Foundation and others. Indeed, the Indological community's touching (occasional) concern for freedom of speech is not erga omnes. And at that point, any similarity with Frawley ends.

'No dissent is tolerated. If you agree with either side, you become rational scientists for them. If you disagree with them, you become fascists—or racists.' Both Frawley and I have written thousands of pages. I offer one symbolic rupee for whoever can find any statement to that brandishing effect. On the other hand, I can point to a number of pages in my own work where I go out of my way to defend the freedom of speech of those conspicuously not in agreement with me, especially Doniger. No special merit, for if you yourself have been the target of enough exclusions, it comes easily.

It seems we are dealing with an attitude that seeks to come out on top during an argument by picking up the quarrel in the middle and pretending that both sides are equal. A very profitable posture, for it also allows for laziness, since you don't even have to study the contents of what the two sides are saying or doing.

Now that our mythographer has gone off track, he extemporizes all at once about 'white knights' with a 'Hindutva obsession', opposing 'multiple truths' and waging a 'crusade against Muslims', out to 'dehumanize' the opposition. Here I confess I simply can't keep up with his cannonade. I think he is referring to himself when he speaks of 'rejecting the model of conversation'.

WRONG!

Yet, I have hardly any quarrel with Pattanaik's conclusion: 'If we have to truly be decolonized, and truly Swadeshi, be it the M.K. Gandhi or the RSS variety, we have to overcome our inferiority complexes, and without succumbing to chauvinism, realize that we Indians, with all our shortcomings, do not really need Europeans and Americans to tell us what Hinduism, Sanskrit or the *Vedas* were, are or should be.'

Well, if you put the issue in those terms, I am all for overcoming inferiority feelings and dependence on others. That is why Indians don't need Doniger's eroticized or Pollock's politicized reading of the *Ramayana*, and why the interiorization of their approach in the late A.K. Ramanujan's or in Pattanaik's own work was a bad idea. Only, I don't think that that is because these august scholars are 'white' or 'Western', or even 'Indologists', but merely because they are wrong.

It is no big deal to be wrong once in a while. Fortunately there are others, conversation partners with a verbal red pencil, who are kind enough to correct you. Vishal Agarwal has published a whole book of corrections to the many errors in Doniger's not-so-banned 'banned book' on Hindu history. I have participated in a whole conference to set Pollock's loaded views of Sanskrit straight. It will not save the world, or even that small part of it that is India, nor that small minority that is still Hindu. But still, it is a good, clean feeling not to have to live amid untruths, whether lies (oh, how I loathe that term) or, more often, mistakes. Myths are another matter.

Symbolism of India's Anthem*

NATIONAL SYMBOLS

When the freedom movement started thinking in terms of a future independent state, then conceived according to the prevailing model of the nation-state, it became aware of the need for national symbols.

For the flag, quite sensibly, it toyed with the idea of reusing Shivaji's saffron flag, as uniformly orange as Moammar al-Qadhafi's Libyan flag was uniformly green. But a movement courting Muslims for support preferred to keep this crystal-clear symbol at a distance. At a 1907 socialist conference in Stuttgart, Mrs Bhikaji Cama introduced a new design featuring the sun and the moon.

But the Congress chose the tricolour, a communal flag of a composite culture with orange on top standing for Hinduism and green at the bottom for Islam, an embodiment of Swami Vivekananda's success formula: 'Vedantic brain and Islamic body.' Like with the green colour in more recent political flags, Hindus need not stick to the communal interpretation of the Muslims and Nehruvians: Long before Islam existed, green was already around and had a natural meaning: opulence, prosperity, as well as nature. Likewise, orange forever remains the colour of fire, of tapas ('heat', asceticism), of spirituality.

The middle strip is white, a colour that plays a role in both (actually, in all) religions and suggests purity. Mahatma Gandhi

---

*This piece has been adapted from the article published on Voice of India, 7 April 2017

tried to adorn it with his pet spinning wheel, but the Nehruvian alternative won through: 'Ashoka's wheel', in blue. Jawaharlal Nehru, 'India's last viceroy', was a champion of both the Moghul and the British colonial cultures and quite ignorant of the native culture, so he did not know that the twenty-four-spoked wheel long predated Ashoka. It was the symbol of the Chakravarti, or the 'wheel turner', the axis in the wheel of the samrajya, 'unified rule', 'empire', a principle already sung in the epics.

Making India into a Chakravarti-kshetra was an old ideal, and Ashoka admittedly came close to realizing it: He was almost a 'pan-Indian' ruler. However, he did not originate this notion. The spoked wheel embodies the relation between a single centre and numerous ('twenty-four') secondary centres on the periphery, i.e., the central authority spreading its umbrella over the several states with their swadharma (ca. 'own mores') and swatantra ('autonomy'). As such, it is a fine symbol of India's federalism, for 'unity in diversity'.

But then, if the belief in Ashoka's identification with this wheel creates enthusiasm among Buddhists worldwide for the Indian republic, so much the better. And on the currency notes, it is really Ashoka's own contribution that we find (together with the face of the poverty-preaching M.K. Gandhi): the lion capital, a shape dug up in Sarnath in 1905.

India's anthem is a song written by Rabindranath Tagore in 1911, *Jana Gana Mana*. It opens by addressing the *Jana Gana Mana Adhinayak* or 'the commander of the people's minds', the *Bharata Bhagya Vidhata* or 'the dispenser of India's destiny'. Who is this?

GOD SAVE THE QUEEN

Before focusing on the Indian anthem and wondering to whom it is directed, we want to remind our readers of some fairly well-known facts concerning the slightly older anthems of a few other countries that acted as role models for the 'anthem' genre. Especially, we will highlight those points that will turn out to provide contrasts, similarities or overlaps. They lay out a framework within which we can evaluate India's anthem.

Britain's anthem is the oldest in the world. The writer is unknown, but the attribution to John Bull ca. 1618 is common. It is addressed to God, but otherwise, it is all about the monarch:

God save our gracious Queen (or King), God save our noble Queen, God save the Queen. Lead her victorious, happy and glorious, ever to reign over us, God save the Queen.

As you will notice, the focus is not at all on the people but entirely upon the monarch, in whom the ideals of victory, prosperity and good governance are embodied. This is the traditional monarchical scheme: the ruler as the embodiment of the nation, with his paramountcy legitimized by religion.

The same tune once provided the anthem to several countries, including even imperial Russia (1816–1833). When devising national symbols, new nation-states just assumed that the tune of the venerable British Empire's anthem naturally and intrinsically was the melody of a national song. Prussia adopted it in 1795, and after its chancellor, Otto von Bismarck, unified the German states (minus Austria and Switzerland) and presided over the founding of the German empire in 1871, the new state adopted as anthem the Prussian national song. Because of its British and Prussian associations, some southern German states did not accept the song.

So, this was set to the tune of *God Save the Queen*, but with the lyrics: *Heil dir im Siegerkranz, Herrscher des Vaterlands, Heil Kaiser dir*. Or 'Hail thee in victor's laurels, ruler of the fatherland, hail to thee, Emperor.' It is not about God and only tangentially about the nation, but mostly about the monarch. Patriotism is lauded, but again only subordinate to the monarchy: *Liebe des Vaterlands, Liebe des freien Manns, gründen den Herrscherthron, wie Fels im Meer,* or 'Love of the fatherland, love by the free man, found the ruler's throne like a rock in the sea.'

In 1918, after losing the Great War, the emperor had to abdicate the throne and the anthem lapsed. As we shall see, the succeeding Weimar Republic would choose a different one, ultimately even more controversial.

'WILHELMUS'

While *God Save the Queen* played a pioneering role in spreading the notion that a state needs an anthem, it was nevertheless not the oldest song to become an anthem. That honour goes to the *Wilhelmus*, with lyrics written ca. 1572, probably by Filips van Marnix van Sint-Aldegonde, mayor of Antwerp, in honour of his friend Willem van Oranje-Nassau (William of Orange-Nassau), the founder of the Netherlands. When the song was written, there was no notion of a national anthem yet, so it was only officially adopted as such in 1932. The tune had only just been composed, in 1568, and had served to animate the Protestant defenders of Chartres in France against their Catholic besiegers. Ideally, after declaring independence from Spain, the Netherlands should have encompassed Belgium (including Antwerp), Luxemburg and a slice of present-day France, but those territories were reconquered by Spain.

William of Orange became the *stadhouder* ('city-holder'), effectively president-for-life, of the Dutch Republic. The song is nonetheless of the monarchical type, viz. about the person of William of Orange. In particular, it describes his profound dilemma between his loyalty to his suzerain, the king of Spain, and his God-given duty to his people. Independence is not always a no-brainer, and this is not mindless patriotism but remains aware of larger issues of conscience. It goes, in translation, like this: 'Wilhelmus of Nassau, am I of German blood. True to the fatherland I remain until death. A prince of Orange I remain, free and fearless. The king of Spain I have always honoured.'

(As for 'German', he came from a town now in Germany, but that is not the reason for this choice of words. At that time, the areas speaking German and Dutch were then one dialect continuum, called Duytsch or Dietsch, literally 'folkish, popular', as opposed to aristocratic French and priestly Latin. To the extent that Dutch/Dietsch already counted as a separate language, it was called Nederduytsch, 'Low German'.)

The central part of the very long song, the rarely performed eighth stanza, likens him to the biblical king David, showing the Bible-solid Calvinist inspiration of its author. The better-known sixth stanza clearly subordinates him to God: 'My shield and trust art Thou, oh God my Lord. On Thee I want to build, don't ever leave me. May I remain pious, Thy servant at all times, and drive away the tyranny that wounds my heart.' It illustrates how Christianity shaded over into nationalism, by likening the worship of 'false gods' to the submission to foreign rulers.

Its tune has also been adopted to turn a different poem into a German national song. In 1814, at the fag end of the Napoleonic occupation, Max von Schenckendorf wrote a poem expressing German patriotism: *Wenn alle untreu werden, so bleiben wir doch treu,* or 'When all become disloyal, even then we remain loyal.' It ends in a pledge to the German Reich, which had long led a ghost existence until it was abolished by Napoleon in 1806 and was only surviving as an ideal.

The poem was soon put to music using the *Wilhelmus* tune and became known as the *Treuelied,* or 'the loyalty song'. More than a century later, it was adopted by the Nazi elite corps SS. In many contemporary sources, you will find it wrongly mentioned as *SS-Treuelied.* In reality, it owed nothing at all to National Socialism, any more than other much older symbols such as the swastika. In Europe, it will nevertheless still take some time before these symbols, tainted by association, can be completely healed and used again without complications. The *Wilhelmus,* though, was never seriously affected. The Dutch have never considered disowning their anthem because of the late and temporary association with the SS. (As we shall see, the topic of possible Nazi associations also pops up around India's anthem.) By contrast, another innocent song, or at least part of its lyrics, was demonized.

'KAISERHYMNE'/'DEUTSCHLANDLIED'

For his birthday in 1797, the Austrian emperor Franz was treated to a new song, with lyrics by leading poet Lorenz Leopold Haschka and music by the famous composer Joseph Haydn. When visiting England, Haydn had been enthused by the ready presence of a good song that everybody knew and that expressed their national togetherness. Though he was composer enough to compose his own tune, he, too, had been inspired by *God Save the Queen* as the model of an anthem. The lyrics, too, were modelled on the British text: *Gott erhalte Franz den Kaiser, unsern guten Kaiser Franz*, or 'God save Emperor Francis, our good Emperor Francis.' And it goes on about: 'Long live Francis the Emperor in the brightest splendour of bliss! May laurel branches bloom for him, wherever he goes, as a wreath of honour', etc. In this *Kaiserhymne* (Emperor's Hymn), it is his well-being that counts, not the nation, though he is posited modestly below God.

Here, too, the defeat of 1918 rendered the song without object, so the lyrics were replaced, but the tune, after a decade of disuse, was revived in 1929. The lyrics had now become thoroughly republican, focused on the nation instead of the head of state, but with God still lurking in the background: *Sei gesegnet ohne Ende*, or 'be blessed without end'. It lapsed in 1938, when Austria was annexed by Germany.

At the end of 1918, Germany became a republic. A new anthem did not have to be devised. The lyrics had been available in a nationalist poem from 1841 by August Heinrich Hoffmann von Fallersleben, since then sung to the tune of the well-known Austrian *Emperor's Hymn*. It was the time of German unification, and the song called on all Germans to put their loyalties to their own local states between brackets and focus on the then-fragmented Germany as a whole. Hence the song's title: *Das Lied der Deutschen*, 'The Song of the Germans', or *Deutschlandlied*, 'Germany's Song'. Foreigners usually know it through its opening line, *Deutschland über Alles*, 'Germany above all'. This sentence had nothing to do with condescension towards non-Germans, only with a hierarchy between Germany as a whole and its parts: Germany above Bavaria, Germany above the Rhineland, etc.

It did not address a monarch, but the German nation. The

liberal nationalists then at the forefront contrasted their own modern liberal and predominantly secular nationalism with loyalty to the erstwhile Holy Roman Emperor and the contemporaneous Austrian emperor. In the revolution year 1848, it represented a rebellion of the people against the transnational nobility. It is for this reason that in 1922, the new German Weimar Republic chose *Das Lied der Deutschen* as its anthem, marking a break with Imperial Germany of the preceding half-century.

Somewhat like *Jana Gana Mana*, the song situated the country geographically, not by listing its component parts ('Punjaba, Sindhu, Gujarata, Maratha...'), but by listing its borders, roughly: *'Von der Maas bis and die Memel, von der Etsch bis an den Belt.* These are the borders, flatteringly but not imperialistically defined, of the German speech area with the French/Dutch, or the Baltic, Italian and Danish speech areas during the mid-nineteenth century. Note that then a unified Germany was still an ideal and its borders were still being debated: It was deemed desirable to include Austria and hence the border would be with Italy. Around 1920 too, the Etsch border with Italy was a realistic proposition, for it was the outspoken desire of the Austrian people to be included in Germany, as is clear from the massive majority that this proposal received in a referendum. (However, France as a victor in the Great War disallowed it.)

The song remained the national anthem when the National Socialists under Adolf Hitler came to power in 1933, including when they occupied much of Europe in 1939–1945. The latter circumstance gave the song a highly negative connotation. Outsiders reinterpreted the opening line as meaning, 'Germany above every other nation in the world.' When Dutch children saw the British bombers fly over their country to drop their load over German cities, they inverted the sentence: *Alles, Alles über Deutschland,* or '(Drop) everything, everything, on Germany'.

After 1945, the same anthem continued, or at least its melody. Of the lyrics, only the third stanza has an official status. It carries the liberal bias of Hoffmann von Fallersleben's unification movement:

Einigkeit und Recht und Freiheit für das deutsche Vaterland, danach last uns Alle streben, brüderlich mit Herz und Hand, 'Unity and Justice and Freedom for the German fatherland, for that let us all strive, fraternally with heart and hand'.

The second stanza is innocent but not deemed dignified enough to serve as an anthem, and the first is frowned upon as seeking the restoration of Germany's pre-1945 borders. With the loss of East Prussia, the Memel River is now hundreds of miles from the German borders, and with the definitive independence of Austria, Germany has lost all pretence of bordering Italy. Now, the listing of these borders has acquired a decisively imperialistic connotation, which originally it did not have.

Many laymen think there is something Nazi about this song (as also about the *Treuelied*). These are not just tamasic Leftists who fill their empty minds with endless Hitler references to assure themselves of a moral high ground, but also the mass of people who are simply ignorant. However, the true story is just the reverse: It is politically liberal, pro-constitution, pro-democracy and emphasizes the non-aristocratic, people-oriented angle of nationalism. It lays no claim to non-German lands and does not contain even a germ of hatred against other nations or communities such as the Jews. When all is said and done, it is just a beautiful song.

'LA MARSEILLAISE' AND 'LA BRABANÇONNE'

After the French Revolution of 1789, the revolutionaries who came to power were first of all nationalists. Today's Leftists prefer to forget it, they advocate open borders, demonize military service and laugh at natalist propaganda, but on the said issues, they are poles apart with their French Revolutionary role models. In 1792, the revolutionary nationalists devised a song, which in 1795 they adopted as an anthem, wherein neither king nor God played a role (*Ni Dieu ni maître*, 'neither God nor master'). The focus was fully on the nation, the tone combative: *Allons enfants de la patrie, le jour de gloire est arrivé*, 'Let's go, children of the fatherland, the hour of glory has arrived'. This set the template for a number of secular anthems in new states the world over. It was rich in energy and self-righteousness, but poor in wisdom. After the temporary restoration of the monarchy and several more regime changes, it remained in force.

La (Chanson) Marseillaise, '(The Song) of Marseille', was written in Strasbourg but was named after volunteers from Marseille who had intoned it while entering Paris. It served as a model for the Belgian national anthem, *La Brabançonne*, '(The Song) of Brabant'. This is the province where Brussels is located, somewhat like 'Kashi' for 'Varanasi'. That song has no God either, but peripherally it does venerate the king, as the new country (°1830) had to make its way in a world where the post-Napoleonic Vienna Conference of 1914–15 had installed a system of monarchical anti-revolutionary regimes. Hence *...le roi, la loi, la liberté*, or '...king, law and liberty'.

Belgium started as an exceptionally liberal country, with freedom of the press and asylum for foreign dissenters. Therefore, its anthem contains the liberal phrase: *het woord getrouw dat g'onbevreesd moogt spreken*, 'true to the word that you are allowed to speak without fear'. But the focus is on the nation itself and its territory: *O dierbaar België, o heilig land der vaad'ren, onze ziel en ons hart zijn u gewijd*, 'Oh precious Belgium, oh holy land of the ancestors, our souls and our hearts are vowed to thee'.

'THE STAR-SPANGLED BANNER'

The anthem of the USA was written in 1814, to the tune of an existing popular song from Britain, by the lawyer Francis Scott Key. He had witnessed an event in the British-American War of 1812 from a rare vantage point: as a prisoner held on a British ship participating in a British naval siege of Baltimore. He had been impressed with the American flag on the tower of a coastal fort, and saw how, after a night of fighting, it was still there in the morning. That, then, is the focus of the song: not God, not the ruler, only tangentially the nation (though in iconic terms, in 'the land of the free and the home of the brave'), but the national flag and the bravery of the American soldiers who defended it. It served as the semi-official anthem for a century, until, in 1931, a law was enacted officially declaring it the anthem.

'JANA GANA MANA'

This survey of the trailblazing European anthems, upon which all other anthems were modelled, indicates three possible foci: God (one or many), the monarch and the nation. Traditional monarchies tend to have anthems focusing on the monarch, either putting him in the shadow of God (*God Save the Queen*, the *Wilhelmus*), or secularly presenting him as the highest authority by himself (*Heil dir im Siegerkranz*). Modern songs emanating from secular elites tend to avoid God, such as the French and German republican anthems, and they have a conspicuous absence of references to the head of state, who is simply one of us, one of the nation that is already being glorified.

In what category does *Jana Gana Mana* fall? What did it mean at the time when it was composed?

The song was written in 1911 by the Bengali poet Rabindranath Tagore in high Bengali bordering on Sanskrit. (Among his other poems, one more was destined to make it to the status of national anthem: *Amar Sonar Bangla*, 'My Golden Bengal', written in 1905. It was adopted as the anthem by Bangladesh in 1971. He also wrote the music for Sri Lanka's anthem.) In a multilingual country, it has the virtue of being understandable to every citizen with even just a smattering of education. It was first performed at a conference of the Indian National Congress, which at that time was working for the interests of the subcontinent, though not for a separate independent state yet.

The song's first performance with the status of national anthem was by Subhas Chandra Bose's troops in Germany. Before his well-known leadership of the Indian National Army under Japanese tutelage in 1943–45, he had commanded a smaller army, recruited from among the Indian soldiers in the British army units taken prisoner at Dunkirk, as part of the Nazi-German war effort in 1941–42. It was on 11 September 1942, in an imposing celebration inaugurating the *Deutsch-Indische Gesellschaft* (German-Indian Association) in Hamburg, that men for the first time stood to attention for *Jana Gana Mana* as India's anthem. That Bose had already elevated the song to anthem status would later predispose India's Constituent Assembly into confirming this status.

THE 'BHARATA BHAGYA VIDHATA' WAS NOT KING GEORGE

The song is frankly nationalist to the extent that it oversees the nation and its territory, of which it enumerates the provinces. However, it principally addresses and glorifies the *Jana Gana Mana Adhinayak,* the 'commander of the people's mind', who is at the same time the *Bharata Bhagya Vidhata,* the 'dispenser of India's destiny'. Does this refer to the country's hereditary, appointed or elected ruler?

We can imagine the vainglorious Jawaharlal Nehru, as prime minister in the 1950s, feeling flattered whenever the crowds in front of him were intoning these words. But then, he was not seriously in the picture yet in 1911. At that time, the British king George V was India's ruler. Moreover, he was about to pay a visit to India only weeks after the song was first performed—at a Congress meeting, where a proper reception for the king was central on the agenda.

By connecting these dots, the British press at the time, and many of its Indian readers, believed that Tagore had composed the song in honour of the king. The claim proved particularly tenacious and is occasionally heard even today. Among RSS activists, the rumour also served as a conspiracy underpinning the suspicion that India had never really become independent. Yet, the poet was to deny it, later in life even vehemently. But the first years, this correction did not reach the public.

The confusion in the British and British-Indian press partly came about due to the existence of another song by an Indian that did genuinely glorify the British king-emperor. This was *Bâdshâh Hamâra*, 'Our King', written in Urdu (or 'Hindustani', as Gandhians prudishly called it) by Rambhuj Chaudhary; it was sung on the same occasion but explicitly in praise of the monarch. At that time, the Congress was still committed only to dominion status within the British Empire, so with King George as its legitimate ruler.

The mistaken belief that Tagore had wanted to praise the British king and thus further legitimize his rule over India had its bright side. It crucially helped in convincing the Nobel committee to award its 1913 prize for literature for the first time to a non-Westerner. *Gitañjali*, Tagore's award-winning collection, is no doubt fine poetry, but to win the Nobel Prize, its author had better satisfy a preliminary condition. Tagore was deemed a loyalist of the colonial dispensation, and therefore a convert to civilization uplifting his own more backward countrymen. He was a link in the chain of 'civilizing the savages', as Europeans in those days conceived of it. From a distance, he counted as what the Belgians in the Congo used to call an évolué, an 'evolved' native who had made the effort to assimilate reasonably well to the level of the colonizers. Now that was the kind of merit to be rewarded.

If questioned, the Swedes on the committee would probably not have opposed or condemned India's nationalist movement. But at the same time, Europe in those days was abuzz with stories of murderous rebels and brave colonials who went there to tame them (cfr. India's 'criminal tribes' or *Thugs*). So, to actually give open support to a rebellious colonial underling would have been too much even for the well-meaning Swedish bourgeoisie. In these circumstances, the mistaken impression that Tagore had put his literary services at the feet of the British monarch came in handy.

THEN WHO IS THE 'BHARATA BHAGYA VIDHATA'?

In a letter dated 10 November 1937, Tagore explained the true story: 'A certain high official in His Majesty's service, who was also my friend, had requested that I write a song of felicitation towards the

Emperor. The request simply amazed me. It caused a great stir in my heart. In response to that great mental turmoil, I pronounced the victory in *Jana Gana Mana* of that Bhagya Bidhata (Bengali pronunciation; "dispenser of destiny") of India who has from age after age held steadfast the reins of India's chariot through rise and fall, through the straight path and the curved. That Lord of Destiny, that Reader of the Collective Mind of India, that Perennial Guide, could never be George V, George VI, or any other George. Even my official friend understood this about the song. After all, even if his admiration for the crown was excessive, he was not lacking in simple common sense.'

Here Tagore already lets on the real identity of this dispenser of India's destiny. As a scion of the Brahmo Samaj, a sect espousing an abstract Hinduism based upon Upanishadic philosophy and frowning upon the variety of colourful god-figures from devotional Hinduism, he avoids mentioning by name any deity. Yet, he leaves no one in doubt that he means the Eternal Charioteer leading the pilgrims on their journey through countless ages of the timeless history of mankind. This clearly refers to Krishna of the *Bhagavad Gita*, who is there as Arjuna's charioteer. Later, he was elevated to the status of the incarnation of Vishnu, deemed to take birth 'in age upon age', whenever dharma has weakened and needs to be strengthened.

Usually, only the first stanza is publicly sung. But if you read on or sing on to the third stanza, it all becomes clear enough. The iconography of Vishnu and Krishna (chariot, conch, the expression *yuge yuge*, 'age upon age') is exuberantly sung there, and the singers describe themselves as yatri, 'travellers' or, in effect, 'pilgrims'. King George, prime minister Nehru or any other worldly ruler is absent—the entire focus is on Krishna, the guide and charioteer. He is said to 'deliver from sorrow and pain', which would be too much honour for a mere state leader; and to be 'the people's guide on the path'. There is nothing humdrum or pitiably 'secular' about this anthem. Hail the *Bharata Bhagya Vidhata*!

As the leading Tamil journalist Aravindan Neelakandan pointed out to us, it doesn't even end there. In the fourth stanza the dispenser of India's destiny is identified as a 'loving Mother', who, 'through nightmares and fears, protected us in Your lap'. This adds to the Hindu vision of the divine. God may manifest as a reliable charioteer, as a loving mother, as Sri Krishna or as Durga Ma, and if the song had been longer, no doubt in other forms as well.

And indeed, why stop there? The fifth and last stanza throws up one more appearance of the Divine Guide. Here, He is identified as Rajeshwara, the 'Royal Lord' or the 'Kingly Shiva', who is the primal teacher or Adi Guru. India would not be India without Him.

IS IT SECULAR?

For a republic that is always praised as 'secular', we might expect a secular anthem, somewhat like *La Marseillaise* or *Heil dir im Siegerkranz*. But whereas these two ignore religion altogether, *Jana Gana Mana* does at most have a passage that could be termed 'secular' in the Gandhian sense, viz. an equally positive recognition of all religions by the state.

India only calls itself secular since 1975, when Indira Gandhi's Emergency dictatorship inserted the words 'secular, socialist' into the Constitutional description of India as a 'democratic, federal republic'. That makes these two words the only ones in the Constitution that never went through a proper parliamentary debate; the least democratic part of it. In the days of the Constituent Assembly, by contrast, Dr B.R. Ambedkar, chairman of the Constitution Drafting Committee, explicitly refused to include 'secular'. When, twenty-eight years later, the term did get inserted, it had acquired the meaning 'anti-Hindu', yet most Hindus accept the term because they naïvely assume it still has the meaning 'secular'.

That word was not in the air when Tagore composed the song. But he did support religious pluralism. In fact, like most Hindus, he took it for granted as self-evident, not in need of being articulated as a separate doctrine. It was in his case vaguely the Gandhian idea of 'equal respect for all religions'. Consider another unsung stanza, the second. To a superficial reader, this might give the impression of espousing religiously neutrality:

> 'We heed Your gracious call.
> The Hindus, Buddhists, Sikhs, Jains, Parsis,
> Muslims, and Christians,
> The East and the West come together,
> To the side of Your throne,
> And weave the garland of love.
> Oh! You who bring in the unity of the people!'

Indian Muslims and Christians still have a lot of un-Islamic or un-Christian feelings in them, inherited from their Hindu ancestors, adopted from their Hindu environment, or simply stemming from universal human nature. Thus, they generally have a strong attachment to their motherland, overruling their tutored orientation to Mecca, Jerusalem or Rome. In that sense, their attachment to India does bring them together with their Hindu compatriots. Most Hindus are not too serious about doctrines, they overlook the specific points which set Islam and Christianity against all other religions, and hence tend to welcome all sects into the Indian fold.

But this stance is not reciprocated. The attitude that takes all sects to be one happy family is emphatically not Muslim and not Christian, for these sects vow only hellfire upon all the others. The spirit of this second stanza is not also-a-bit-Muslim, nor also-a-bit-Christian, it is not a bit of everything; while (or even because of) welcoming every one regardless of beliefs, it is thoroughly Hindu.

Does that mean every true Indian should believe in a being up there who watches over India's destiny? Hinduism is pluralistic and has room for different interpretations. Several orthodox as well as heterodox schools of Hindu thought are non-theistic and treat the gods as mere projections of ideas in the human mind, existing only because we feed them our mental energy. Fine, treat the Dispenser as a mental projection—but do feed Him or Her your mental energy.

TERRITORIAL DEBATE

Secularists and Pakistanis, not too surprised to find themselves in the same bed once more, object to the inclusion of Sindh among India's provinces. Of course, the song was written when Sindh was fully included in British India, no less than Utkala (Odisha) or Banga (Bengal). It had not been partitioned off yet, not even from the Bombay Presidency, let alone from India when Pakistan was formed. Come to think of it, West Panjab and East Bengal also failed to be taken out.

Well, the fathers of Pakistan had better adapt their plans to the geographical enumeration of regions in this song. They should not have tried to sever these provinces from India. Now they are stuck with a state of which most of the territory properly belongs to another state, another civilization, of which the remnants are still found in their soil, from Mohenjo-Daro on down. For it is entirely apt that Sindh, West Panjab and East Bengal still find mention in India's anthem. Just like Gilgit and Baltistan are rightly called 'Pak-Occupied Kashmir', Pakistan and Bangladesh are nothing but 'Islam-occupied India'. When a Pakistani leader lamented to Murli Manohar Joshi that 'Pakistan is not complete without Kashmir', Joshi finished his sentence: '... and India is not complete without Pakistan.'

When Germany put the first stanza of its anthem on the back-burner, it was because it wanted to prove it laid no claim on the territories between the post-1945 borders and the Memel River (which would mean most of Poland and Lithuania). Those territories were not, even if there exists such a thing, 'intrinsically' German. They had been conquered and forcibly Christianized in the Teutonic Order's crusade centuries after the German state (in full: the 'Holy Roman Empire of the German Nation') had come into existence. That they were lost again could be a pity, but not a strike at Germany's heart. By contrast, Sindh, the province around the lower Indus River, happens to be the root of the name 'India' itself, derivative from the Greek river-name Indos, from the Persian form 'Hindu' of Sanskrit 'Sindhu', i.e., the Indus river. It contains Mohenjo-Daro, with the Priest King, the Dancing Girl and Shiva Pashupati, famous icons not of '5,000 years of Pakistan' but of Hindu civilization. Of course, Sindh deserves to return to India. One day, when Pakistan has lost its reason for existing, it will.

ALSO RAN

When the freedom movement and later the Constituent Assembly deliberated upon the choice of an anthem, there were three serious candidates. *Sâre Jahân se Acchâ Hindustân Hamâra*, 'Of the whole world, the best is our Hindustan', was an Urdu song by Mohammed Iqbal, composed in 1904. Having studied in Germany, he may well have been inspired by *Deutschland über Alles*, but with the wrong, though now common, idea that this means 'Germany is superior to the rest'. At any rate, his opening line said in so many words that India is superior to the rest.

Whatever the merits of the lyrics and the melody, any choice of an Iqbal song came to leave a bad taste in the mouth when, a few years before his death in 1938, he became the spiritual father of the fledgling Pakistan movement. That best-in-the-world country India was suddenly not good enough any more; he wanted the Islamic-dominated territories to separate from it.* Nonetheless, it has never ceased to enjoy a certain recognition within the Indian Army.

Another option was *Vande Mâtaram*, 'I salute thee, Mother', meaning Mother India. It was drawn from a novel by Bankim Chandra Chatterjee, *Ânandamath*, 'Abbey of Bliss' (1882). Covertly, the story appealed to its readers to rise up against the colonizers, at that time the British. But in its explicit narrative, it was set in an earlier age, when the occupiers against whom to revolt were Muslims. Here is a little complication, as the story

*See e.g. Bhai Zakir, '"Sare Jahan Se Achcha" poet Mohammed Iqbal remains pariah in India', *Pakistan Defence*, 9 November 2012

is meant to take place in 1771, when Bengal was already under British control (since 1757). Yet, the Muslims were still treated as the enemy while the sword against the British was blunted, probably to let the novel pass under the British censor's radar. As was to be expected, Muslims and Nehruvian secularists objected to this anti-Muslim background.

Moreover, and perhaps even more decisively, Muslims proposed a theological objection: This veneration of the Mother Goddess, easily recognizable as the warrior-goddess Durga, was idolatry, pure and simple. Only Allah should be worshipped. To the extent an anthem with all its pomp and ceremony was acceptable at all (the Jehovah's Witnesses reject it), it should emphatically not deify the nation, nor any symbol or deity associated with it. Till today, some Muslims boycott public performances of *Vande Mâtaram*. Thus, an article* quotes a Barelvi cleric: 'It is un-Islamic to sing the national song'; and a Muslim law scholar explains the reason: 'There are some objectionable words in Vande Mataram.'

This throws a different light on *Jana Gana Mana*. The anthem's 'Dispenser of India's Destiny' unambiguously signifies the Beloved Guide Krishna, the Combative Mother Durga, the Eternal Guru Shiva. According to certain prophets, these are all 'false gods', if not impersonations of Satan. If *Vande Mâtaram* is 'communal', so is *Jana Gana Mana*. And that is what is good about it.

While the song is large enough to encompass all of India throughout its history, united or divided, Aryan or Dravidian, tribal or urban, monarchical or republican, without distinction, it still does take an ideological stand. It is not nihilistic, no liberal-anything-goes here, no Islamic monolithic caliphate, nothing that negates or oppresses the native civilization. Instead, this song welcomes a dharmic umbrella for all the varieties of India's children.

---

*'Muslim clerics differ on singing Vande Mâtaram, big setback for CM Adityanath', *India Today*, 14 August 2017

MOTHER INDIA

Recently, the secularists have looked hard and deep for more objections to *Vande Mâtaram*. And yes, they found something. In a later stanza, not usually sung, it is asked (in a translation by Sri Aurobindo):

> 'Who hath said thou art weak in thy lands,
> When the swords flash out in seventy million hands
> And seventy million voices roar
> Thy dreadful name from shore to shore?'

When the novel was written, the results of the first census were well-known. 'Seventy million' was not the population of India, which then must have been approaching 300 million. Instead, it was very nearly the population of Bengal, and suggests that the book did not envisage a rebellion by all Indians, but one by all the inhabitants of Bengal. This could be used by the secularists and all their *Breaking India* allies as proof that even the nationalist Bankim Chandra Chatterjee did not think of India as a political unit: He was more of a Bengali nationalist. Indeed, their revered British role models would have been right in asserting that they themselves had 'created' India, which, until then, had been (in Winston Churchill's words) 'no more a political unit than the equator'.

Conversely, the poem has to be read in the context of the novel, and there we find the freedom fighters worshipping *Bhârat Mata*, 'Mother India'. The poem itself, as quoted above, defines the Motherland geographically as 'from shore to shore', clearly India rather than Bengal. They saw no contradiction between love of Mother India and love of Golden Mother Bengal. So, this secularist discovery is little more than a storm in a teacup.

CONCLUSION

India's founding fathers may have made their choice based on incomplete information. Apparently, most voting members were unaware of the God-talk in *Jana Gana Mana*'s third, fourth and fifth stanzas. Alternatively, they may have considered it as not really part of the national anthem anyway, which officially it wasn't. Or they may not have cared for secularism. At any rate, when including these stanzas, the song is emphatically God-oriented and Hindu.

India's anthem is not ruler-oriented like *Heil dir im Siegerkranz*. It is not ruler-and-God-oriented, like the *Wilhelmus*, the *Kaiserhymne* or *God Save the Queen*. It is not secularly nation-and-state-oriented, like the *Brabançonne* or *Das Lied der Deutschen*. It is not nation-and-army-oriented, like the *Marseillaise* or the *Star-Spangled Banner*. It is emphatically nation-and-God-oriented, God in this case probably being identifiable as Krishna, or more abstractly, the idea of the divine involving itself in this world whenever dharma requires it.

The song does not commit itself to a specific political system, such as monarchy, by glorifying the ruler. It merely expresses love for the nation through all its variegated landscapes and experiences—which goes hand in hand with, and follows naturally from, a veneration of the Divine Guru. According to Tagore, and according to all Indian citizens who intone or honour his anthem, India is not complete without a heaven-oriented, sacred dimension.

Down with 'Nationalism'*

For once, the secularists have it right. The nationalism by which the Hindutva crowd swears is a Western invention. Feelings for your home country are universal, and natives of India will need no prodding, nor any foreign or native ideology to defend their country when necessary. Nationalism is just there, as a gut feeling, not in need of any promotion or defence. But as an ideology, it is the creation of the modern West, hardened in the fires of the First World War. Of the secularists, we already knew that they always ape the West (or what they assume to be Western), but for champions of native civilization, it is worth noticing.

Long before I learnt about India, I already knew that national provenance is not very useful as an explanation of anything in politics. I remember how as a child I saw the TV news report ca. 1970 of a public speech by Canadian Prime Minister Pierre Trudeau. Suddenly he was interrupted by a bearded young man in the audience, loudly scolding him. Trudeau singled him out for an improvised reply: 'You have been swayed by those bogus progressist ideas from the US, from Chicago and Los Angeles. Get Canadian, man!' Similarly, the Flemish politician Eric van Rompuy (younger brother of the later European Union President Herman van Rompuy) criticized Leftist-inspired innovations as 'counter to the Flemish national soul'. As if there can be anything Canadian or non-Canadian, anything Flemish or non-Flemish, about ideas.

---

*This is based on an article in Hindu Human Rights, London, October 2017

NATIONALISM IN A CHANGING WORLD

In the 1920s, because of the freedom struggle, loyalty to some form of Indian nationalism was the obvious choice for self-respecting people in India. And because of the British presence and influence on the curriculum, European ideological influence was larger than life, absorbed by nationalists even while they were opposing it. Just at that time, after the First World War, nationalism was at its peak. When theorizing the national struggle, Hindu activists had little choice but to take inspiration from European thinkers like Giuseppe Mazzini, mastermind of Italian reunification and translated by Vinayak Damodar Savarkar.

The construction of Hindu concerns in terms of 'Hindu nationalism' (effective meaning of 'Hindutva', a term marginally attested since ca. 1880 but launched on the political stage by Savarkar) was understandable. So, it is not our aim to berate freedom fighters like *Hindutva* author Savarkar, Hindu Mahasabha co-founder Swami Shraddhananda or RSS founder Keshav Baliram Hedgewar.

However, they could have looked to Hindu history to see that one of the central concerns of all nationalists was completely lacking there: homogenization. India was the champion of diversity. States were rarely linguistically homogenous and rulers didn't care to make them so. Loyalty was less to one's state (which could easily change) but to a more lasting and more intimate identity: one's caste. As B.R. Ambedkar's grandson, Prakash Ambedkar, said: 'Every caste a nation.' States had only limited power and were hardly present in the lives of their citizens. By contrast, modern nation-states sought to involve its citizens in the state project, for example, by military conscription, and to insinuate itself in their lives—see the example of Otto von Bismarck's creation of social security to cement Germany's new-found unity. In traditional India, one's community, in many cases meaning one's caste, served as one's social security.

If the Hindutva stalwarts per se wanted to look to 'civilized'

Europe, they could have taken inspiration from a number of multinational empires there. In Savarkar's student days in London, the Russian and Austro-Hungarian empires still flourished and were characterized by a state religion (Orthodoxy or Roman Catholicism), just as Hindutva stalwarts had in mind for India, whereas ethnic nationalism favoured secularism—for example, German unification deliberately downplayed the Catholic/Lutheran dichotomy. Another example of how nationalism and religiosity are naturally antagonistic was provided by Turkey: While Atatürk abolished the Ottoman Empire's religious bias, his secular-nationalist republic created the Turkish-Kurdish conflict. The old empires had a dominant language (Russian or German), but along with a certain unequal tolerance to minority religions, they also left room for minority languages and made no attempt to impose a single language. This could be contrasted with the then purest example of nationalism, the French Third Republic (1871–1940), where the minority languages, still spoken by half the French population in the nineteenth century, were being destroyed and the state 'religion' of secularism aggressively promoted.

True, with the First World War, the aforementioned empires disappeared, but another example even closer at hand survived: the United Kingdom. Few people realize how the specific status of each part of the UK differed: the Isle of Man, the Channel Islands, Wales, etc., all had and still have a different relation with the British Crown. The Welsh and Gaelic languages were not supported by the state, but there was no active campaign to weed them out either. In spite of a rising level of tolerance, there was a state religion and all traditional customs and institutions were upheld. All while struggling for their sovereignty, perhaps Hindus could have learnt something from their colonizers? (For starters, they could have realized that Britain was centred on Brigid, the fire-clad goddess whose name is related to Bhrgu, the Vedic Ur-seer who introduced the fire sacrifice.)

Back to reality. The Hindutva pioneers opted for the then-prestigious model of the nation-state and tried to cram Hindu political aspirations into it. Rightly or wrongly, this is what happened, so let us start from there. The normal course for a political doctrine is to take in feedback from evolving reality, and to improve with the times. A speech by a Marxist leader today will sound very different from one by his predecessor a century ago. But in the case of Hindutva, the reverse development took place. It froze in its tracks.

This way, important international developments passed without registering on the RSS radar. Nationalism lost its lustre and even became a term of abuse. First there was the circumstance that the German and Japanese imperialists of the Second World War had sworn by stalwart nationalism (many of the Resistance fighters too, for example, Charles de Gaulle, but that has been forgotten), whereas their Soviet enemies called themselves internationalists. This way, nationalism came to connote both evil and defeat. Secondly, the more recent wave of globalization turned nationalism into a nostalgic past-oriented attitude, something for village bumpkins who had missed the latest train to progress.

Yet, the Sangh Parivar remained blind to these developments and kept swearing by interbellum nationalism. It continued to take inspiration from its first leaders, Hedgewar and his successor Madhav Sadashiv Golwalkar. If you don't know their voices and you listen to a tape-recorded speech by Hedgewar and one from his current successor Mohan Bhagwat nine decades later, you wouldn't know who is who: The thoughts they express are interchangeable. That does not reflect on Hedgewar, who was a child of his time and contributed the best he could to the Hindu cause. But it reflects quite negatively on the course the Sangh Parivar has taken since then.

'NATIONALISM IS HINDUISM'

In one sense, the word 'nationalism' is defensible from a Hindu viewpoint. For the overseeable past, Hinduism has been native to India, whereas Christianity and Islam are irrevocably of foreign origin, with their founding histories and sacred places located outside India. Other factors remaining the same, Hindus will always identify with India in a way that Christians and Muslims cannot.

On this reality, V.D. Savarkar based his definition of Hindu as 'one who has India as both his fatherland and his holyland'. Applying this insight, M.S. Golwalkar came up with his oft-quoted suggestion that, if India were to be a Hindu state, Christians and Muslims could only stay there as guests, not as citizens. This deduction followed logically from the premise that India would be a state of the Hindus.

Golwalkar's rhetoric was notoriously clumsy, but the point to retain is that he made a distinction between Hindus, howsoever broadly defined, and non-Hindus. Whether or not that distinction should have any juridical consequences, the fact is that Hindus and non-Hindus were deemed different in respect of nationhood. That was a non-secular vision. In a secular state, religion wouldn't matter, but Golwalkar opted for a state in which religion would determine citizenship.*

A comparison with Israel comes to mind, where any Jew worldwide can claim citizenship. Some non-Jews are citizens because they already lived there before the creation of the Zionist state or because they are spouses of Jewish immigrants, but, as a class, they cannot claim citizenship. And indeed, both Savarkar and Golwalkar did invoke Zionism as an inspiring example.

To sum up, nationalism can be loaded differently from the religiously neutral meaning given to it by the Nehruvians. For now we should make abstraction of the anti-Hindu discriminations instituted by Jawaharlal Nehru and his partisans, and merely take them at their word when they dishonestly pontificate that in India, secularism means religious neutrality. That neutrality, at any rate, is not what Savarkar and Golwalkar had in mind.

Note the contrast with the current thinking in the RSS and even more in the BJP. For decades now, and with increasing

---

*http://cpiml.org/commentary/citizenship-amendment-bill-2016-a-covert-step-towards-golwalkars-india/

oblivion of their earlier view, they have been erasing the distinction between 'Hindu' and 'Indian'. Now they claim that 'anyone who lives in India is a Hindu'. I see no further need to point out once more how mendacious this view is; let us merely settle for the observation that it is impolite: No account is taken of the general Muslim's or Christian's rejection of his own unasked-for inclusion in the 'Hindu' category. And if half-baked politicians insist that their mendaciousness is necessitated by political expediency, let us then maintain standards and remind them that at least they should distinguish the lies their mouths speak from the views their brains actually believe in: If you think you really must tell a lie, at least stop believing your own lies (which are meant to fool the enemy, not yourself) and remain aware that 'Hindu' is not the same as 'Indian'.

As the author of a book called *Decolonizing the Hindu Mind*, I take objection to the recent organization of a Hindu nationalist forum called 'Decolonizing the Indian Mind'. There is a lot to be decolonized about Hindu society as such, which is still exploited and belittled, though now mostly by Indians, but nothing at all to be decolonized about 'India'. The country became independent in 1947. Any lingering British influence in India, including the official use of the English language, has been a free and conscious choice by Indian politicians. Similarly, the present Americanization has not been imposed by any outside forces, in spite of their eager desire, but has been allowed in and welcomed by Indian politicians, most of all by the BJP.

Long live India, down with 'India'. Admittedly, in some cases the latter term has innocently been used as interchangeable with dharma ('Hinduism'), as in the name of S.R. Goel's publishing house Voice of India. But increasingly, it has become a weasel word to disown Hinduism.

PARTITION

As the decades went by, the Hindutva movement kept calling itself 'nationalist'. In the 1940s, the emphasis came to lie on the unity and territorial integrity of India, against the Partition project designed by MA Jinnah's Muslim League. Advocates of the Partition were also called nationalists: 'Muslim separatists', in Congress parlance, but they saw themselves as 'Muslim nationalists'. One man's separatism is another man's nationalism, and these men argued that the Indian Muslims had every attribute of a nation. They gave in somewhat to the then-fashionable trends of democracy (hence the importance of numbers, so that rule by 24 per cent Muslims would not be legitimate) and nationalism. In this case, modern nationhood thinking could be made to continue seamlessly where Muslim theology had spoken of *umma* and recent Muslim (particularly Ottoman) history had thrown up *millat*, meaning 'religious community', as an equivalent of 'nation'.

Lined up against them within the Muslim community were the so-called 'nationalist Muslims', meaning that minority among Muslims who rejected Partition because they ultimately wanted to gobble up the whole of India, not just a part of it. Their spokesman was Maulana Azad, veteran leader of the Khilafat movement, who even managed to convince Mahatma Gandhi to prevent Partition by handing all of India over to Jinnah and thus realize Muslim minority rule (but they were overruled by Congress, see my book *Why I Killed the Mahatma*). They were not impressed with the nationalist idea that the world should be divided into sovereign territorial units belonging to nations. At most these could be administrative units within the really sovereign unit, the caliphate, intended to comprise the whole world. Nor were they impressed with the modern fad of democracy.

As Pakistan's spiritual father Mohammed Iqbal said: 'Democracy is a system in which heads are counted but not weighed.' He only gave in to the force of numbers because of awe for modernity and the British-created power equation. But the Khilafatists believed that this novelty of democracy was but a paper tiger and that like in the Middle Ages, Muslims should just grab power. Later, Muslim power could always see to it that Muslims *become* the majority. Since Gandhi and Nehru had always been called nationalists, Muslims who sided with them against Partition in order to keep their option of all-India conquest open were also called nationalists, though what they really hoped for was a reunification of the Muslims in a new caliphate where they would lord it over the unbelievers.

Do keep in mind that both parties had the same goal: Islamic world conquest. The wrongly called 'nationalist Muslims' went straight for it, largely because the modern world was unfamiliar to them, while the separatists made temporary concessions to the new circumstances and first wanted to consolidate Muslim power in Pakistan. Initially they were even willing to settle for Dr BR Ambedkar's proposal to exchange populations, so that no Muslim would stay behind in remainder-India. They couldn't believe their luck when, on this score, India's hands were tied by Gandhi and Nehru, who insisted on blocking this rational and peaceful formula. The Muslim League's assessment was that while the Paki Hindus had to flee, the Indian Muslims could stay where they were, thus forming a fifth column for the next phase of Islamic expansion.

INTEGRAL HUMANISM

Forty years later, ca. 1965, Deendayal Upadhyaya adopted the promising term 'integral humanism', in Hindi *ekatmata manavavad* or *ekatma manavadarshan*. This seemed to transcend the division of mankind in box-type nations. Moreover, unlike nationalism, it did not seem to have been borrowed from the West, in spite of appearances. In the 1930s, the French Catholic political thinker Jacques Maritain had launched the notion of *humanisme intégral,* the ideological core of what was to become the dominant post-war movement of Christian democracy. But it is unlikely that that is where Upadhyaya had the term from: At that time, there was still a large barrier between the French and the Indian public spheres, and the term had been used cursorily by Indian writers as well, being a rather evident concept.

Let us nonetheless note the parallel: In 1930s' France, there was a militantly secular regime, the Third Republic, and the advancing threat of communism, exactly like in 1960s' India. Both were effectively atheist but called themselves 'humanist', which had the effective meaning of 'non-religious'. Against these two arms of atheism, the core counter-insight from the religiously committed side was that 'a humanism which denies man's religious dimension is not an integral humanism'. Materialism amputates the natural religious dimension from man, and it has to be restored.

So, in name, 'integral humanism' had a touch of genius. It sounds so innocent and positive, something that nobody can object to. That is why, in spite of being the official ideology of the RSS and the BJP, in which every member is trained, it is never mentioned in textbooks by 'experts' on Hindutva. Out of an unscholarly political activism, these 'experts' prefer to push more negatively sounding terms, of which 'Hindu nationalist' is still the kindest. It is unthinkable to read a textbook on the Labour Party without coming across the word 'socialism', yet so noxious is the intellectual climate in both India and India-watching that it is entirely the done thing to write expert introductions on the RSS-BJP without mentioning its actual ideology.

Alas, once Upadhyaya went beyond the basics, he relapsed into talk that can only be explained as nationalistic. The central concept in his system is chiti, the 'national soul'. This notion had been dear to Johann Herder, the Romantic theorist of nationalism ca. 1780. Last winter in Pune and Mumbai, the heartland of Hindu nationalism, during Upadhyaya's centenary, I noticed that this rather simplistic ideology went through a revival, with some convivial symposiums but few new ideas. It was again around this nationalist notion of chiti that the main churning took place.

The concept of a 'national soul' could make sense as a purely descriptive attempt at encapsulating the statistical tendency of a 'nation' towards a certain mentality. But even as a statistical average, it is susceptible to serious evolution.

One example. The ancient Romans were known for their organizing power, and this is what allowed them to defeat the fearless but less organized Gauls and Germans. But then Arminius, a German mercenary in the Roman army, learnt these organizing skills, returned to his country, organized a German army and defeated the Romans. It was the first time the Germans got associated with organizing skills, a great tradition of theirs ever since. By contrast, after holding out as great organizers for several more centuries, the Italians became proverbially chaotic, great artists but lousy strategists or politicians. They know all about cuisine and *amore*, but you wouldn't entrust any organizational task to them. The 'national soul' is an entity subject to change.

While not very precise as a descriptive term, chiti is even worse as a normative concept. The stereotype of 'the drunken Irish' may have a grain of truth to it, but for Irish nationalists, it is hardly a value worth defending. I don't know what the Hindu/Indian national soul is (the first European travellers in Asia, not colonialists yet, had stereotypes of 'the violent Muslims', 'the indolent Buddhists', 'the perverse Chinese', and yes, 'the deceitful Hindus'), but I imagine it may also have some less desirable traits, not really worth upholding. In Upadhyaya's day, communism was a major concern, but it was not wrong because it failed to accord with the Indian chiti—it did not accord with the Russian or Chinese chiti either. Any serious critique of communism or other challenging ideologies can perfectly be made without reference to the 'national soul'.

Here again, chiti serves as a secular-sounding escape route from a religious category. That, after all, was part of Upadhyaya's agenda. Alright, his term 'integral humanism' was bright, and the best possible secular-sounding approximation to a perfect translation of the Hindu term 'dharma'. What Upadhyaya was really getting at was that Indians have a mentality in common that oozes out from Hinduism. The 'idea of India' that secularists like Shashi Tharoor or Ramachandra Guha like to preach about is but a secular nod to the unmentionable term 'Hinduism'. However, rather than being proud of his Hinduism as the source of integral-humanist values, Upadhyaya, like most Sanghi ideologues ever since, was in the business of downplaying and hiding this Hinduism behind secular terms. His 'integral humanism' ended up as the equivalent of the secularists' 'idea of India'. He pioneered what was to become 'BJP secularism'.

AYODHYA

During the Ayodhya controversy around 1990, the RSS-BJP professed loyalty to the 'Indian hero' Rama and indignation towards the 'foreign invader' Babar. In reality, his geographical provenance had nothing to do with demolition of temples. The Greeks, Scythians, Kushanas and Huns had been foreign too, as were the British, yet they had not been in the business of temple-destruction. By contrast, Malik Kafur had been a native but as much of a temple-destroyer as Babar, after he had converted to Islam. So, in reality, there had been a religious conflict between Hinduism and Islam, the religions of the 'Hindu hero' Rama and the 'Muslim invader' Babar, but Sangh Parivar escapists had tried to clothe it in nationalist language of 'Indian' versus 'foreign'.

When Prophet Mohammed and Ali entered the pagan pilgrimage site, the Kaaba in Mecca, they were not foreign invaders. They were of the same gene pool, skin colour, language, food habits, literary inheritance and anything else that may define a nation, as the people from whom they were about to rob the temple. And then they removed the idols, just as the Muslim invaders did in India—as well as in West and Central Asia and in the Mediterranean (see e.g. my book *Ayodhya, the Case against the Temple*).

Conceptualizing Islamic iconoclasm in terms of 'national' versus 'foreign' is completely mistaken. In the case of the contemporary Sangh Parivar, it has moreover become a wilful mistake, an act of escapism. It thinks it can escape the label of 'religious fanaticism' and earn the hoped-for pat on the shoulder from the secularists by swearing it is not Hindu. It now claims to be wedded to secular 'nationalism', not realizing that this term also invites contempt, at least in the West and, therefore, also among the Westernized intelligentsia.

However, its continued loyalty to 'nationalism' could be

dismissed as only a publicity mistake. It seems to me that its ever-more-pronounced shame about its historical sobriquet 'Hindu' is more serious. Though once calling themselves 'Hindu nationalists', and still called that by all media, they are now only nationalists, and they repeat this over and over again to secularist interviewers, thinking this will earn them their approval. 'Nationalism' has gotten absolutized at the expense of dharma, and now serves the Sangh, and especially the BJP, as a conduit for secular nationalism, dropping any Hindu concerns altogether.

BJP SECULARISM

We are currently witnessing the incumbency of 'BJP secularism'. This non-ideology was already taking shape with the Nehru imitator A.B. Vajpayee's increasing dominance in the later Jana Sangh and the early BJP. It became evident in the Ayodhya events, which the BJP leadership eagerly distanced itself from after reaping the rewards in the 1991 elections. When Hindu activists defied the BJP leadership to demolish the disputed structure on 6 December 1992, BJP leader L.K. Advani called it 'the blackest day in my life'. Yet, in the larger scheme of things, this act greatly expedited a solution to the controversy, thus saving thousands of lives.

The Vajpayee government of 1998–2004 did strictly nothing about the list of Hindu priorities, not even the version laid down in the forty-point Hindu agenda of another Sangh branch, the VHP. The late Pramod Mahajan realized (possibly purely as a matter of electoral calculus) the untenability of the contrast between the BJP programme and the BJP performance: He wanted the BJP to raise certain of these Hindu demands. It they were to be vetoed by the allies, or defeated in the Lok Sabha, they would form excellent stakes in the election debates; and if they were to pass, the BJP could take them as trophies to the campaign. But Vajpayee was adamant about going to the voters with a purely economic programme, and though India's growth figures were then at its peak, he got soundly defeated.

The current BJP government is repeating this performance. The Supreme Court judgment against triple talaq (divorce through instant repudiation of a wife) was used as a fig leaf, somehow proving that the BJP was slowly inching towards the abolition of the separate Islamic family law system and towards a common civil code, an old election promise. In reality, the case had been brought by a few Muslim women. That the BJP happened to be in power was merely a coincidence (though its follow-up, viz. to consolidate the verdict by trying to enact it into law, is commendable and contrasts favourably with Rajiv Gandhi's 1985 move to overrule the progressive Shah Bano verdict on alimony rights with a more sharia-compliant law).

Similarly, the private Bill proposing to abolish anti-Hindu discrimination in education and temple management is just that: private, emanating only from BJP MP Maheish Girri, not from the party or the government. *(Postscript February 2019: Later a more comprehensive Bill was proposed by BJP MP Satyapal Singh, but in spite of Hindu activist support, it likewise came to nought.)* Like Jawaharlal Nehru, like the erstwhile RSS ideologue Nana Deshmukh (theorist of the Vajpayee line), like all the NGOs meddling in Indian affairs, like every capitalistic or socialistic materialist, the BJP swears exclusively by 'development' (vikas). It gladly ropes in the Hindu votes through the Hindu image that the secularists keep giving it, but makes no commitment any more to anything Hindu.

Not that it will ever receive the much-hoped-for pat on the shoulder from the secularists. In their circles, the done thing is still to throw texts from the 1960s or 1920s full of Hindu rhetoric at the supposedly Hindu party, as if these could tell you what the party is about today. So long as this pat on the shoulder is an unreachable goal beckoning in the distance, the RSS-BJP will sacrifice anything, including its professed ideology, to get it. For, in its universe, the secularists still lay down the norms that it tries to live up to.

MISCONSTRUCTION

Time and again I get to see how the nationalist paradigm distorts issues. Thus, the missionary challenge is no longer a matter of Western intrusion into India. Most missionaries are now Indian, and even the Evangelical sects teleguided from America will make sure to send a native to any inter-faith meeting or TV debate. Missionaries are not CIA agents plotting against India; they have their own agenda since centuries before the CIA or the colonial enterprise even existed, and their target is not some nation or state, it is all pagan religions—in India, principally Hinduism.

Two examples from my own experience. A Hindu who used to like me turned his back on me after I uttered my scepticism of a certain guru called Gurunath who claimed that the enigmatic character, Babaji (a normal form of address for any ascetic), described by Lahiri Mahasaya and Swami Yogananda as a Himalaya-based yogi of indeterminate age, is the same character as Gorakhnath, who lived a thousand years ago. He found that I was unimpressed by his assurance that this Gurunath is 'enlightened'. I happen to have met a big handful of people deemed 'enlightened', and I have concluded that their yogic power and knowledge, in itself superior to our humdrum lives, does not magically confer on them a superior knowledge of worldly matters. At that mundane level, their knowledge and opinions are no different from those of any other man from the same background and circumstances. Therefore, if this Gurunath wants to make eccentric claims such as of a man living for millennia, then he has the same burden of proof on him as any ordinary man. After that, my Hindu friend cut off the debate and decided that I was insufferably attached to a 'Western' prejudice. As if numerous Hindus don't have a similar healthy scepticism of paranormal claims, and as if, conversely, there aren't equally gullible Westerners in great number. The division between 'Indian' and 'Western' is very often a curtain behind which to smuggle beliefs that cannot withstand the normal light of reason.

In another discussion, Hindus were arguing that the Partition was the doing not of the poor, hapless Muslims, but of the British, who had it in for the Hindus, so much so that they even committed 'genocide' on them. Well, 'genocide' implies murderous intention, and Hindus only flatter themselves if they attribute this to the British, who merely wanted to make money and thus instituted economic policies with an enormous collateral damage, but didn't care one way or the other whether the natives lived or starved. When the Muslim League launched the Partition project, the Brits initially rejected it (though taunting the Congress with it as proof that the Congress did not represent India) and only came around when Muslim violence had made it seem inevitable and the beginning Cold War made them see its benefits. The Partition was a 100 per cent Muslim plan, only assented to by the British at the same time and in the same spirit as the conversion to its acceptance by many Congress politicians, ultimately even Mahatma Gandhi (June 1947) who had sworn 'Partition only over my dead body'.

Moreover, while no Hindu says it openly, it is so obvious to any observer that they only want to play hero against the long-departed Brits because they have interiorized the fear that they might offend the Muslims, with whom they still have to deal. What S.R. Goel called 'the business of blaming the British' is a trick of misdirection, popular among stage magicians, which only a buffoon would believe.

Anyway, during the discussion, I used the Indian word 'tamasic' rather than the English equivalent 'deluded' and 'slothful'. Immediately, one of them flared up and warned all the Indians present that I was equating 'Indian' with 'tamasic'. And then all through a number of altercations, he went on with this line of deluded discourse. Political delusions are as common among Westerners as among Indians, and appeasement of Islam has become just as big in Europe as in India. Conversely, people who are sceptical of the faux-heroic attitude against long-dead colonialism as a cover for cowardly Muslim appeasement exist as much in India, starting with the late S.R. Goel, an impeccable patriot.

Falling back on the nationalist paradigm makes Hindus

misunderstand issues. It is, of course, far easier to separate people by skin colour than by ideology, very appealing to the lazy, tamasic mind. But it is sure to make you mistake enemies for friends, and friends for enemies. If you think you can afford that on a battlefield, suit yourselves.

CONCLUSION

When you are on a battlefield, not because you choose to but because your enemies impose this confrontation on you, it is a matter of life and death to be supremely realistic. You simply cannot afford to misconstrue the reasons and stakes for the battle, nor the nature and motives of your enemies. It is but rare that the ideological stakes coincide with national ones, as they did in the Indo-Pak confrontation during the Bangladesh war, a truly 'just war' (*dharma yuddha*), if ever there was one.

A Hindu yoga master whom I know once made the effort of disabusing some European yoga aspirants from their fascination with India: 'India is not that important, India will disappear one day.' India is not absolute, not sanâtana, 'eternal'. India is relatively important as the cradle of yoga, and secondarily as the cradle of many other cultural riches. But what is important is its culture, sanâtana dharma. If a party of Hindu travellers get stuck on an uninhabited island without the means to escape from there, they can still set up their 'Ram rajya' in this new territory. Maybe they won't have coconuts and marigolds there to reproduce their rituals, but to those new circumstances too they can adapt their sanâtana dharma.

Finally, let me state that nationalism, not as a pompous ideology but as an intimate feeling, as what a better word calls patriotism, is just natural. Certain ideologies try to estrange you from it, but Hindu dharma accepts and nurtures it. Every penny spent on RSS propaganda for nationalism is a penny wasted. Every effort to rewrite textbooks in a nationalist sense is an effort misdirected. A feeling for your motherland is simply normal and doesn't need any propaganda. For the Vedic seers, the motherland was only the Saraswati basin in Haryana; King Bharat never heard of the subcontinent named after him, but for today's Indians, that subcontinent is a lived reality. It is that expanse to which they are attached, and that we should uphold.

In the modern age, when the state is far more important than in the past, the Indian republic is a necessity to defend Hindu civilization. In that sense, it is only right to be an Indian patriot. But that national feeling goes without saying.

Pishacha Vivaha and Rakshasa Vivaha: On the Notion of a 'Lesser Evil'*

A culture war that has raged in Christian countries before, and is bound to rock Muslim countries in the coming decades, concerns 'reparation marriage'. Once in a while, a case of such an arrangement makes headlines, followed by arguments pro or, mostly, contra.

On Twitter, a lady friend protested against a judicial verdict in a case where a Muslim man had raped a Hindu girl, who, as a consequence, gave birth to a child. A judge okayed a 'solution', viz. that he marry her. We won't discuss the particular case, but the very principle of treating rape as less consequential if the victim agrees to marry the perpetrator.

PATRIARCHAL

The lady had counselled us not to 'communalize' the issue, as it happens as well in cases where only Muslims or only Hindus are involved. Well, there is, of course, a communal angle, in that the Prophet, as per his biographer Ibn Ishaq, explicitly condoned rape of non-Muslim hostages after caravan raids**, according to Islamic

*Published on Pragyata.com, 27 January 2018

**http://cemsg.org/wp-content/uploads/2015/11/AliSina-Understanding Muhammad4th.pdf law, non-Muslim women, in certain circumstances, are up for grabs (cfr. the Islamic permission to take infidel women as 'captives of the right hand', in Q.4:3, 4:24, 23:1-6, 33:50, 70:30). To be sure, in many earlier societies, this was also the relation between the upper classes and the despised classes, and that is precisely the point Islamic law intends to make: Muslims are the upper class, unbelievers must be subservient to them. However, while this communal angle is really there, it is not our concern here.

She alleged that the judge's leniency towards rape if followed by marriage is 'patriarchal'. She could have called it unjust, she could have called it a refusal to apply the law, she could have called it a dereliction of duty by the judiciary, but she chose to call it something deemed worse nowadays, viz. 'patriarchal'.

Lately I notice that many Hindus who really mean to serve the Hindu cause, many of whom are indeed labelled 'Hindu fanatics' by their secularist colleagues, have taken to using this concept. Last week, a *Swarajya* article about the proper Hindu reaction to the galloping Muslim demography (with a Kerala Muslim community of 26 per cent having 42 per cent of new births) warned that Hindus should not think of forcing their wives to have more children, as that would be 'patriarchal'. That would turn them into 'breeding machines', the approved progressive term for 'mother'. This was not just a terminological problem: It bought into the whole presupposition that women are being instrumentalized and that they have no agency themselves, and certainly no 'communal' agency, in wanting to counter the Muslim demographic offensive. Apparently, women can't want anything, certainly not survival as a community.

Another week earlier, I attended a Mahabharata conference in Delhi, with many traditionalists participating, where a young lady gave a paper on Draupadi. She had been through the mill of liberal indoctrination, so her paper was full of American feminist buzz words, such as 'patriarchy' and 'empowerment'. There exists a much wiser and more rooted Indian women's advocacy movement, pioneered by Madhu Kishwar's *Manushi*, one area where India can teach the world, not in the past but today. Unfortunately, meanwhile, the American conflict-oriented (because at heart cultural-Marxist) variety is gaining ground. I don't expect any Hindu revival to go very far if Hindus keep swallowing the enemy's narratives like this.

But let all of that pass. No matter what terminology and hence what conceptual framework we use to make sense of this practice of marriage after rape, we all agree that there is something wrong with it. Or to use more social-'science' jargon: It should be 'problematized'.

AN INTERNATIONAL PROBLEM

Many cultures that knew the institution of marriage, and that considered rape as a punishable offence (whether out of respect for the woman's violated autonomy or for her male guardian's violated 'property'), showed themselves lenient if the woman came forward agreeing to marry the man standing trial. In medieval Europe, it was the done thing. Cases are known of many a man standing trial for rape and being saved from punishment by his victim offering to marry him.

As I write this, I receive an e-mail from the liberal advocacy forum Awaaz, calling for solidarity with a girl called Lubna, a rape victim in the Arab world forced to marry her rapist. But then, I learn that Jordan has just outlawed the practice, and that Egypt and Tunisia have also done this in recent years. In other Muslim countries, the practice persists, and in Personal Law, India since Jawaharlal Nehru tries to provide its Muslims with a Muslim environment.

In the more backward parts of Europe, the practice was also known until recently. Thus, Franca Viola (°1948), a farmer's daughter from rural Alcamo in Sicily, got engaged to Filippo Melodia, nephew of a rich mafia don, with her parents' assent. Shortly after, he was arrested for theft and mafia membership, and because of this, Franca's father called off the engagement. Her family got threatened but persisted. At 17, Franca was abducted and raped by her rejected fiancé. Her father was contacted by Filippo's family for a meeting to settle the matter, namely with a 'reparation marriage', to 'repair' her and her family's honour. In 1965, Italy still had its Article 544 of the penal code, which turned rape into mere premarital sex, frowned upon but not punishable, and even annulled an earlier conviction for this rape, if a marriage between perpetrator and victim ensued.

Thanks to the coordinates given for the proposed meeting, he could send in the police, have her liberated and her abductors arrested. In the court case against Filippo, the defence tried to portray the abduction as voluntary on the girl's part. This so-called *fuitina*, 'escape', was the usual scenario in love marriages not wanted by the girl's family. The girl presented her father with an accomplished fact: First violating the family's honour, then restoring it through marriage. But the *fuitina* defence did not help: Filippo was imprisoned for ten years. (Data borrowed from Philip Roose: "Franca Viola en de afschaffing van het 'herstelhuwelijk' in Italië", *Doorbraak*, 3 August 2017)

The trial and its outcome gave a boost to the legal recognition of women's rights. In 1981, Article 544 was abolished. In 1996, rape was redefined as a violation of personal integrity, no longer as a violation of public morality or family honour. In my own country, Belgium, this change took place in 1989, not very long ago either. That Jordan abolished the 'reparation marriage' only in 2017, and that Tunisia outlawed all violence against women the same year, is hardly proof of being 'backward' when we consider how recent these developments are in Europe. Which is not to deny that India, backward or not, had better catch up with these developments.

GLOBAL HUMAN CULTURE

What missionaries and other so-called secularists attack in Hinduism is usually an attack of something brought forth by mankind and now (or within living memory) only surviving in Hinduism. Thus, to culpabilize Hinduism, they berate sati (a widow's self-immolation on her husband's funeral pyre), a very minoritarian practice among ancient Hindus, now non-existent. It was limited to the warrior castes, and counselled against in the *Rig Veda*, where the very first mention of the practice is where a widow intends to commit it but gets dissuaded. On the other hand, it has been attested among the aristocracy of the ancient Chinese, Mongols, Egyptians, Celts and Scandinavians. Contrary to feminist analysis, it was not a measure of the contempt in which women were held: Among the Greeks, women had a lowly status and had no 'honour' to defend by committing sati, whereas among the Celts, where women had a higher status, there was plenty of sati.

The secularists attack the Purusha Sukta ('Hymn of the Man'), the late-Vedic foundation stone of social differentiation ultimately yielding the caste system, as if similar myths did not exist in China, in Rome, in Scandinavia and, indeed, in the New Testament. There, Saint Paul likens the social classes to body parts, unequal but condemned to cooperate. This became the basis of the social teachings of the Catholic church, better known as corporatism, i.e., 'body-like worldview'. The church has always defended a layered society with inequality against the rising tide of socialism and egalitarianism. (This does not only count for the Catholic church of the nineteenth-twentieth century, but also for Martin Luther's opposition against the German peasants' rebellion, Russian Orthodoxy's support for serfdom, the Southern Baptist support to slavery in the US or the Afrikaner Calvinists' support to apartheid.)

When the missionaries are taking Hindus by the nose and pointing it towards the 'social evils of Hindu society', they are cleverly pointing it away from the skeletons in the cupboard of Christian society. So, contrary to secularist- missionary designs, Hindus need not be village bumpkins only aware of their own traditions. The knowledge of foreign traditions will go a long way in relativizing any 'evils of Hindu society', even if real.

Meanwhile, it is incontestably true that the Hindus' own legal tradition, as laid down in the Dharmashastras, does equally contain the recognition of marriage consequent on rape. Dharmashastra is a field in its own right, and proper experts can say a lot more about it, but let us already point to a general fact of consequence to our topic.

DEMONIC MARRIAGES

The Dharmashastras recognize a series of different marriage forms, usually eight. These are all legally binding and confer a number of enforceable rights and duties, but they are not equal. On top of the list are several forms of arranged marriage, where both families involved are in consensus. To the moderns' objection about the marriage partners' feelings, let us briefly say that a start with neutral feelings (often between youngsters who had never met) means that it can only get better, especially with the bond conferred by common children; whereas a love marriage starts with intense feelings which tend to diminish, mostly slowly but sometimes dramatically. Among older Hindus, the consensus used to be that emotion-driven love marriages decided on by immature youngsters end in disaster.

In modern India, the arranged marriage has become a compromise between the parents' considerations and the youngsters' preferences, often at their own suggestion of a prospective partner they have met in university or on the job. Even where the parents introduce them to a partner they have sought out, the smartphone gives the engaged couple opportunities to get to know each other that were unthinkable in the past. In those days, in the Hindu as in many other cultures, newly-weds often met for the first time before the altar. Often, it was the love of their parents and the confidence in the latter's choice (even when seemingly harsh or irrational) that gave newly-weds the determination to see the initial difficulties through.

Moreover, nurture and nature conspire to make children take after their parents, so the parents' choice of a son/daughter-in-law may not have been too different from what those youngsters at a riper age would consider likeable in a partner. Very recently, an older woman confided to me that her mother had warned her about the fiancé she had chosen: 'Of course she had seen it correctly, as I was to find out later, but since I was young and headstrong, I ignored her advice.' Modern forms of online (especially psychologically assisted) dating try to combine the advantages of mutual attraction with those of the premeditated arranged marriage.

A lower type is where the compatibility of the partners or their families is not considered. Thus, a rich candidate comes to buy your daughter, offering a bride-price, as is still common in the Muslim world and among African tribes. This type was named after a foreign people deemed hostile yet rich and powerful: the Asuras. It is common to name negative things after foreigners; for example, when the native American venereal disease syphilis spread in Europe through seamen and their encounters with prostitutes, the French called it 'the Spanish disease', Germans called it 'the French disease', and the Poles called it 'the German disease'.

Another respected foreign tribe, a bit farther removed and less the object of hostilities, were the Gandharvas, known mostly as musicians. They gave their name to the artsy form of marriage now common, heavily propagated in modern anti-traditional literature and films, first in the West, now in India: the love marriage.

Two other foreign tribes were treated with hostility but also with contempt: the Râkshasas and the Pishâchas. The former are the 'bear people', hence 'demons'. The latter have been described by Panini as a warrior tribe in the Afghan-Pak mountains, thought to be cannibals, and whose name has indeed survived with a similar connotation as 'cannibal', or, again, 'demon'. After them, the two lowest forms of marriage were named. The first is violent abduction and rape, against her family's and her own will. (This must be distinguished from the love marriage that sometimes takes the form of a staged abduction, but with the woman's consent, the above-mentioned *fuitina*). The second is seduction with intoxicants, where the woman is in no position any more to give or withhold her consent.

History is rife with episodes where women were abducted and forced into marriage. Far more often than is thinkable today, they also acquiesced in the situation as the lesser evil, especially as soon as children came and stabilized the forced marriage. That set their mind on something relatively more positive, the absorbing business of raising children who, after all, were also their own. The classical example here is the abduction of the Sabine women by the Romans.

During the Partition there were numerous cases of Hindu women abducted and raped by Muslims. After a semblance of peace had returned, a lot of them rejoined their families, but many others preferred to stay with their abductors (where they would at least be honoured as the women who gave their parents-in-law grandchildren) rather than go back to their families and to a life of being reviled as carrying the stain of defilement. Something of the same problem resurfaced when Yezidi women were abducted en masse by the Islamic State in 2014–15. Yezidi tradition was very harsh on a raped woman, but since it had now happened on such a scale, the community elders decided to lift the otherwise usual status of defilement and dishonour, and welcome the victimized women back with full honour.

RATIONALE OF DEMONIC MARRIAGES

The remarkable thing about the Shastric arrangement is that all these scenarios, including those sternly disapproved of, are treated as valid marriages. Naïve moderns ('blushing virgins') and the ever-superficial secularists will object to this arrangement with holy indignation: 'See how evil Hindu scripture is! It legalizes rohypnol-induced seduction and even plain rape!' Worse, they might even call it 'patriarchal'.

As pointed out by my erstwhile supervisor at BHU, philosophy professor Kedar Nath Mishra (I signed up for a Ph.D. programme there, which I could not pursue due to family circumstances, but Mishra and I remained in contact and later he invited me for lectures in Varanasi), it made good practical sense to extend the recognition of the married state even to such crime-originated unions. The Shastra writers were less into pure principles and more into the good of society, less concerned about the individual and more about the large number. Thus, unlike modern self-centred liberals, they cared about the child that might spring from such unions. It was no pleasure to grow up as a bastard (reason why 'bastard', 'son of a bitch', 'harâmzâda' and other synonyms were the ultimate swear words), and this arrangement ensured that they had a father. It might not be the mother's favourite partner, but then, the child was half him as much as half her.

But for the mother too, this was the best possible outcome after unfortunate events had befallen her. As she had become 'impure' in the eyes of society, including her own family, she risked being expelled and finding herself alone and defenceless out on the street. The best chance she still had was to become the keep of some rich man, treated as an inconsequential and invisible backstreet girl but nonetheless cared for, at least as long as she was sexually desirable. More likely, her only possible livelihood would be prostitution, and her child, even if a boy, would soon fall prey to sexual predators too and probably never reach adulthood. Further, her whole family, having been tainted by her 'impurity', her siblings' chances on the marriage market would also be affected. That would turn the one-time misfortune of being raped into a lifelong disaster extending beyond her own person. But declaring her legally married to her rapist would give her and her child a leg to stand on vis-à-vis him and his family. It would also restore her honour somewhat in the eyes of her family and of society at large.

All this makes sense only in a society with a 'patriarchal' valuation of the roles of men and women and the life-styles open to them. But that is the society in which the Shastra writers had to design their rules. In practice, they generally could not make the affected women fall back on the state's social security (though the self-same Shastras impose upon kings also the duty to provide for such women), and certainly not restore her 'honour'. They dealt with reality, not with wishful thinking in air-conditioned parlours, as American feminists do. What they ensured was the best possible outcome for all concerned *in the circumstances.*

In feminist eyes, all men are essentially rapists anyway, so the woman's 'choice' of life partner didn't make much difference. In the jaded feminist view of marriage, even the most romantic wedding only leads to a life of oppression and estrangement, so a straightforward rapist is not so different from the subtle rapists that most husbands are.

MODERNIZATION

In today's society, this arrangement need not be continued. The Shastras themselves provide for the possibility of change, especially for allowing the letter of the law to be changed by senior people well versed in the laws and careful to preserve their spirit. In this case, changing values in society and the availability of other support structures than the family, such as modern women's full access to the labour market, do indeed occasion and justify such changes. The extant Hindu Marriage Act, modernized in the 1950s, has introduced new attitudes and doomed the practice.

In Hinduism, such reforms need not be seen as a Western encroachment on native tradition, not even where formally they are just that. Essentially, they fulfil Hindu tradition's own capacity for what modern Catholics would call *aggiornamento*, 'updating'.

Among Muslims, with their more backward Sharia, it still persists. But even there, it is on its way out, as witnessed in the reforms in several Middle Eastern countries. The Indian Muslim community is called upon to follow suit.

CONCLUSION

To sum up: On the occasion of a 2017 verdict ordaining a reparation marriage, and not knowing the details of this specific case sufficiently, we have merely wanted to observe in general that the reactions of indignation clothed in feminist jargon bespeak a poor sense of history and a defective sense of proportion. This type of verdict, sanctioning the marriage of a rapist with his victim, may and indeed does call for a correction in a modernizing sense; but as an age-old practice, it is understandable in context.

As happens so often, and more so among our culturally illiterate contemporaries, we notice the typical projection of contemporary norms emanating from a prosperous equal-opportunity society on to an ancient arrangement fit for a traditional society. This is a narrow-minded and self-centred thought habit and had better be corrected. Yet, regardless of these intellectual niceties, we may nonetheless agree that the days of the reparation marriage are over for good.

Standing Up for the Purusha Sukta*

This article starts as a book review, but then shifts the focus to a defensive passage in the book concerned, significant for the whole Hindu psychology resulting from the Hindu situation of being besieged.

Anuradha Dutt's novel *Redemption* (Evolutes Publication, Gurgaon, 2017) is the story of the Chaudhury family from Dhaka, but also the analysis of a recent piece of Indian sociocultural history. The one large-scale event at its centre is pregnant with dramatic potential, and has indeed brought dramas and tragedies to the lives of millions: the Partition. This family avoids the worst by moving out in time to what was then called Calcutta. But even in peacetime, that city of the dark goddess Kali is full of religious zeal and social friction, enough to fill a good novel with. And then the children move out to Varanasi, to Delhi, and again become part of the main episodes of post-Independence history.

I won't take away the suspense: The reader eager to know the destiny of the Chaudhury family will have to read the book for himself/herself. If only for the sake of the many ancient mythic motifs made relevant by getting tied in with modern events, and in a more authentic way than in the new wave of myth-based novels, this book is simply a good read. Reviewing novels as such is not my specialism anyway, but here, the historical background

---

*Published on Pragyata.com, 26 February 2018

is legitimate prey for my searchlight, so allow me to comment on that.

Both an introduction and a plethora of off-hand references interspersed throughout the novel explain numerous aspects of Hindu society relevant to the narrative, especially caste. Indeed, for most Hindu laymen, it is the best summary of the relevant data they will ever encounter. So, do read this book, but nonetheless, also pay attention to the following remarks. These concern only a few lines in the whole book, but they are consequential.

CASTE POLITICS

When Hindu activists are confronted with the officially propagated view, thought up by communist leader M.N. Roy, that Islam made many converts thanks to popular resentment against the caste system, they often counter this by alleging that, instead, Islamic rule hardened caste relations and other inequalities (especially between the sexes) and strengthened the hand of orthodoxy over the other Hindus. That is indeed the position taken in *Redemption*. In itself, it is correct, but it is not the whole story: Caste undeniably started earlier, before any Muslim appeared on the scene.

Similarly, Dutt gives a good overview of the British uses and manipulations of caste as they appear from both public statements and candid references in private correspondence. Yes, the British did conduct policies calculated to maximize caste consciousness, often with a deliberate intention to 'divide and conquer'. But then, they could only manipulate what was already there.

The colonizers did not invent (or 'concoct') caste. Caste was already there when they arrived, just as it was a thousand years earlier, when the Muslim invaders arrived. Yet it had not been eternal, and there, too, we agree. Caste had a history, including a genesis, a time of flowering and, at present, a stage of decline. But then, where and how did it really originate?

AVESTAN 'COLOURS'

In the writer's opinion, the Avestan four pistras, 'colours', are the origin of the Indian varnas, 'colours' (p.xi). These are known from the Denkart, a book written down after the Muslim invasion of Iran had started, when the Zoroastrian priests realized that the very survival of their religion was under threat. It is based on oral tradition, till then kept from being defiled by writing, and no doubt very old, though not necessarily unchanged. The book itself could not possibly have influenced India's social structure, even when the Parsi refugees brought it into India shortly after. We are then talking about the ninth century AD, some 2,000 years after caste considerations make a number of appearances in the *Mahabharata*, the life of the Buddha and other old sources.

Rather, the Iranian division of society has a similar origin as the same division in Indian society. The Iranians came from India, as Shrikant Talageri has convincingly demonstrated. Moreover, the division is a natural one, present in every society. It may be tempting to push responsibility far from you, preferably to a foreign source, but in this case the Iranian option doesn't fulfil your wish. Their status of 'foreigner' is ambiguous, given that they came from India and are one of the 'five peoples' alongside the Vedic tribe: They are deemed to descend from the two brothers Anu and Puru, two of the five sons of Yayati. Iranians are quite present in the *Vedas*, such as through the sages Bhrigu and Cyavana.

Hindus ought to give up this defensive stand of trying to appease critics. Yes, Christian missionaries, themselves veterans of much oppression and representatives of a culture that practised slavery till recently, do find fault with Hindu casteism, and with anything else they can lay their hands on, like sati. So, lots of Hindus react by agreeing with them—yes, casteism is bad, Sir—and then trying to salvage Hinduism by disconnecting it from caste. (Or likewise, trying to disconnect it from sati, alleging that this was caused by the Muslim invasions or so.) This only makes your critics laugh and is totally counterproductive. The result is that they multiply these argumentative tactics—for example, today they have taken to saying that Hinduism is anti-ecological, so that flying kites on Uttarayana kills birds, bursting crackers on Diwali pollutes the air, the colours thrown on Holi are full of toxic chemicals, etc. The only thing left for Hindus is to wind up their whole noxious religion and convert.

Instead, you should assume responsibility for your entire history—and make your critics do the same. So, the missionaries, along with the mullahs, carry the burden of slavery with them, and of lots of misogyny, superstition, iconoclasm and the rest, and Hindus uncontestably carry the burden of more than 2,000 years of casteism. First, there are the facts: No matter whether caste is bad or has some good features, the fact is that caste has for long been closely bound with Hinduism. Stop trying to explain away this fact. Then comes the work of finding out how and why this happened. And at the end, if caste is found to be a bad thing, assume the responsibility of remedying it. Let missionaries and mullahs set their own house in order, instead of coming to trouble you, and do likewise yourself.

Look at me: My Celtic and Germanic ancestors practised human sacrifice. Near my place, there is a pond where, thanks to the composition of the soil, dead bodies are well preserved. They have dug up bodies there of people bearing ritual marks who had been drowned on purpose in the pond as sacrifice to the gods. So what? We don't do that any more, and if we did, I make bold that I would be among the abolitionists striving to stop this practice. But I find no virtue at all in denying it as a fact of history. So, please stop these attempts to wimp out from the ethically challenging parts of your own heritage. Hindu dharma is good enough to exist and to continue, even if it has some stains to wash off.

PURUSHA SUKTA: INTERPOLATION?

The author also declares that the Purusha Sukta (*Rig Veda* 10:90), the earliest metaphor for caste society as a body where all parts are doomed to cooperate even if different, was 'a very late interpolation in the *Rig Veda* and clearly based on Avestan ideas' (p.xi). How would she know?

As for the Avestan origin: See above, plus the fact that after the Rig Vedic period, once Iranian culture had relocated to the far side of Afghanistan and ultimately to Iran, no meaningful contact with the Iranians is reported any more. There is no indication for this Avestan origin of so central a Vedic hymn as the Purusha Sukta, and the perfect sameness of the body metaphor in the *Vedas* and Avesta rather points to a common origin. And this is not unlikely, given that the same metaphor is found in the Germanic myth of Ymir and the Chinese myth of Pangu.

As for the hymn being an interpolation, that is indeed a widely held belief, at least among nineteenth-century orientalists, from whom Dr B.R. Ambedkar copied it. And who, nowadays, would dare to go against Ambedkar?

Ostensibly, the hymn is from the final stage of Rig Vedic composition, shortly before Veda Vyasa's final editing of the hymns into the fully formed *Vedas*. It soon became the Vedic bedrock of varna doctrine and gets reproduced or quoted to that effect in younger Vedic writings, including the *Atharva Veda* and the *Yajur Veda* (so, there also interpolations?), the *Panchavimsha Brahmana*, *Taittiriya Aranyaka*, the *Mahabharata* and the *Bhagavata Purana*.

Linguistically, nothing sets the hymn apart from the others in the Tenth Mandala of the *Rig Veda*, though it may and does differ from the Family Books, the ancient core, centuries older. Thus, Friedrich Max Müller speculates that the word vasanta, 'spring', is un-Vedic, because it doesn't appear in the whole *Rig Veda*, 'except in another hymn of Book 10'. So, clearly, the word had come into use in the long intervening period, and is, in the final period of Vedic composition, no longer a *fremdkörper* ('foreign body') necessitating an interpolation from an even later period.

He, like H.T. Colebrooke, is also struck by the philosophical depth of this hymn, which both deem uncharacteristic of the *Rig Veda*. We need not even highlight the philosophical depth of early hymns like Dirghatamas' Riddle Hymn (1:164), we need only point to contemporaneous (Tenth Book) philosophical hymns such as the Nasadiya Sukta. Philosophical depth was not beyond the late Vedic poets.

The whole idea of interpolations into the *Vedas* sounds very improbable. The *Aitareya Brahmana* does list some interpolations, and the Purusha Sukta is not among them. The *Vedas* are a very stable body of texts, a virtual 'tape-recording' of actual recitations from thousands of years ago (says Harvard Sanskritist Michael Witzel), and were not easily trifled with. The defensive apologetic attempt to disown caste as 'totally un-Hindu' or at least 'totally un-Vedic' exists at least since the late nineteenth century, with the Arya Samaj. It has never convinced anyone who was out to fix the responsibility for caste on Hinduism; they only see it as transparent hypocrisy of the wily Brahmins.

Yet, because the Purusha Sukta was used to confer Vedic legitimacy on a later practice, it stands to reason that the hymn could have been a later interpolation. But in that case, the interpolators would have made sure to include occupational heredity and endogamy into it. These are the two aspects of caste which, no doubt, parents regularly had occasion to convince recalcitrant sons and daughters of, so that some Vedic authority would have been useful to them. Instead, the hymn can serve as testimony of an earlier (viz. late-Vedic) age when these practices were not yet part of the budding caste system.

To sum up: It is an understandable and honourable hypothesis that the Purusha Sukta was an interpolation, but it is unproven and probably untrue.

PURUSHA SUKTA: CONTENTS REGARDING CASTE

In any case, it makes no difference, for Hindu tradition has assumed this hymn even if it were younger than the *Vedas*, have given it Vedic ('revealed') authority and regarded it as the bedrock of varna ideology for some 2,000 years. Nitpicking about its literary status as possibly an interpolation can't undo this. Hindus have amply owned it up, and now have the responsibility to deal with it.

Yet, this dealing with caste does not mean dealing with the Purusha Sukta. There is something problematic about caste, even if it cannot be reduced to that, but there is nothing actually problematic about the hymn.

If you read more carefully than done by the traditionalists of centuries past and the Ambedkarites of our own time, you find that the hymn says nothing about caste. It only describes four functions in a developed society: priest, warrior, entrepreneur and worker. It does not say that these functions are discreet, and among animal husbandmen (as the Vedic tribe apparently was), they were not. They overlapped, and initially, any householder could perform as priest, he could take up arms to defend his village, he could, of course, tend his cattle and he could repair his utensils and do other menial work. The hymn doesn't say jobs were allotted to one specific birth group; nor that by birth you are predetermined to doing that profession, the same that your father did (of which the *Vedas* itself provides counter-examples). It doesn't say you can only marry someone from the same birth group.

Indeed, centuries later, we see the Buddha uphold the idea that caste is purely patrilineal, a son is Kshatriya because his father was and regardless of what his mother was. His friend Prasenajit, by contrast, disappointed because his wife turns out to be non-Kshatriya, already espouses the norm of caste endogamy, which must then have been an innovation. At any rate, endogamy as a defining trait of the historical caste system is not yet present in the Purusha Sukta.

Meanwhile, the same body-parts metaphor for the social classes is paralleled not just in writings of ancient Scandinavia and China but also in two sources definitely familiar to nineteenth-century orientalists: the Roman administrator Menenius Agrippa and the New Testament author Saint Paul, considered the real founder of Christianity. In their case, the metaphor does not pertain to the correspondence between body parts and parts of the universe, only to that between body parts and societal classes (where the Purusha Sukta has both). If those worthies could think up the corporatist metaphor, so could the Vedic sages. The said Greco-Roman authors used the simile to deduce that everyone should know his place on the social ladder and be satisfied with it—just the conservatism and lack of social mobility that the missionaries and Leftists object to in the case of Hindu caste society. And again, even if this trait of keeping everyone in his place was an aspect of the full-grown caste system, it was not part of the Purusha Sukta.

CONCLUSION

Hindus have learnt to look at their own classics through the eyes of their enemies. Thus, they are very ashamed and embarrassed about their legal codes, the Shastras, because these do, indeed, contain some iniquitous casteist verses—thus doing injustice to the rest of those books, often very inventive or lofty. They are even ashamed of their Purusha Sukta, which the enemy claims is casteist, but in fact is not casteist at all.

And here, too, there are other, non-controversial parts that get overlooked. Thus, the hymn opens by saying that the Universal Man (Purusha) has a thousand heads. That means: The Universal Man is a community of ordinary individual men. Hindus sometimes felt the need for a leader, but hey, the Purusha Sukta rightly prescribes: We together are that leader. When we put our limited heads together, we together become the Cosmic Man. Isn't that profound? If I were a Hindu, I would be proud of my Purusha Sukta. I would never want it to be a mere interpolation from an obscure foreign source.

Index